The Final Year of
Anne Boleyn

The Final Year of
Anne Boleyn

Natalie Grueninger

PEN & SWORD
HISTORY

First published in Great Britain in 2022 and reprinted in 2023 by
Pen & Sword History
An imprint of
Pen & Sword Books Ltd
Yorkshire – Philadelphia

ISBN 978 1 52677 698 3

A CIP catalogue record for this book is
available from the British Library.

Typeset by Mac Style
Printed in the UK by CPI Group (UK) Ltd, Croydon, CR0 4YY.

Pen & Sword Books Limited incorporates the imprints of Atlas,
Archaeology, Aviation, Discovery, Family History, Fiction, History,
Maritime, Military, Military Classics, Politics, Select, Transport,
True Crime, Air World, Frontline Publishing, Leo Cooper, Remember
When, Seaforth Publishing, The Praetorian Press, Wharncliffe
Local History, Wharncliffe Transport, Wharncliffe True Crime
and White Owl.

For a complete list of Pen & Sword titles please contact

PEN & SWORD BOOKS LIMITED
47 Church Street, Barnsley, South Yorkshire, S70 2AS, England
E-mail: enquiries@pen-and-sword.co.uk
Website: www.pen-and-sword.co.uk
or
PEN AND SWORD BOOKS
1950 Lawrence Rd, Havertown, PA 19083, USA
E-mail: Uspen-and-sword@casematepublishers.com
Website: www.penandswordbooks.com

For Anne,

May your story continue to inspire and connect people through the ages, and long may you reign in our hearts.

Contents

Try me good king, but let me have a lawful trial, and let not my sworn enemies sit as my accusers and judges... My last and only request shall be, that myself may only bear the burden of your grace's displeasure, and that it may not touch the innocent souls of those poor gentlemen, whom (as I understand) are likewise in strait imprisonment for my sake. If ever I have found favour in your sight; if ever the name of Anne Boleyn hath been pleasing in your ears, let me obtain this request.

(A letter to King Henry VIII from the Tower, attributed to Anne Boleyn)

Foreword

As the light gently fades of an evening in the Great Chamber of Hever Castle, where Anne Boleyn spent much of her youth, the rippling moat which surrounds the fortress casts glittering reflections onto a sixteenth-century tapestry hanging in that space. Visitors to Hever have spent hours searching for the elusive face of Anne Boleyn in that tapestry, for it was believed to illustrate the wedding of King Louis XII of France to Princess Mary Tudor: Henry VIII's sister. The wedding was an event that Anne Boleyn may well have attended in 1514, when she entered the French court. As the twilit luminescence dances across the many faces woven into the tapestry, one could be forgiven for believing that they had momentarily awoken from their inanimate state. However, just as light play can change our perception of an historical object, so too can the study of that object's history and construction.

When the tapestry was expertly restored by The Textile Conservancy Company in 2016, it became evident that significant alterations had been made to it. Patches had been discreetly sewn in where the original edges had frayed, and where key segments had eroded over time. They had, no doubt, been added by its earlier conservators to mirror that which had been lost. Soot from exposure to the smoke from hundreds of years of open fires had obscured a significant part of the tapestry's story, calling into question our understanding of what is depicted. Layers of dirt had cloaked an original woven inscription upon the bride's gown, identifying her not as Mary Tudor, but as Queen 'Esther'. The smoke and mirrors of time had provided us with a seemingly complete picture of the past, despite the significant losses to that image since its creation.

While this tapestry could have been created to allegorically depict both the marriage of Mary Tudor *and* the biblical marriage of Queen Esther to King Ahasuerus, it is also possible that it was erroneously linked to Mary Tudor years later. While looking for the face of a youthful Anne Boleyn in the wedding congregation, we have been blinded to a more troubling connection between the tapestry and Anne's story. In the final days of her queenship, Anne was making very public and dangerous allegories of her own. It was the story of Queen Esther and her triumph over King Ahasuerus's wicked advisor, Haman, which was evoked by Anne's almoner, John Skipp, in his Passion Sunday sermon of 1536. It was a bold and dangerous move, played before king and court, and it laid bare the increasingly fraught relationship between Anne Boleyn (Esther), and Henry VIII's chief advisor, Thomas Cromwell (Haman). It was not the queen who triumphed in Anne's case, for she wasn't married to a 'gentle' King like Ahasuerus.

A thundering storm of speculation, hearsay and misinformation about Anne Boleyn's downfall has rolled about her empty throne since the brief, bloody days that marked the end of her life. Henry VIII's frenzied efforts to wipe all memory of his wife from earth were, mercifully, only partly successful. What we are left with, however, is a body of evidence reminiscent of partial, damaged fragments of a once complete set of tapestries. Many fine efforts have been made in the past to meddle in Anne's cause and make sense of these often incomplete and, at times, embellished sources. Efforts that have resulted in a kaleidoscope of conflicting theories as to why Anne Boleyn fell.

This exceptional, scholarly study of Anne Boleyn's final year forensically and fearlessly challenges many of the conclusions that have been previously made. No footnote has been left unchecked and no source has been left unscrutinised. By removing the many patches of misinformation, and by washing clean the accumulation of myth, the true horror of Anne's downfall is presented to us in the most lucid and compelling account to date. We will never be able to recover the full tapestry of Anne Boleyn's life, but Natalie Grueninger has presented us with what is undoubtedly the most cogent and vivid picture of why her life was taken. It is an extraordinary achievement, and it does Anne justice.

Dr Owen Emmerson
Historian and Assistant Curator, Hever Castle

Prologue

On the morning of Friday, 19 May 1536, a large crowd of Englishmen and women filed into the Tower of London to witness an event never before seen in the country – the execution of an anointed queen of England. The star of this macabre show was Anne Boleyn, the woman King Henry VIII had ardently pursued for seven years and turned his world upside down to marry. Anne had been tried by a jury of her peers and, despite her eloquent defence, found guilty of adultery, incest and conspiring the king's death. Her five alleged lovers and co-conspirators, consisting of her younger brother George, Viscount Rochford; Sir Henry Norris, the king's Groom of the Stool; Sir Francis Weston and Sir William Brereton, both gentlemen of the Privy Chamber; and the court musician Mark Smeaton, had been dispatched by an axeman in a public display of the king's supposed justice at nearby Tower Hill two days earlier. Anne's sentence, however, was to be carried out within the confines of the Tower, far from the prying eyes of any foreigners who might be touched by the plight of the fallen queen and spread favourable reports of her final moments across Europe.

The onlookers, many of whom may have also witnessed the bloodbath on Tower Hill, gathered around a newly erected scaffold, draped in black, which stood on the north side of William the Conqueror's White Tower. Among the spectators were men Anne knew well: Thomas Audley, the Lord Chancellor; 16-year-old Henry Fitzroy, the Duke of Richmond and Somerset and the king's illegitimate son; and Charles Brandon, the Duke of Suffolk, who had known Anne since she was a child. Also present, the Lord Mayor and Alderman of London, with the sheriffs and most of the king's Council, including Thomas Cromwell, Henry's right-hand man, who within two months of Anne's fall, succeeded her father as Lord Privy Seal, one of the highest ranking offices at court, and was raised to the peerage as Baron Cromwell.

The impatient crowd did not have long to wait. At around 8.00 am, the Constable of the Tower, Sir William Kingston, followed by the ladies who had served Anne during her imprisonment, escorted the queen from the Queen's Lodgings, where she had been kept for the last seventeen days, to her place of execution. The sombre procession made its way past the Great Hall – where Anne feasted in splendour on the eve of her coronation less than three years before, and, more recently, the setting of her and her brother's sensational trials – under the Cole Harbour Gate and along the west side of the White Tower to the open ground beyond, where the crowd caught its first glimpse of her.

The queen selected an English hood for the day's spectacle, as opposed to the French style that she so often favoured, and dressed with the utmost care, donning a grey damask gown edged with fur, over which she wore an ermine mantle. Adept at using clothing to promote her interests and emphasise her royal magnificence, Anne used her final public appearance to send a very clear message – in her eyes she would die every inch the English queen.

An executioner from Calais, renowned for his deftness and precision with the sword, stood aside discreetly as, following Tudor scaffold etiquette to a tee, Anne addressed the hushed crowd. She did not protest against the king or the unjust sentence:

> For according to the law and by the law I am judged to die, and therefore I will speak nothing against it... I pray God save the king and send him long to reign over you, for a gentler nor a more merciful prince was there never, and to me he was ever a good, a gentle, and a sovereign lord.

Anne was well aware that any open criticism of the king or his laws would inevitably lead to more suffering for her parents and the fiery-haired toddler she was leaving behind. While she had not publicly protested her innocence, neither had she confessed to any great sin or admitted to having wronged the king in any way. It's what Anne failed to say that had the most impact, especially on a Tudor audience skilled at reading between the lines. Anne Boleyn subtly proclaimed her innocence and went to her death with the same courage she had shown in life. The queen was beheaded with just one stroke of the sword, and despite Cromwell's order to ban foreigners from the Tower, news travelled quickly around London and abroad that Anne Boleyn had died 'boldly'.

The speed with which these extraordinary events unfolded sent shock waves through the Tudor court. It had been a mere nineteen days since the first arrest, and in that brief period, six people, all bar one prominent members of the king's inner circle, had been detained, tried and beheaded, and their families and loved ones left shell-shocked and bereft. The question, though, remained. How had it come to this?

The answers lie in the twelve months that preceded Anne's downfall – a year that one eyewitness would later refer to as 'the year of marvels'.

Part I

Spring 1535

Chapter 1

The Subtle Game

As spring 1535 dawned across the land, a chorus of birdsong and the scent of fragrant blooms filled the crisp morning air with the promise of new life – something England's queen, Anne Boleyn, wished for more than anything. Since her marriage to Henry VIII and her coronation on 1 June 1533, Anne had given birth to a daughter, the future Elizabeth I, and suffered at least one miscarriage or possibly a stillbirth in late June 1534.[1] Their healthy and precocious daughter offered the couple hope, however, the primary role of a queen consort was to bear sons, a duty Anne had not yet been able to fulfil. Their lack of a male heir was an obvious concern for the royal couple, but there were other pressures on their relationship. Opposition to their marriage continued both at home and abroad, and disquiet and confusion reigned in the hearts of their subjects, many of whom refused to accept Anne as their rightful queen.

Despite the years that had passed since the annulment of Henry VIII's marriage to his first wife, Katherine of Aragon, she remained as popular with the people as ever, as did her 19-year-old daughter, the Lady Mary. Support for the ousted queen and former princess was not restricted to England. Katherine's familial links abroad gifted her with influential and vocal allies. Among them was the man who ruled over the most powerful empire in Europe, her nephew Charles V, the Holy Roman Emperor, who, in 1526, married Katherine's niece, Isabella. To further complicate matters for Henry and Anne, following the death of Francis I's first wife, Claude – whom Anne served for almost seven years – the French king married Charles V's sister, Eleanor. Thus, even the friendships Anne had forged during her time in France with women such as Francis I's sister, the spirited Marguerite de Angoulême, were now strained by family loyalty. Loyalties that Katherine of Aragon called on at every opportunity.

From her exile at Kimbolton Castle in Cambridgeshire, Katherine wrote to her nephew Charles V on 8 April 1535 to thank him for 'the good he has done in getting the Pope to give a definitive sentence in the matter between the king and her.'[2] The sentence she was referring to was given by Clement VII on 23 March 1534 – the very day that Parliament passed the First Act of Succession. At a secret consistory, he declared Katherine's marriage to the king valid.[3] The declaration, however, had not improved Henry's treatment of either mother or daughter. Katherine implored Charles to do something to remedy the situation, especially considering Mary's fragile health and ill-treatment at the hands of her father, which, according to Katherine, 'would suffice to make a healthy person ill'.[4] Mary's illness had been the subject of several communications between Eustace Chapuys, the Imperial ambassador since August 1529, and his master, Charles V.[5]

On 9 February 1535, Chapuys reported that at a meeting with Henry's Council, he had been told by Thomas Boleyn, 'as he spoke French the best', that Mary was 'dangerously ill'.[6] The following month she was sick again with her 'usual illness'.[7] Katherine suspected foul play and a broken heart, and wanted to personally nurse Mary back to health, but Henry would not allow it, as he feared this would give them the perfect opportunity to conspire against him and bring war to his doorstep. Chapuys, who stayed in regular communication with the erstwhile queen via her physician, worked tirelessly to have Katherine and Mary reunited.[8] He interceded for them at every opportunity, petitioning Thomas Cromwell and requesting audiences with Henry on a regular basis. He was, however, not the only person pressuring the king.

Since Henry's break with Rome, Pope Clement VII and his successor Paul III had been trying to persuade him to discard Anne and return to his first wife and the Roman Catholic fold. On more than one occasion, the king was threatened with excommunication and later with a Bull of Deprivation, which, if published, would deprive Henry of his kingdom and discharge his subjects of their allegiance.[9] The Pope, however, needed powerful rulers to enforce the sentence and, despite Katherine's implorations, it transpired that neither Charles V nor Francis I were willing to do so. But in 1535, the threat of an invasion by the combined Catholic powers remained a real possibility. 'The Pope, the Emperor, and all other Christian kings, France excepted, are preparing a great army and navy against England, which has few friends in Europe', warned Andrew Boorde in June 1535.[10] Boorde was a physician, traveller and writer, and just one of Cromwell's vast network of informers who kept the king's principal secretary abreast of all the important developments in domestic and foreign affairs. There was little that went on without Cromwell knowing about it.

Henry realised that a full-scale invasion would require a Franco-Imperial alliance, so he did his best to block it while taking care not to alienate either party. By March 1535, negotiations for a match between the Princess Elizabeth and Charles, the Duke of Angoulême, Francis I's third son, were well under way.[11] At the same time, Thomas Cromwell, presumably at Henry's behest, worked behind the scenes to improve relations between the king and the emperor, who, for much of the second half of 1535, was occupied with his conquest of Tunis. This suited Henry as it meant the emperor lost interest in the rebellion that had broken out in Ireland in June 1534, which was causing Henry significant headaches. It was rumoured that Charles hoped to use the situation to pressure Henry into reconsidering his separation from his aunt.[12] The delicate diplomatic dance, or 'subtle game' as Chapuys called it, continued.[13]

The threat of invasion and the Irish revolt were not the only things casting a shadow over Anne and Henry's marriage. The king feared that with the help of her royal cousin, the emperor, the Lady Mary would try to flee England.[14] His concerns were not unfounded. According to Chapuys, Mary 'desired nothing else' and thought ceaselessly about how it might be arranged.[15] At first, the ambassador advised caution and informed Charles of the many hazards associated with such an enterprise, but it wasn't long before he was feeling more confident: 'As to getting her away from here… it could be accomplished by having a pinnace on the river and two armed ships at the mouth of the river; at least I could find means to get her out of the house almost at any hour of the night.'[16] A report of local support for the enterprise spurred the ambassador's enthusiasm:

> A score of the principal lords of England and more than a hundred knights were quite ready to employ their persons, goods, friends, and dependents if they had the smallest assistance from your Majesty, and that as aforesaid the time is most favourable, because the people are every day more dissatisfied at the taxation, for the levying of which they are beginning to depute commissioners to enquire the value of every one's goods and assess them accordingly.[17]

The source of this information is unknown. Chapuys heard it from 'the gentleman of whom I lately wrote to your Majesty', therefore, its veracity is questionable. Nevertheless, it does illustrate the uncertainty and instability of the times, if it appeared plausible to Chapuys – a perceptive and experienced diplomat whose job it was to provide accurate information to his master. When the ambassador included rumour in his communique with the emperor, he often included his assessment of its credibility for the emperor's benefit. To purposely lead Charles astray would risk his own reputation, but also that of his masters. If there were any principal lords or knights involved in this plot to whisk Mary away, then they were putting their necks on the line.

For supporters of Katherine and the Lady Mary in England, it was an increasingly dangerous time. The Succession Act of 1534, among other things, formally recognised Anne Boleyn as queen, forbade the king's subjects from appealing to Rome and pronounced the king's children from his marriage to Anne as the lawful heirs to the throne. It also stipulated 'that the said Lady Katherine shall be from henceforth called and reputed only dowager to Prince Arthur and not queen of this realm'.[18] If Katherine had never really been queen, then Mary was obviously illegitimate. It also outlined the penalties for contravening the Act or speaking out against the king, queen, their marriage or any of their issue.

In order to further secure the succession, the Act also required all the nobles of the realm, 'both spiritual and temporal', and all the king's subjects if summonsed, to swear an oath that they shall maintain 'the whole effects and contents of the present Act'.[19] Anyone refusing to take the oath would be guilty of misprision of high treason, 'and the offender therein to suffer such pains and imprisonments, losses and forfeitures, and also lose privileges of sanctuaries.'[20] This was a lesser crime than high treason but one which nonetheless landed Thomas More, Henry VIII's former Lord Chancellor, and John Fisher, Bishop of Rochester, in the Tower of London in April 1534, where they remained until their executions fourteen months later. The devout Catholics, both stalwart supporters of Katherine of Aragon, were imprisoned for refusing to swear the oath. The exact form of the oath tendered to More and Fisher is unknown, as it was not included in the original Act. However, accepting the 'whole effects and contents of this present Act' meant accepting that Henry and Katherine's marriage was null and void and 'against the laws of Almighty God', something their consciences would not allow them to do, for it implied a rejection of papal authority. After all, it was the Pope who had granted Henry and Katherine a dispensation to marry in the first place and who had, more recently, declared their marriage valid. 'The Act', More affirmed, 'is like a sword with two edges, for if a man answer one way it will destroy the soul, and if he answer another it will destroy the body.'[21]

A further piece of legislation passed by Parliament in November 1534, The Act Respecting the Oath to the Succession, specified the oath that all subjects were required to take in order to uphold the Act of Succession:

Ye shall swear to bear faith, truth, and obedience alonely to the king's majesty, and to his heirs of his body of his most dear and entirely beloved lawful wife Queen Anne, begotten and to be begotten, and further to the heirs of our said sovereign lord according to the limitation in the statute made for surety of his succession in the crown of this realm, mentioned and contained, and not to any other within this realm, nor foreign authority or potentate: and in case any oath be made, or has been made, by you, to any person or persons, that then ye [are] to repute the same as vain and annihilate; and that, to your cunning, wit, and uttermost of your power, without guile, fraud, or other undue means, you shall observe, keep, maintain, and defend the said Act of Succession, and all the whole effects and contents thereof, and all other Acts and statutes made in confirmation, or for execution of the same, or of anything therein contained; and this ye shall do against all manner of persons, of what estate, dignity, degree, or condition soever they be, and in no wise do or attempt, nor to your power suffer to be done or attempted, directly or indirectly, anything or things privily or apartly to the let, hindrance, damage, or derogation thereof, or of any part of the same, by any manner of means, or for any manner of pretence; so help you God, all saints, and the holy Evangelists.[22]

This went further than the original Act as it required all subjects to renounce the power of any 'foreign authority or potentate' and to repudiate any oaths previously made to 'any person or persons'. This may have been the form of the oath presented to More in April 1534 because he later told his daughter Margaret that he was committed to the Tower 'for refusing of this oath not agreeable with the statute' and complained that they 'by their own law are unable to justify my imprisonment'.[23]

During the November 1534 session of Parliament, the Act of Supremacy was also passed, which recognised Henry as 'the only supreme head on earth of the Church of England'.[24] To ensure its stability, a new Treason Act followed, which stipulated that anyone who did 'maliciously wish, will, or desire, by words or writing, or by craft imagine, invent, practise, or attempt any bodily harm to be done or committed to the king's most royal person, the queen's, or their heirs apparent...' was guilty of high treason. To deny the royal supremacy or to call the king a 'heretic, schismatic, tyrant, infidel, or usurper of the crown' was now a crime punishable by death.[25] Whereas in the past 'treason had required some overt act against the monarch's authority', now spoken or written words that expressed some desire for harm to come to the king, queen or the heir to the throne was all that was needed.[26] This was met with anxiety by members of Parliament.

In early 1535, Robert Fisher, MP for Rochester, visited his brother John Fisher in the Tower of London and brought him news of the Acts of Supremacy and Treason. During questioning, Fisher's servant, Richard Wilson, later revealed that Robert Fisher had informed his brother that 'speaking is made high treason, which was never heard of before', and marvelled that words could now constitute high treason. He told him that there was 'never such a sticking at the passing of any Act in the Lower House as was at the passing of the same'.[27] He also noted that the words must be spoken 'maliciously'. But in reality, when would an insult directed at Henry or his family not be considered malicious? Those speaking out against the royal family would be pursued with indefatigable vigour.

The draconian penalties, however, were not enough to silence all of Henry's subjects. Throughout 1535, reports of people speaking treasonous words about Henry and Anne regularly reached the king's ears. Bishops reported their clergymen, masters their employees, and friends, family and associates reported each other. A mere slip of the tongue was all it took to bring you to the chief minister's attention, as an elderly Dr Carsley, canon and residentiary of Wells Cathedral, discovered in February 1535. While delivering a sermon, and 'after a very honourable mention of the king's highness', wrote John Clerk, Bishop of Bath and Wells to Cromwell, Carsley said, 'that, according to our most bounden duty, we should pray for his grace, and for the Lady Catherine the queen; and also, by express name, for my Lady Elizabeth, their daughter.'[28] The bishop immediately reproved him. At first, Carsley denied ever having mentioned the old queen, however, he soon publicly acknowledged his error and expressed sorrow for his mistake: 'I call God to record that I thought not of the Lady Catherine: I meant only Queen Anne, for I know no queen but her.'[29]

Other incidents were more deliberate. On 11 February 1535, Margaret Chanseler, a spinster from Suffolk, confessed to having said that the queen had had a child by the king, which was 'dead-born', (possibly a reference to the miscarriage or stillbirth Anne had suffered in 1534), and she prayed that she would never have another. She also called Anne a 'naughty whore' and, according to two witnesses, 'a goggle-eyed whore'. Margaret ended her name-calling spree by asserting 'God Save Queen Katherine', England's righteous queen and one whom she trusted to see back on the throne soon. When questioned, she alleged that an excess of alcohol was to blame, and possession by an evil spirit.[30]

Later in the month, Sir Francis Bryan wrote to Cromwell about one George Taylor, of Newport Pagnell in Buckinghamshire, who claimed that 'the King is but a knave and liveth in avowtry, and is a heretic and liveth not after the laws of God'. In addition, he boasted that if he had the king's crown, he would play football with it.[31] Taylor denied the accusation and confessed only to drunkenness. Nevertheless, he was promptly imprisoned, and Bryan told Cromwell that his expedient execution by hanging, drawing and quartering, the standard penalty for men convicted of high treason, would serve as a great example to the people.

Richard Tydder, a tailor from Blisworth, was put in the stocks for attempting to rob his master's house. In the presence of the king's watchmen, he claimed that 'the King liveth in avowtry, and so hath done all the days of his life' and said that he trusted to see the king's head run upon the ground like a football.[32] Some witnesses asserted that Tydder was heavily intoxicated when he made the remarks and had no memory of what he had said the following morning. Edward Knightly, sergeant at law, told Cromwell that he deserved to be executed for the attempted robbery alone, but noted that he was a clerk and could speak Latin and write very well.

Another outspoken subject, Margery or Margaret Cowpland, allegedly called the king 'an extortioner, knave and traitor' and Anne Boleyn 'a strong harlot'.[33] It turns out, however, that one of her accusers, John Wynbok, whom Margaret had raised since a child, was involved in a dispute with her about the lease of a mill, so it's possible that the accusation was false and motivated by Wynbok's desire to discredit her and obtain the mill for himself. Margery vehemently denied the charge, however, Sir Walter Stonor, who had examined all the witnesses, told Cromwell that he believed it was true because 'she is a marvellously drunken woman… and her husband is out of his mind.'[34] The fact that she was elderly, the sole carer of her sick husband, and, according to Stonor, 'lacked wits' herself, did not save her from imprisonment at Wallingford Castle. This case shows just how dangerous words had become for all of Henry's subjects, especially considering that accusations of treason might be prompted by malice and greed, rather than a genuine desire to uphold the law.

Not all rants, however, were fuelled by alcohol or family feuds. Guilliaum Cowschier, a skinner from St Omer, felt 'that our sovereign lord king Henry was a wretch, a caitiff and no Christian man, having two wives and a concubine.'[35] His friend Nicholas Delanoy was just as disapproving: 'Pity it was of the King's life to forsake the noble blood of the Emperor and to take a poor knight's daughter.'[36] Christopher Ascheton alerted the authorities after his business associate 'began to rail on the king' and said that 'neither his Grace nor his servants should long prosper.'[37] One disgruntled, unnamed priest was detained after 'bidding a vengeance on the king' for the first fruit and tenths tax, which required the clergy to pay the first year's revenue from their benefice and thereafter a tenth of their income annually to the Crown.[38] He was sent to Cromwell, along with a woman who claimed 'that since this new queen was made there was never so much pilling and polling in this realm.'[39]

In this atmosphere of distrust and suspicion, rumours thrived, as did the fear that drove them. In April 1535, during the interrogation of a number of Carthusian and Bridgettine monks, including Richard Reynolds, a monk from Syon Abbey, it emerged that John Hale, Vicar of Isleworth, had had conversations with one Sir Thomas Mody about an old rumour that had resurfaced about the king and Elizabeth Boleyn, which claimed that 'the King's grace had meddling with the Queen's mother.'[40] Despite the story's popularity, the king himself had denied the rumour even before his marriage to Anne. When it was put to him that he had slept with both Anne's sister and her mother, Henry responded, 'never with the mother'.[41] In his monumental biography of Anne Boleyn, Professor Eric Ives reminds us that John Hale 'was part of a cell which Reynolds had been feeding with gossip about the morals of the Boleyn family and the falseness of Henry's claim to be supreme head.'[42] During questioning, Hale reported further gossip. He said that one Mr Skydmore had told him that Henry Carey, son of Mary Boleyn and her first husband William Carey, was in fact the king's son: 'Mr Skydmore did show to me young Master Carey, saying that he was our sovereign Lord the King's son by our sovereign Lady the Queen's sister, whom the Queen's grace might not suffer to be in the Court.'[43] This tale is not as easy to dismiss. The paternity of Mary Boleyn's children remains a hotly debated issue, even though the official line was that they were the children of Mary Boleyn and her first husband, William Carey.[44] Importantly, Henry did not acknowledge either child, as he had done with Henry Fitzroy, his son by his known mistress, Elizabeth Blount. While most of the rumours circulating were unfounded and spread by supporters of Katherine and Mary and the old faith, Hale was right about one thing – in 1535, Mary Boleyn was not at court with her family.

The queen's sister had been sent away in around September 1534, after it was discovered that she had married William Stafford, a second son of a minor gentry family, without Anne's knowledge or approval.[45] Following Anne's elevation to the throne, she had become the Boleyn family's accepted head and, as such, would have expected to play a leading role in arranging a suitable second marriage for her sister.[46] The fact that Mary had failed to consult Anne, at a time when so many people were publicly challenging the legitimacy of Anne's position, incensed the Boleyns. It was a breach of protocol the queen could simply not ignore. To add insult to injury, Mary was pregnant. This must have made Anne's own recent devastating loss all the more distressing. (It's worth noting that the sources are silent when it comes to the fate of Mary's baby, which suggests that the pregnancy may have ended in a miscarriage or stillbirth, or, if the child was born alive, that it did not survive to adulthood.) So why did Mary disregard her sister's authority and make such an obvious *mésalliance*, which was not only injurious to her and her new husband's future prospects at court but also to her family's reputation? She did it, Mary confessed, for love.

In the wake of her banishment, Mary penned a moving and desperate letter to Cromwell, begging him to intercede with Anne and Henry on her behalf and to restore her husband's position at court. This lengthy letter is worth quoting in full because it offers a unique and illuminating glimpse into the mind of its author, a woman who makes only fleeting appearances in the contemporary accounts and documents. It also offers a glimpse into what it may have been like for Mary to forever live in the shadow of her accomplished sister.

> Master Secretary,
> After my poor recommendations, which is smally to be regarded of me, that am a poor banished creature, this shall be to desire you to be good to my poor husband and to me. I am sure it is not unknown to you the high displeasure that both he and I have, both of the king's highness and the queen's grace, by reason of our marriage without their knowledge, wherein we both do yield ourselves faulty, and do acknowledge that we did not well to be so hasty nor so bold, without their knowledge. But one thing, good master secretary, consider, that he was young, and love overcame reason; and for my part I saw so much honesty in him, that I loved him as well as he did me, and was in bondage, and glad I was to be at liberty: so that, for my part, I saw that all the world did set so little by me, and he so much, that I thought I could take no better way but to take him and to forsake all other ways, and live a poor, honest life with him. And so I do put no doubts but we should, if we might once be so happy to recover the king's gracious favour and the queen's. For well I might have had a greater man of birth and a higher, but I assure you I could never have had one that should have loved me so well, nor a more honest man; and besides that, he is both come of an ancient stock, and again as meet (if it was his grace's pleasure) to do the king service, as any young gentleman in his court.
> Therefore, good master secretary, this shall be my suit to you, that, for the love that well I know you do bear to all my blood, though, for my part, I have not deserved it but smally, by reason of my vile conditions, as to put my husband to the king's grace that he may do his duty as all other gentlemen do. And, good master secretary, sue for us to the king's highness, and beseech his highness, which ever was wont to take pity, to have pity on us; and that it will please his grace of his goodness to speak to the queen's grace for us; for, so far as I can perceive, her grace is so

highly displeased with us both that, without the king be so good lord to us as to withdraw his rigour and sue for us, we are never like to recover her grace's favour: which is too heavy to bear. And seeing there is no remedy, for God's sake help us; for we have been now a quarter of a year married, I thank God, and too late now to call that again; wherefore it is the more almones [alms] to help. But if I were at my liberty and might choose, I ensure you, master secretary, for my little time, I have tried so much honesty to be in him, that I had rather beg my bread with him than to be the greatest queen in Christendom. And I believe verily he is in the same case with me; for I believe verily he would not forsake me to be a king.

Therefore, good master secretary, seeing we are so well together and does intend to live so honest a life, though it be but poor, show part of your goodness to us as well as you do to all the world besides; for I promise you, you have the name to help all them that hath need, and amongst all your suitors I dare be bold to say that you have no matter more to be pitied than ours; and therefore, for God's sake, be good to us, for in you is all our trust.

And I beseech you, good master secretary, pray my lord my father and my lady to be so good to us, and to let me have their blessings and my husband their good will; and I will never desire more of them. Also, I pray you, desire my lord of Norfolk and my lord my brother to be good to us. I dare not write to them, they are so cruel against us; but if, with any pain that I could take with my life, I might win their good wills, I promise you there is no child living would venture more than I. And so I pray you to report by me, and you shall find my writing true, and in all points which I may please them in I shall be ready to obey them nearest my husband, whom I am most bound to; to whom I most heartily beseech you to be good unto, which, for my sake, is a poor banished man for an honest and a godly cause. And seeing that I have read in old books that some, for as just causes, have by kings and queens been pardoned by the suit of good folks, I trust it shall be our chance, through your good help, to come to the same; as knoweth the (Lord) God, who send you health and heart's ease. Scribbled with her ill hand, who is your poor, humble suitor, always to command,

Mary Stafford.
To the right worshipful and my singular good
friend, Master Secretary to the king's highness,
this be delivered.[47]

Mary's letter is revealing on many levels. Her claim that she was 'in bondage', suggests that prior to her marriage she felt trapped, presumably by familial obligation and the many challenges of being a widow in a patriarchal society. Interestingly, her comment 'that all the world did set so little [store] by me and he so much' shows how unimportant and unloved she felt. Living in the shadow of Anne's quick wit, charisma and sparkling intellect had obviously taken its toll on Mary and goes a long way to explain why William's love and respect meant so much to her, and why, ultimately, she chose to 'take him and to forsake all other ways, and live a poor, honest life with him.' While Mary accepts that as the queen's sister, she could have made a much more advantageous match, she touchingly asserts that she would not give up her loving relationship for any worldly titles or riches, not even to become 'the greatest queen in Christendom'. Perhaps this declaration alludes to the sacrifices Anne had made to reach such dizzying heights. Despite Mary's obvious love and admiration for her husband, she acknowledges that a life without Anne's favour would be a burden 'too heavy to bear', which suggests that at one time the sisters had shared a close bond. But the fact that Mary felt that without the king's support, Anne would never forgive them, betrays just how hurt the queen was and how complicated their relationship had become. It's also a testament to Anne's sheer determination and perhaps hints at some remaining affection between Henry and Mary, if the king was the more likely to take pity on the couple.

Mary's letter also confirms that her parents, Thomas and Elizabeth Boleyn, were equally displeased, and that her maternal uncle, Thomas Howard, Duke of Norfolk, and her brother George were vehemently against the match. There's little doubt that Anne saw her sister's hasty marriage as a terrible betrayal, one which could not have come at a worse time. It wasn't long before another important familial tie was close to being severed. As the country's mood became increasingly volatile, so too did the queen's behaviour.

In January 1535, Chapuys gleefully reported that Henry Percy, Earl of Northumberland, appeared to be turning against Henry and his ministers, and had even spoken to his physician of 'the arrogance and malice of the King's lady'. Anne was said to have 'spoken such shameful words to the Duke of Norfolk as one would not address to a dog.'[48] Admittedly, later in the month, the ambassador confessed that he had been advised to take the earl's words with a pinch of salt, as 'he was very light and hasty.'[49] Anne's deteriorating relationship with her uncle, however, was again alluded to in Chapuys' despatch the following month. According to the ever-watchful ambassador, sometime in early February 1535, Norfolk left court and returned to his house 'very ill-pleased'. Prior to his departure, he complained to Henry, Lord

Montagu, that he was held in no esteem.[50] We might dismiss these stories as the fabrication of her enemies, if it wasn't for the fact that Anne's sharp tongue is well documented. Moreover, the extreme stress she was under only enhanced her irritability. Anne's outspokenness was only part of the problem. The conservative Duke of Norfolk had become increasingly uncomfortable with his niece's reformist leanings. This tension between Anne and her uncle was a telling sign of the religious turmoil that was tearing the country apart.

Following the break with Rome, some traditional Catholic devotional practices and the doctrines that underpinned them came under fire and reforms were implemented over time. There were some issues that were too contentious to tackle early on, so, in April 1534, Archbishop Thomas Cranmer forbade preachers to mention these in their sermons: 'no preacher for a year to preach either for or against purgatory, honouring the Saints, marriage of priests, justification by faith, pilgrimages, miracles.'[51] The ban, however, as Eamon Duffy points out, was disingenuous.[52] Evangelicals, backed by Thomas Cromwell and conservatives alike, continued to take to the pulpits to defend their beliefs, and the English people were left utterly confused. In order to bring an end to the 'diversity in opinions' and ensure 'the profit, tranquillity, and quietness' of the realm, in the summer of 1536, Convocation agreed on a set of articles, which not only addressed religious doctrine, but also ceremonies and rites.[53] The articles were published with a preface in the king's name in which he styled himself, 'Henry the Eight, by the Grace of God, King of England, and of France, Defender of the Faith, and Lord of Ireland, and in Earth Supreme Head of the Church of England', a title he had adopted in January 1535.[54] The king urged his subjects to follow his articles in order to 'attain that most charitable unity and loving concord, whereof shall ensue your incomparable commodity, profit and lucre'. Their obedience in the matter would also encourage 'us [Henry] to take further travel, pains, and labours for your commodities in all such other matters, as in time to come may happen to occur.'[55] Duffy notes that these Ten Articles 'were the first official doctrinal formulary of the Church of England'.[56] They reflected the struggle between conservatives and reformers, but they also reflected the religious confusion that existed at the time. The Ten Articles did little to settle some of the most controversial debates. For example, on the question of purgatory, prayers and masses for the dead, which might relieve souls of 'some part of their pain', were deemed commendable forms of Christian charity. However, in regards to the details, it was fairly ambiguous:

> But forasmuch as the place where they be, the name thereof and kind of pains there, also be to us uncertain by Scripture; therefore this with all

other things we remit to God Almighty, unto whose mercy it is meet and convenient for us to commend them, trusting that God accepteth our prayers for them, referring the rest wholly to God, to whom is known their estate and condition.[57]

The article did, however, condemn the belief that 'through the Bishop of Rome's pardon, souls might... be delivered out of Purgatory, and all the pains of it'. This and other 'abuses' like the popular 'Scala Coeli' indulgence were denounced.

In regards to the veneration of images, as they were 'representers [*sic*] of virtue and good example' it was acceptable for them to be displayed in the churches, however, the bishops and preachers were to teach the people that idolatry was forbidden by God. As for the custom of censing the images and kneeling before them, this was permitted as long as the people were taught that regardless of whose image they knelt before, they were worshipping only God and not the image.

Henry hoped that his articles would help unite his people and quell the debates, but in fact they only served to further divide his subjects. As Peter Marshall reminds us, the fact that modern historians can't agree on whether the Ten Articles was a victory for the conservatives or the reformers 'mirrors the confusion of contemporaries'.[58]

Up until this point, it's been argued that all Henry had done was 'in effect, create an English Catholic Church'.[59] Even after 1536, the king remained fairly conservative and his religious policies were 'neither thoroughly Protestant nor thoroughly Catholic'.[60]

By the time the articles and the injunctions that followed were issued in the summer of 1536, Anne was already in her shallow grave in the Tower of London. Nevertheless, they spotlight the issues that were being discussed and debated during her lifetime, discussions that Anne undoubtedly took part in. The religious tug of war was a great source of confusion, but other difficulties loomed.

Excessive rainfall led to failing crops and famine, which further intensified the unease and disgruntlement, and with the warmer weather came pestilence. Against this turbulent backdrop, Anne Boleyn navigated the sunlit peaks and desolate valleys of the final year of her life.

Chapter 2

She is my death and I am hers

The court greeted the arrival of spring at Hampton Court, where the violets and primroses were just beginning to bloom. Situated on the banks of the River Thames, upstream of Westminster, the palace was originally built for Cardinal Thomas Wolsey, as a place for entertaining royalty, foreign ambassadors and dignitaries. Following Wolsey's fall from favour, for failing to secure the king an annulment of his marriage to Katherine, the king took possession of the palatial residence and embarked on an enormous building campaign that would transform it into one of the most magnificent royal residences in the country, as attested to by the diaries of a number of foreign visitors who toured the palace in the mid- to late sixteenth century. In August 1554, Pedro de Hoyo, concluded that it was 'the finest house in the country and some say the world', a sentiment echoed by Jacob Rathgeb, secretary to the Duke of Württemberg.[1] In 1592, he noted in his diary that 'this is the most splendid and magnificent royal palace that may be found in England or indeed in any other kingdom'.[2]

It was, of course, a palace that Anne knew well. She had her own accommodation there as early as 1529, when a pane of glass was mended in 'mistress anne boulleyns lodgyng', and had stimulated Henry's interest in architecture from these early days of their relationship.[3] Her position as queen allowed her to directly influence the development of the palace, something Anne had taken full advantage of. For the last two years, workmen had been building lavish new rooms expressly for her, and there is little doubt that Anne was 'intimately involved' in their planning.[4] The queen's new apartments were built on the east side of a new courtyard, overlooking the park, and decorated in the latest fashion. To the north stood a gallery that connected the queen's lodgings to the king's, and to the west was another gallery. The quadrangle was completed by the king's long gallery on the south side, which overlooked the privy gardens and the river beyond. All four sides were raised up on arches and encircled a knot garden, hence the seventeenth-century name for the quadrangle, Cloister Green Court. Thanks to the decades-long research conducted by Dr Simon Thurley, we have an idea of the internal arrangement of the interconnecting rooms built for Anne. The new queen's lodgings contained a 'watching chamber', with an adjoining page's chamber;

a 'presence chamber', which doubled as the queen's dining room and had two 'jakes' or toilets attached to it; a 'withdrawing chamber', also referred to in the records as a 'raying chamber', with an adjoining closet; a 'bed chamber'; and a 'jewel chamber'. Situated beneath the lodgings was a privy kitchen and larder, a wardrobe for the queen's clothing and a nursery, which the royal couple hoped would soon resound with the cries of a lusty Tudor prince. A door from Anne's presence chamber led to a room for the queen's ladies-in-waiting.[5]

Anne's apartments were not completed until early 1536, therefore, it's unlikely that she would have stayed in them during the March visit. On this occasion, she was probably accommodated in the old lodgings built for her predecessor. While she may not have lived to make use of her lavish new suite, she did get to enjoy the palace's stunning gardens, which, in time, would become almost more lauded than the palace itself.

By March 1535, two orchards grew on the north side of the palace and the king's new gardens were laid on the south side. Among other notable features, the southern gardens consisted of a private area for the monarch, known as a privy garden; a triangular-shaped garden containing ponds, called the Pond Yard; and a garden containing a mound, known as the Mount Garden. The latter was home to four double-storey brick 'herbers' or arbours, where the royal couple could enjoy intimate banquets – an after-dinner course of sweet dishes and other delicacies – and a principal banqueting house for more formal occasions. Each compartment was enclosed by tall brick walls, and the earth banks or terraces that ran around the inside perimeter of the walls offered guests splendid views over the gardens and surrounding landscape. The gardens at Hampton Court were both ornamental and practical, as they provided an abundance of fruit and herbs for the royal kitchens, including apples, pears, strawberries and mint, as well as flowers cultivated to flavour sweets and desserts, like marigolds, violets and roses. In the warmer months, this outdoor space was considered an extension of the palace, and important guests were often received and entertained outside. In inclement weather the gardens could also be enjoyed from the palace galleries above.

Hampton Court was built to inspire awe and was designed to showcase the Tudor dynasty's power and magnificence. Foreign dignitaries, whom Henry was always keen to impress, were a constant presence at court. The French ambassador, Charles de Solier, Sieur de Morette, whom Hans Holbein the Younger immortalised in an astoundingly lifelike portrait, and Palamedes Gontier, the Treasurer of Brittany, were with the king at Hampton Court from 24 February until 2 March.[6] They were at court to discuss the proposed marriage between the Princess Elizabeth and Francis I's son, Charles, the

Duke of Angoulême, and a possible treaty between Henry and his 'best beloved brother', Francis.

Relations between the two nations had become strained following a disastrous French embassy to England the previous year, headed by Philippe de Chabot, Count of Brion and Admiral of France. Both Henry and Anne were under the impression that the purpose of the admiral's visit in November 1534 was to renew amicable relations with France, by negotiating a marriage between the Princess Elizabeth and the Dauphin, Francis I's eldest son, Francis. This match would show the world that the king of France accepted the legitimacy of Henry's marriage to Anne and acknowledged that Elizabeth, and not Mary, was the king's rightful heir. Imagine the royal couple's disappointment when the admiral proposed a match between the Dauphin and Mary instead. To make matters worse, the architect of this proposal was none other than Charles V himself, who, in October 1534, sent Henry, Count of Nassau, to France with the suggestion.[7] Needless to say, Anne was furious. The proposal implied that Francis, the man whom Anne had long considered her patron, believed that Mary had a better claim to the throne than her own daughter. After the years Anne had spent promoting French interests in England, this was a blatant and hurtful insult. The fact it was 'noted by several persons' that during the visit the French ambassador failed to show Anne the courtesy which her position demanded only exacerbated the problem.[8] Henry responded with a proposal of his own – a marriage between the Princess Elizabeth and the Duke of Angoulême, which was received with callous indifference.[9]

Despite the obvious tension, the admiral was lavishly entertained by the Dukes of Norfolk and Richmond, and on the eve of his departure, the king honoured him with a grand feast. Anne's behaviour on this occasion betrayed her emotional fragility. According to Chapuys, while dancing with the French envoy, Anne 'burst into a fit of uncontrollable laughter without any occasion'. The admiral thought Anne was laughing at him, but Anne explained that she was laughing 'because the King had told her he was going to ask for the Admiral's secretary [Gontier] to amuse her, and that the King had met on the way a lady who made him forget the matter'.[10]

Anne feared that the loss of French support for her marriage would be detrimental. At her next meeting with Gontier, the admiral's secretary, in February 1535, Anne confessed her fears and urged him to persuade Chabot to act. The delay in answering the king's counter-proposal had sparked doubts in the king. The secretary described the rest of the encounter in a letter to his master:

She said the Admiral must think of applying some remedy, and act towards the King so that she may not be ruined and lost, for she sees herself very near that, and in more grief and trouble than before her marriage. She charged him to beg the Admiral to consider her affairs, of which she could not speak as fully as she wished, on account of her fears, and the eyes which were looking at her, her husband's and the lords' present. She said she could not write, nor see him again, nor stay longer. She then left him, the King going to the next room, where the dance was beginning... without the said Lady going thither. As far as he can judge, she is not at her ease on account of the doubts and suspicions of the King, which he has mentioned before.[11]

By Anne's own admission, she was in a very precarious situation. She had spent her formative years in France. She probably spoke with a French lilt and was considered by the English 'wholly French – in style and elegance, in dress, in sympathy and in culture'.[12] This, coupled with her exotic looks and fierce intelligence, is why she had stood out when she first arrived back at the English court in late 1521, and it's why Henry became captivated by her. But now, with relations between the two nations deteriorating and Henry's suspicions mounting, being 'wholly French' was a huge liability.

Despite the challenges, negotiations continued. The ambassador and Gontier departed Hampton Court, armed with Henry's answer to the French proposal, and went to London to see Cromwell, who had for more than a fortnight been 'vexed with an ague' that had left him with a swollen eye and cheek.[13] The king, meanwhile, busied himself responding to letters from Philippe de Chabot, Count of Brion. He explained why he was unable to agree to the propositions made by the treasurer and responded to each 'article of his charge *seriatum*'.[14] He laced his demands with flattery and reminded Francis that 'there is nothing we desire more than that our friendship should be indissoluble'.[15] Cromwell rallied to pen his own letter in which he expressed the hope that the admiral would 'do his best to remove all suspicion, and prevent their enemies from having any cause to suspect the interruption of their friendship'.[16] There can be no doubt that what Henry and Anne wanted was for Francis to make a public commitment to their cause. The king even went as far as providing Francis with a declaration, which he pressed him to confirm:

The French king, having been informed by the most learned of his kingdom of the discussion concerning the pretended marriage of the king of England and the princess dowager Katharine, and the validity of the dispensation for the said marriage, and having considered the King's

present marriage and the sentence given by pope Clement, promises
to maintain the said second marriage of the king of England with his
present queen Anne as legitimate and immutable, and the issue therefrom
legitimate and capable of inheriting England, and the daughter of the
first marriage to be illegitimate; that he will maintain the sentence given
by Clement, and any others given in the future, to be contrary to human
and divine law, and he will endeavour to procure their revocation. If, by
reason of this marriage, the king of England, his heirs or successors, are
molested, Francis will give them aid against any one attacking them.[17]

In the end, Henry suggested that as he 'was the first inventor of that knot'
– the proposed marriage – he would send representatives to Calais to
negotiate the conditions around Whitsuntide.[18] Importantly, many of the
original documents pertaining to the marriage negotiations contain passages,
additions and corrections made in the king's own hand. As Seth Lerer has
noted, 'the king loathed writing, hated even signing his own name', rarely
personally wrote to other men, and only occasionally reviewed and corrected
official proclamations and ambassadorial exchanges.[19] That he did so on this
occasion shows how deeply invested Henry was in these negotiations.

Copies of the letters sent to the king from France were mailed to Anne's
father at Hever Castle, who happily declared that 'matters are in very good
train, and I reckon he [the king] will have of the Admiral there, if he be well
used, a sure servant for all his affairs there'.[20]

Regardless of the mounting challenges, Anne was still Queen of England
and, as such, had to attend to the running of her household, including
overseeing the provision of livery for her staff. Sadly, virtually nothing is
known of its appearance, although in general terms, 'livery was clothing
marked with sewn or embroidered badges'.[21] Servants dressed in Anne's livery
could be easily identified as part of her household and, as Michelle L. Beer
has noted, 'amplified the queen's presence at court, serving as visual proxies
for the queen wherever they went'.[22] The livery for Anne's household may
have been embroidered with Anne's own personal emblems, including the
crowned white falcon. The only mention of it appears in the *Lisle Letters*,
an illuminating collection of the personal and official correspondence of the
household of Arthur Plantagenet, Viscount Lisle, who was an illegitimate
but acknowledged son of Edward IV and, thus, an uncle of Henry VIII. He
and his wife, Honor Grenville, Viscountess Lisle, regularly corresponded
with their family, friends and associates in England and abroad, offering an
unparalleled window into daily life in the period. The letters, which date
from 1533 to 1540 when Lisle was Lord Deputy of Calais, survive because

they were confiscated by Henry following his uncle's arrest in 1540 on suspicion of treason. Of the circa 3,000 letters that make up the collection, John Husee, their London agent, is responsible for 515 of them.[23] On 12 March 1535, he wrote to inform Lady Lisle that 'the Queen's Grace liketh your kersey specially well'.[24] Kersey was a woollen fabric that varied widely in cost and quality. It was used to make 'hose, petticoats, stockings, linings, [and] cloaks', and, at the time, was the material that all adult elite women would have used to make their hose.[25] Presumably, the kersey that Lady Lisle had sent Anne was of the very best quality. Husee also mentioned that 'Mr. Receiver', whom we shall shortly meet, 'saith your ladyship shall have a livery'. A month later he noted, 'touching your ladyship's kirtle of the Queen's livery, your Ladyship shall be assured thereof before midsummer.'[26] In the end, it wasn't until 18 March 1536 that Thomas Warley, another of Lisle's retainers, happily reported that he had the kirtle, 'which is of cloth of gold paned'.[27] While we don't know the details of the livery issued to Anne's household during her reign, we do know that in December 1530, when the Crown's bid to have Henry's first marriage annulled moved sluggishly towards its goal, Anne briefly adopted the haughty motto, *Ainsi sera, groigne qui groigne* ('let them grumble, that is how it's going to be'), which she may have learned from Margaret of Austria, and had it embroidered onto her household's livery.[28] This defiant act speaks to Anne's assertiveness, but it also shows how strain could bring out her reckless side.

Apart from overseeing the activities of her Wardrobe, Anne would have also devoted time to responding to petitions. On 8 March, she wrote to Thomas Cromwell asking him to intercede on behalf of one John Baptist, the king's dyer:

> Trusty and right well beloved we greet you well, desiring you to give firm credence unto our trusty and right well beloved Councillor George Taylor squire our receiver in those things as he hath in commandment of us to show unto you concerning our well beloved John Baptist the King my lord's dyer. Given under our signet, at my said lord's manor of Hampton Court on the 8th day of March.[29]

George Taylor was Anne's receiver general, a position which carried a generous yearly salary of £50.[30] He had been in her service since at least 1528 and continued in her employ until her death.[31] His position primarily involved making and receiving payments on Anne's behalf, but, as the abovementioned letter shows, he also conducted other business. On this occasion, his visit to Cromwell was a success. The following month, John Baptist received a full pardon for all the penalties he had incurred by 'using the art of calendering of worsteds'.[32] In 1533, an Act of Parliament was passed, which specified that 'dyers of worsteds shall not calender them'. This particular offence carried a penalty of 40 shillings, about a month's wage for a skilled labourer, and forfeiture of the cloth.[33] Anne's intervention would have undoubtedly earned the gratitude of the king's dyer and forged a bond of loyalty with her subject.

In this instance, we see Anne successfully fulfilling the long-established queenly role of intercessor and mediator of patronage. Queenly petitions could be elaborately staged events, like when in May 1517, Katherine of Aragon pleaded for the lives of a number of young apprentices, who were awaiting execution for participating in the 'Evil May Day' riots, against foreigners residing in London. According to Francesco Chieregati, Pope Leo X's representative in London, 'our most serene and most compassionate Queen, with tears in her eyes and on her bended knees, obtained their pardon from his Majesty, the act of grace being performed with great ceremony.'[34] Anne's letter to Cromwell, however, shows that many requests were handled in private, by the queen and her councillors as part of the daily running of her household.

At around the same time as Anne's receiver general delivered the queen's letter to Cromwell, he received another, from an equally resolute woman – Katherine of Aragon. The letter is fascinating for a number of reasons, including its extremely personal tone established from the very opening line, which begins, 'Special friend'.[35] The other intriguing thing is that it's written in Spanish. This is precisely why it's been largely dismissed by historians, who have assumed that Cromwell did not speak Spanish, and therefore could not have been the intended recipient of Katherine's letter. But as Professor Diarmaid MacCulloch has noted in his biography of the king's chief minister, Cromwell 'had a gift for learning languages'.[36] He was fluent in Italian and French, understood Latin, and could at the very least read Spanish, as evidenced, not only by Katherine's letter, but by a letter penned by Chapuys following his recall in early 1539.[37] After a decade of friendship, the ambassador chose to write his farewell letter to Cromwell in Spanish – proof beyond doubt that the chief minister was comfortable with Katherine's native tongue. Katherine's original letter, which is undated, is recorded under September 1534 in *Letters and Papers*, but its content suggests that it belongs to March 1535.[38] MacCulloch observed, 'that rather unusually in Cromwell's correspondence', he had Katherine's letter carefully translated into English, probably for the benefit of other councillors, or even the king himself.[39] While Cromwell is not identified in the salutation, there can be little doubt, as we shall shortly see, that he was indeed the intended recipient.

Special Friend,

You have greatly bound me with the pains, that you have taken in speaking to the King my Lord concerning the coming of my daughter unto me. The reward you shall trust to have of God. For (as you know) in me there is no power to gratify that you have done, but only with my good will. As touching the answer, which has been made you, that his Highness is contented to send her to some place nigh me, so as I do not see her; I pray you, vouchsafe to give unto his Highness mine effectual thanks for the goodness, which he sheweth unto his daughter and mine, and for the comfort, that I have thereby received: and as to my seeing of her, you shall certify, that if she were within one mile of me, I would not see her. For the time permitteth not that I should go about sights; and, be it that I would, I could not, because I lack provision therefore. Howbeit you shall always say unto his Highness, that the thing, which I desired was to send her, where I am, being assured that a little comfort and mirth, which she should take with me, should undoubtedly be half a health unto her. I have proved the like by experience, being diseased of the same infirmity, and know, how much good it may do, that I say. And since I desired a thing so just and reasonable, and so much touched the honour and conscience of the King my Lord, I thought not it should have been denied me. Let not (for my love) to do what you may, that this may be yet done. Here have I among others heard, that he had some suspicion of the surety of her ['*alguna sospecha de la seguridad de ella*']. I cannot believe, that a thing so far from reason should pass from the royal heart of his Highness. Neither can I think that he hath so little confidence in me. If any such matter chance to be communed of, I pray you say unto his Highness, that I am determined to die (without doubt) in his realm, and that I from henceforth offer mine own person for surety, to the intent, that if any such thing should be attempted, that then he do justice of me, as of the most evil woman, that ever was born. The residue I remit to your good wisdom and judgement, as unto a trusty friend, to whom I pray God give health.[40]

While Katherine was obviously pleased that Henry had agreed to move Mary closer, with the proviso that she not see her daughter, she did not conceal her utter disappointment at Henry's refusal of her request to have Mary live with her, which was, of course, Katherine's greatest desire. Her remark about Henry's suspicions surrounding Mary's security – and her passionate denial of any such threat – are a testament to how far Katherine was willing to go to protect her interests. Katherine was well aware that Chapuys and the emperor had considered plans for Mary's 'escape'. Not only was she aware, but she had long been tacitly urging her nephew to do something to improve their situation. It's clear that this was not a letter to Chapuys or to any one of her other Imperial supporters. This was a letter that Katherine knew would reach Henry's distrustful eyes. However, the question remains, if Cromwell is not mentioned by name in the original letter, how do we know it was meant for him? From the contents, it's clear that the recipient was a man close to the king, one who understood Spanish and whose position enabled him to discuss such delicate and personal matters. Who else but Thomas Cromwell?

A letter from Chapuys to the emperor, written on 4 March 1535, provides further evidence and firmly dates Katherine's letter to this period:

> He [Cromwell] assured me he had forgotten nothing of what was said between us, and had obtained permission of the King that the Princess should be placed in some house near her mother for the convenience of the physician and apothecary. He had not gained leave for the Queen to see her, but by degrees all would be accomplished.[41]

While Katherine was astute enough to understand the importance of keeping the king's right-hand man on side, she also knew better than to trust in his promises. Later in the month, she warned her ambassador 'not to show himself either distrustful or very friendly, because he will be deceived' and advised him to 'practise reserve'.[42] Evidently, Chapuys was well aware of the need for caution because, in April, he confessed to the emperor that although Cromwell had always spoken of his loyalty to Mary, he had done little to prove it.[43]

Even though Katherine had offered 'her own person for surety' if Mary would only be permitted to reside with her, and proclaimed that she was determined to die in England, it did little to assuage Henry's fears. On 19 March, after being informed that his eldest daughter was once again ailing, the king left Hampton Court and visited Elizabeth and Mary's household at Greenwich. Mary's own household had been disbanded in November 1533, at which time she was forced to join her half-sister's, where precedence was, as one would expect, given to Princess Elizabeth.[44] To add to Mary's humiliation, Anne Boleyn's paternal aunt, Lady Anne Shelton, and her husband, Sir John Shelton, were put in overall charge of the establishment.[45] When Chapuys bravely broached the subject of Mary's awkward situation with the king and asked that, at the very least, Margaret Pole, Countess of Salisbury – a devout Roman Catholic and close confidante of Katherine of Aragon – be restored to her position as Mary's governess, he responded by saying that the countess was 'a fool, of no experience'.[46] Elizabeth's care was entrusted to

Lady Margaret Bryan, Anne's mother's half-sister. At first glance, Anne may appear solely responsible for this appointment. Understandably, she wanted to surround her daughter with people whom she could trust – with family. However, Lady Margaret Bryan had previously served as lady mistress to Mary during her infancy, so the choice must have been Henry's.[47] Moreover, as Professor Ives concluded, when it came to major decisions concerning Elizabeth's upbringing, 'Henry and his council had the last word'.[48]

Upon the king's arrival at Greenwich, he enquired about Mary's health and spoke to her governess and other members of the household. When one of the physicians tried to speak to the king of the seriousness of Mary's illness, Henry accused him of disloyalty. As far as he was concerned, it was all a ploy to convince him to allow Mary to see her mother, something he declared he would never permit, because Katherine, 'being so haughty in spirit', might use the opportunity to 'raise a number of men, and make war' as boldly as her mother Isabella had done. During his overnight stay, Henry did not see Mary, nor did he send her any comforting words. Instead, he sent Lady Shelton to tell her that 'he had no worse enemy in the world than her, and that she was the cause of mischief to the greater number of Christian princes'. He ended his tirade by accusing Mary of encouraging 'conspiracy against him'. Before his departure, he instructed Lady Shelton to continue to receive the Imperial ambassador's servants, but to not allow them to see Mary, 'as they might conspire to carry the Princess [Mary] off'.[49]

There's no record of the king having visited Elizabeth while at Greenwich, although it's entirely possible that he did. There's also nothing to suggest that Anne joined the king on this occasion. Regardless, Anne bore the brunt of public opprobrium. It was much easier to lay the blame for Mary's ill-treatment at Anne's feet, instead of accepting that in this matter, Henry needed no coaxing. As this incident illustrates, the king was incensed at his daughter. Like her mother, Mary had obstinately refused to submit to the king's will. She had refused to accept the king's supremacy, the invalidity of her parents' marriage and, thus, her own illegitimacy. This disobedience, especially from one's own daughter, Henry found unnatural and intolerable. Chapuys had difficulty reconciling the king, who often warmly and graciously received him at court, with the man who refused to allow his poorly daughter the company of her mother. While he was adamant that Anne was the cause of all the troubles that had befallen his two favourite ladies, he was under no illusions about Henry's character. In a letter to the emperor he observed: 'I considered the King of such a nature that he did not like to be conquered by another, either by words or otherwise… he desired only to conquer himself and do things of his own free will.'[50]

When it comes to Anne's treatment of her teenage stepdaughter, Chapuys' correspondences are littered with tales of Anne's lurid and murderous threats against Mary. In February 1534, he warned the emperor that 'a gentleman told me yesterday that the earl of Northumberland told him that he knew for certain that she [Anne] had determined to poison the Princess'.[51] According to another of his unnamed sources, Anne also instructed Lady Shelton to ban Mary from using the title of Princess and, if she disobeyed, to 'box her ears as a cursed bastard'.[52] The following month, he confessed to his master that he feared 'the Lady' intended, by any means possible, to 'bring down the pride of this unbridled Spanish blood'.[53] In June, 'a person of good faith' informed the ambassador that if, as expected, Henry went to Calais to meet Francis I and Anne was made regent, she would take the opportunity to put Mary to death, 'either by hunger or otherwise'. When Anne's brother, Lord Rochford, reminded her that this would anger the king, she supposedly declared that 'she did not care even if she was burned alive for it after'.[54] If we are to believe Chapuys, Anne constantly spoke of Katherine and Mary as rebels and traitors deserving death, and was willing to resort to poison if needed. She even allegedly 'suborned a person to say that he has had a revelation from God that she cannot conceive while the said two ladies are alive.'[55]

What to make of all of this? As we've already noted, Chapuys was not in the habit of intentionally misleading his master, however, caution is called for because his unabashed loyalty and devotion to Katherine and Mary made him a natural ally for Anne's enemies at court. It's likely that on some occasions he was fed misleading information about Anne and the Boleyns, which, despite his experience and discernment, he reported in his letters. It's also important to bear in mind that there is only one recorded instance of Chapuys and Anne ever coming face to face, therefore, all of the ambassador's information about Anne came from other sources, most of them hostile to the queen.[56] At the very least, the portrait that Chapuys painted of Anne was heavily skewed and we need to look to other sources to balance it.

This is not to say that Anne was faultless. On the contrary, her fiery temper is well documented and her actions could often be counterproductive, especially when she was under undue stress. While Anne was capable of very sophisticated thinking, she was impulsive and prone to ranting when she felt threatened. Her innate outspokenness adds weight to Chapuys' reports, but the evidence also clearly demonstrates that the threats were borne out of sheer frustration and distress, rather than hatred. If Anne did make death threats against Mary, the lack of any corroborating sources or actual incriminating evidence other than hearsay, must lead us to conclude that Anne was blustering.

On at least three separate occasions, the queen extended the hand of friendship to Mary, only to be very publicly rebuffed. The first was in early 1534 when, on a visit to see her infant daughter, a pregnant Anne offered to reconcile Mary with her father, if only she would visit her and accept her as queen.[57] Not even the promise of being 'as well or better treated than ever' helped soften Mary's resolve. She retorted 'that she knew no queen in England except her mother', but that if the king's mistress, 'Madame Anne de Bolans', would do her the favour of interceding with her father, she would be much obliged. Despite the very public insult, Anne repeated her offer of friendship, but to no avail. Understandably, the rejection left Anne feeling indignant, and, as we've already noted, she vowed to 'bring down the pride of this unbridled Spanish blood'.[58]

That April, Sir William Kingston penned a letter to Lord Lisle in which he happily reported that 'this day the King and the Queen was [*sic*] at Eltham, and there saw my lady Princess, which is a godly child as hath been seen, and her Grace is much in the King's favour, as a godly child should be.'[59] It was probably during this visit that Anne, whose swelling belly was now visible for all to see, made another attempt at reconciliation.[60] What follows was recorded in *The Life of Jane Dormer* by Henry Clifford. Again, caution is required as it was written by an English Catholic hostile to Anne and Elizabeth, and was not begun until after Jane Dormer's death in 1613. Although Jane was born two years after Anne's execution, she did go on to serve Mary during her queenship – and later married an influential Spanish nobleman, the Duke of Feria – so it's possible that she heard this story directly from Mary, whom, by all accounts, she became close to. Henry Clifford collected the information for his biography during the years in which he resided in Jane Dormer's household. We pick up the story in the chapel of Eltham Palace, where Anne found herself with Mary:

> At the end of Mass, the Lady Mary made a low courtesy and went to her lodging; so did the Lady Anne, then called queen. When she came to her quarter, one of her maids told her that the Lady Mary at parting made reverence to her, she answered that she did not observe it; and said, 'If we had seen it, we would have done as much to her;' and presently sent a lady of honour to her, to excuse it; adding that the love of none, should be dearer nor more respected than hers, and she would embrace it with the kindness of a true friend. The lady that carried the message came when the Lady Mary was sat down at dinner. When admitted, she said; 'The queen salutes your grace with much affection and craves pardon, understanding that at your parting from the oratory, you made a courtesy

to her, which if she had seen, she would have answered you with the like; and she desires that this may be an entrance of friendly correspondence, which your grace shall find completely to be embraced on her part.' 'It is not possible,' answered the Lady Mary, 'that the queen can send me such a message; nor is it fit she should, nor can it be so sudden, her majesty being so far from this place. You would have said, the Lady Anne Boleyn, for I can acknowledge no other queen but my mother, nor esteem them my friends who are not hers. And for the reverence that I made, it was to the altar, to her Maker and mine; and so they are deceived, and deceive her who tell her otherwise.' The Lady Anne was maddened with this answer, replying that one day, she would pull down this high spirit.[61]

Anne's anger is understandable, for this was no ordinary family feud. By refusing to acknowledge Anne as queen, and by denying Elizabeth's precedence, Mary was effectively stating that she was still the heir to the Tudor throne. At every opportunity, she relished in snubbing her half-sister. Whenever they were being relocated, she refused to walk by Elizabeth's side or share a litter with her sibling. She would not pay court to her unless, as Chapuys recounts, she was 'compelled by sheer force', in which case she would then publicly protest against the violence used. Mary even went out of her way to ensure that she got the best seat on the royal barge.[62] Even the Imperial ambassador felt that she went too far, informing Charles V that 'I should never have advised the Princess to go to such an extremity for fear of her over-irritating the King, her father, and giving him occasion and excuse for treating her worse than he is doing at present.'[63] He strongly advised her to maintain 'her usual modesty, to speak boldly and show good heart, and yet not to carry things to such extremity as to oblige her guards to use violence'.[64] Mary's behaviour, however, had her mother's stamp of approval: 'the Queen, her mother, and some of her friends, have for some time been thinking that it was better for the Princess to act thus, and show her teeth to the King.' Chapuys disagreed with Katherine and feared that Mary's inflexibility would 'further damage her cause', but such was his loyalty that he was 'ready to soften down, for her honour and advantage, the rather rigorous terms I have lately used respecting the Princess's treatment'.[65]

Even though the Act of Succession had illegitimatised Mary and vested the succession on Henry and Anne's children, canon law stipulated that 'a child born to a couple who at the time were apparently lawfully married, remained legitimate even if it was subsequently found that the union had been invalid.'[66] Mary's parents had been married for almost twenty-four years, so if anyone could argue that they had been born in *bona fide parentum*, it was Mary. For this reason, her continued endorsement of her mother's right to the crown and insistence on using the title of princess greatly alarmed and frustrated Anne. These were not just the rebellious acts of a stubborn teenager; they were the studied actions of a rival claimant to Elizabeth's throne. When conciliatory gestures failed to win Mary over, Anne's apprehensiveness drove her to make violent threats. Ultimately, Anne knew that to settle the matter of the succession once and for all, Mary needed to concede her claim, or Anne needed to give birth to a healthy son. She reached out one final time in January 1536. By that time, Katherine was already in her grave and Anne was once again with child. The queen offered to be like another mother to Mary and obtain for her anything that she desired. She even promised that if Mary came to court, she would be exempt from 'being her train-bearer, and might walk by her side'.[67] Still, Mary would not budge. Instead, she responded that she 'would rather suffer a hundred deaths than change her opinion, or do anything against her honour and conscience'.[68] This bitter battle of wills was exhausting. It's little wonder that in the end Anne declared, 'She is my death and I am hers.'[69]

Following Henry's overnight stay at Greenwich, he returned to Hampton Court, where preparations were well under way for the court's removal to Richmond Palace for Easter. On Tuesday, 23 March, Anne boarded the royal barge with her ladies, her mind perhaps wandering to her daughter's establishment, which on the very same day was being moved to Hunsdon House in Hertfordshire.[70] Unbeknownst to the queen, this visit marked her last extended stay at the riverside mansion. The monumental building campaign that encompassed many areas of the palace, not just the new eastern courtyard, prevented the court from returning until May 1537, by which time Anne was but an unspoken memory. She returned for a brief sojourn in April 1535, forced to flee to Hampton Court, as John Husee recounted in a letter to Lord Lisle, 'by reason one of her gentlewomen sickened of the measles'.[71] But she would never again witness the birth of spring from its splendid galleries.

Chapter 3

Perseverance

Approaching Richmond Palace from the river, the royal party took in the splendid facade of the state apartments, built in white stone and rising three storeys high from the banks of the Thames. The appeal of the riverside exterior was greatly enhanced by a series of picturesque towers, surmounted by cupolas and gilded gold weather vanes. The building stood on the site of two former royal houses: the first, known as Sheen or Shene Palace, was enlarged and beautified during the reign of Richard II, who lived at Richmond with his wife, Anne of Bohemia. While the couple were in residence, the queen fell ill and died suddenly in June 1394. Overcome by grief, the king ordered that the palace be demolished.[1] The second royal house, commenced by Henry V in 1414 and completed under Henry VI, was largely destroyed by fire in 1497, after which time, Henry VII embarked on a rebuilding programme.[2] The stone donjon, which formed the nucleus of the Lancastrian palace, was retained by Henry and served much the same purpose as during the rule of his predecessors – it was 'the heart of his building'.[3] The interior was reconstructed and transformed into luxurious apartments for the royal family, which boasted a series of fine rooms spread across three storeys. The second and third floors were occupied by apartments for the queen and king respectively, which overlooked the galleried gardens – the first of their kind in England – while the lower level contained the privy kitchen and wardrobe, and other service rooms. Other new additions included a great hall, chapel and outer courtyard, and a magnificent orchard, which, in 1501, was home to 'many marvellous beasts, as lions, dragons, and such other of divers kind, properly fashioned and carved in the ground'.[4] Like Hampton Court, Richmond was a pleasure palace and, as such, the gardens contained many recreational facilities, including 'pleasant galleries and houses of pleasure to disport in at chess, tables, dice, cards... bowling alleys, butts for archers, and goodly tennis plays.'[5]

The enclosing galleries also provided access to the adjoining Observant Franciscan friary, founded by Henry VII in 1502. According to G.W. Bernard, 'they were among the most rigorous of monastic orders in early Tudor England'; therefore, it's not surprising that they were among the first to openly and publicly disapprove of Henry VIII's desire for an annulment.[6]

In these luxurious surroundings, the king and court spent Easter 1535, with the exception of Palm Sunday, also known as Passion Sunday, which marked the start of Holy Week.[7] As Maria Hayward explains, 'on Palm Sunday the priest blessed the palms or branches brought by the congregation in remembrance of the palms spread before Christ on the entry into Jerusalem'.[8] Presumably, the court observed this practice at Hampton Court as they only arrived at Richmond on Tuesday, 23 March.[9] It was one of a number of important court rituals in which the king processed under a cloth of estate or canopy to the chapel.

Another of the principal religious practices attached to Easter was the *pedilavium*, the ritual washing of the feet of the poor on Maundy Thursday, sometimes called Sheer Thursday. This ceremony, which took place on the day before Good Friday, had been part of the church service for many centuries. It commemorated the Last Supper where, at the end of the meal, Christ washed the feet of his twelve disciples and instructed them to imitate his charity: 'If I then, your Lord and Master, have washed your feet, ye also ought to wash one another's feet. For I have given you an example, that ye should do as I have done unto you.'[10] According to Professor Carole Levin, Edward II was the first English monarch to hold a Maundy in the nineteenth year of his reign, when he washed the feet of fifty poor men.[11] While previous monarchs had been involved in the Maundy, typically by distributing alms to the poor, Levin argues that given Edward's political problems at the time, he may have taken a more active role in the ceremony to enhance his prestige.[12] Its association with medieval monarchs continued and gradually it became customary 'for the sovereign to provide a meal and to also give gifts of clothing, food, and money to the poor people involved.'[13]

As it was considered a day of mourning at the Tudor court, and also an occasion for crown-wearing, the monarch dressed in either blue – the official royal colour of mourning, as Henry VII wore at his Maundy observances in 1503 – or violet, which was also associated with mourning.[14] While the king took centre stage at this important court ritual, the Tudor queens were also involved. In March 1502, Richard Pain, Elizabeth of York's almoner, provided her with money to distribute to thirty-seven poor women at her Maundy.[15] (It was common practice for the number of poor people to equal the monarch's age or the monarch's age plus one.) Like her mother-in-law, Katherine of Aragon also distributed alms to poor women, as well as gifts of clothing. In 1520, Katherine's 'wardrobe bought 96 yards of cloth for the gowns of 35 poor women, in addition to smocks for a total cost of £16 9s 5d.'[16]

Frustratingly, while we know that Anne also participated in the Royal Maundy ceremonies, there is no direct evidence of how many poor women were involved – a detail that would, of course, have helped settle the long-standing debate over Anne Boleyn's year of birth.[17] Nevertheless, like her predecessors, Anne displayed her piety through almsgiving. While there are no eyewitness accounts of the 1535 Maundy Thursday observances at Richmond, Anne's Chaplain, William Latymer, furnishes us with the details of Anne's involvement on 'a certain Maundy Thursday' during her reign, which sheds some light on the practice. Latymer wrote his 'chronicle', a short biographical sketch of the queen, during the reign of Anne's daughter, and while it's not known whether his account was ever presented to Elizabeth, that was certainly the intention, 'as it's prefaced by a dedicatory epistle to Elizabeth I'.[18] Therefore, as Eric Ives warned, 'caution is needed, as with all Elizabethan material about Anne, because of the risk of anachronistic embroidery intended to present her as a Protestant heroine'.[19] However, contemporary evidence of Anne's charitable giving and participation in this important ritual lend credence to this particular anecdote. In the words of William Latymer:

> It hath been an ancient custom time out of mind that princes of this land should distribute on Maundy Thursday to the relief of the divers poor people a certain sum of money; which custom continuing to her grace's reign, she observed with no less reverence than liberality. For upon a certain Maundy Thursday, after she had most humbly (humbly, I said, because kneeling on her knees she washed and kissed the feet of simple poor women) embased herself to perform the ceremonies of that day, she commanded to be put privily into every poor woman's purse one George Noble, the which was vis viiid, [6s. 8d.], over and besides the alms that wonted was to be given.[20]

After the ceremony, one of the 'poor women' returned to the queen's almoner, presumably John Skipp, to ask whether the purse she received was indeed meant for her, as she had never received such a generous sum before. The incident is used to highlight Anne's largesse and Katherine's miserliness, since Latymer states that the woman had received royal alms before and was 'well acquainted therewith'. While it's obvious that Latymer was attempting to paint Katherine in an unfavourable light, it does appear that Anne spent significantly more on her Maundy ceremony than her predecessor. In 1536, the Queen's Maundy cost £31. 3s. 9½d, equivalent to around £14,000 in today's money. This sum would have included the gifts of money and clothing for the poor women, as well as other goods needed for the Royal Maundy, including aprons, towels, tubs, bowls and transport costs for ferrying the goods from place to place.[21] That Anne felt a responsibility to the poor is undeniable, but

Katherine also took her role of almsgiver very seriously, so much so that she was unwilling to give it up, even when commanded to.

On Monday, 22 March 1535, Sir Edward Chamberlain and Sir Edmund Bedingfield, the men whom Henry had entrusted with the unenviable task of watching over the exiled Katherine at Kimbolton, informed Cromwell of the following:

> We have just learnt that the Princess Dowager intends to keep a Maundy, in spite of the King's order of last year to the contrary. She says she will keep it secretly in her chamber, and wishes to know if she may go to the parish church, where we think she will try and keep it if prevented from doing so privately. Advertise the King of this, and send answer to arrive here by 9 or 10 o'clock, at the latest, on Thursday, 25 March.[22]

As Michelle L. Beer argues, the *pedilavium* and almsgiving on Maundy Thursday were a profound statement of Katherine of Aragon's sacred status as anointed queen and reaffirmed her high estate and partnership with the king.[23] By the same token, Anne's participation alongside Henry reinforced her authority and elevated status. For these reasons, despite the king's express orders, Katherine refused to give the practice up. Once again, Chapuys laid the blame for the king's decision solely at Anne's door. In April 1534, he remarked to the emperor, 'Your majesty may imagine the severity used towards the Queen in other things, when on Holy Thursday she was not allowed to hold her Maundy to the poor according to custom, and orders are given not to allow poor people to come near her, because the Lady [Anne Boleyn] says that the alms she has been accustomed to give have attracted the love of the people'.[24] These acts of personal charity endeared the sovereign to their subjects, so Anne's concerns were well founded. Furthermore, the royal couple understood the 'spiritual authority and moral capital' that this powerful ritual bestowed, which is why it was a privilege reserved for the king and queen alone.[25]

In the end, the king agreed that Katherine could observe a Maundy, but only if she 'keep her Maundy in her chamber in the name of the princess Dowager', not as queen. If she dared do otherwise, Henry made it clear that 'she and all her officers and such as receive it will be guilty of high treason'.[26] This incident reaffirms that while others could hold Maundies, only the king and queen were permitted to do so in a public ceremony. In 1535, the royal chapel at Richmond Palace served as the magnificent backdrop to the solemnities.

The royal couple would have started their day by attending mass. It's probable that a sword was carried before the king on his way to chapel, as it was on other occasions. On 15 May 1539, John Worth informed Lord Lisle that on Holy Thursday the king had processed about the court at Whitehall

Palace, 'and my Lord Cobham bare the sword before the King's Grace, with all other nobles a great multitude. And the high altar in the chapel was garnished with all the apostles upon the altar, and mass by note, and the organs playing, with as much honour to God as might be devised to be done.'[27]

As customary, later in the day, Anne and Henry returned to the chapel. Dressed in violet, they would have processed from their apartments to the lavishly decorated chapel in state, where tradition dictated the king should kneel on a cushion, in full view of the congregation, while the altars were stripped and washed. After the Gospel had been read, the *pedilavium* was performed, followed by the distribution of alms, some of which may have been provided by the lords and nobles who witnessed the event.[28]

The chapel at Richmond Palace stood in the central or inner courtyard opposite the great hall and measured about 96 feet long and 30 feet wide internally.[29] The chequered plaster and timber ceiling was painted azure, 'having between every checker a red rose of gold or a portcullis'.[30] The walls were adorned with statues of past kings who had achieved sanctity, including Edward the Confessor, King Cadwallader and Saint Edmund. On the west side, elevated at first-floor level, was a privy or holyday closet for the king, which overlooked the main body of the chapel. It was spacious and lavishly decorated and contained rich hangings that screened the monarch's devotional space from the rest of the closet. On the opposite side was a similar closet for the queen. Rowland Lockey's painting of Lady Margaret Beaufort, Henry VIII's grandmother, in a holyday closet gives us a good idea of the furnishings of a royal closet.[31] While Lady Beaufort is depicted at prayer, kneeling beneath a canopy of state, the closet served an additional purpose. Given its privacy, it was the perfect place for its royal occupants to conduct business and catch up on correspondence, while mass was being said below.[32]

As Maundy Thursday was one of the most important feast days of the year, the leading members of the nobility and of the king and queen's households were present and permitted to accompany the royal couple into the chapel. Other members of the court would have lined the processional route to the chapel or congregated in the palace's more public spaces, like the great hall, where jostling courtiers and foreign ambassadors vied to catch a glimpse of the king on his way to mass. This custom was not only reserved for high feast days, it occurred every Sunday, when, according to Chapuys, 'everybody is at Court'.[33]

Among those present at Richmond Palace was Edward Seymour, eldest son of Sir John Seymour and Margery Wentworth, who, in September 1530, was made an esquire of the body to the king.[34] Edward was not the only member of his family in royal service. His younger sister, Jane, had served Katherine of Aragon before finding a place in Anne's entourage.[35] In January

1534, she received a New Year's gift from the king, along with a number of other members of the queen's household, including Anne Gainsford, Lady Zouche; Elizabeth Holland, the long-time mistress of Anne's maternal uncle, Thomas Howard, Duke of Norfolk; and Madge Shelton, daughter of Anne's paternal aunt, Anne Shelton.[36] While we have no direct evidence for the whereabouts of Anne's parents at the time, we do know that the queen's brother, George Boleyn, was in London, and so it's likely that he was by his sister's side during the Easter festivities.[37] As previously mentioned, Anne's sister, Mary, had been sent away from court in 1534, but there was another notable absence – the queen's sister-in-law, Jane. According to Chapuys, who is our only source for this event, Jane had been banished from court not long after Mary. In October 1534, he informed Charles V:

> The wife of Mr. de Rochefort [George Boleyn] has lately been exiled from Court, owing to her having joined in a conspiracy to devise the means of sending away, through quarrelling (fasherie) or otherwise, the young lady to whom the King is now attached. As the credit of this latter is on the increase, and that of the King's mistress on the wane, she is visibly losing part of her pride and vainglory. The lady in question has lately sent a message to the Princess, telling her to take good heart; that her tribulations will come to an end much sooner than she expected; and to be assured that, should the opportunity occur, she will show herself her true friend and devoted servant.[38]

Never one to back away from a challenge, Anne responded to her husband's flirtation with the unidentified 'young lady' by demanding her immediate removal from court. The queen complained that the said lady did not treat her 'with due respect in words or deeds'.[39] However, Anne's forwardness only served to infuriate Henry, who is said to have left their meeting 'in a great passion, complaining loudly of her importunity and vexatiousness'.[40] When appealing directly to her husband failed to get Anne the outcome she desired, she took matters into her own hands and, as we've already heard, enlisted Jane's help. They came up with a daring plan to rid themselves of Anne's rival, but this too failed dismally, and in an ironic twist of fate, Jane was the one sent away from court. While this incident exemplifies Anne's boldness and perseverance, it also betrays her insecurities. Anne feared that Henry would do to her exactly what he had done to Katherine and worried that an innocent flirtation with one of the ladies at court might lead to something more enduring and genuine, as it had in her case. She knew that convention dictated that she should look the other way, as her predecessor had done for decades, so why didn't she? Pride must have played a part, but fear appears to be the most likely answer. Katherine's behaviour had always been beyond reproach, even in the face of her husband's infidelities, because her position was secure and uncontested. She did not feel the need to compete for Henry's favour. Anne, on the other hand, was well aware that opposition to her marriage and title loomed around every corner, therefore, 'she was in the contradictory position of being expected to behave as a queen, but having to continue to challenge as a mistress'.[41]

This episode is also evidence of a close relationship between Anne and her sister-in-law. There's no doubt that Jane understood that her fate and fortune were inextricably linked with those of the Boleyns. Should they fall from favour, she would swiftly follow. Jane and Anne bore the brunt of Henry's anger, but the king was well aware that the Boleyn family operated as a team. If Anne had confided in Jane, then it's almost certain that George was also privy to their plan. Chapuys noted that following Jane's dismissal from court, George was 'unfavourably treated by the King in a question or dispute he had with Master Bryan', however, he prefaced this comment by glumly remarking that 'there [aren't] any further signs of the King's ill-humour towards the Lady's relatives'.[42] The Imperial ambassador wisely concluded that Anne and Henry's arguments were 'merely lovers' quarrels', and advised the emperor not to read too much into the king's dalliances, as there was no guarantee that they would last, 'considering the king's fickle and capricious humour'.[43]

We do not know where Jane spent her enforced exile because she disappears from the records, only resurfacing again in late 1535. As for 'the young lady who was lately in the king's service', by February 1535, she too had faded into obscurity, and according to Chapuys, 'there has succeeded to her place a cousin german of the concubine, daughter of the present *gouvernante* of the Princess'.[44] This 'cousin german' was Margaret (or Madge, as she is more commonly known) Shelton. Yet her time in the limelight, if ever there was any, was fleeting. It appears that what Henry was doing was offering his 'knightly services' to ladies of the court as part of the game of courtly love.[45] Nonetheless, this was anything but a game to Anne. While public opposition to her marriage continued, she would fiercely defend her position. Smiling through gritted teeth at her husband's amours was simply not an option.

It may have been while the court was at Richmond that one of Anne's ladies fell ill with the measles, forcing the queen to flee to Hampton Court. On 8 April, the king was at Hackney, probably at a royal residence known as 'the King's Place', which he had recently acquired from Henry Percy.[46] It wasn't long, however, before the royal couple were reunited and the court was once again on the move. The destination on this occasion was a Tudor perennial favourite, Greenwich Palace.

Chapter 4

The Die is Cast

The splendid red-brick riverside palace in Greenwich held many warm memories for Anne. Most notably, it was where on 7 September 1533, she had brought her daughter, Elizabeth, into the world. Records of some of the preparations made for her lying-in survive. Also known as 'taking her chamber', this was a custom in which noble or royal women took leave of the court and of the world, and remained secluded through the last weeks of their pregnancies, with only other women for company. They would not resume their normal lives until they had been 'churched', which usually occurred around a month after delivery. Arrangements for Anne's first lying-in followed the established protocol for royal births. In July 1533, William Lord Mountjoy, Katherine of Aragon's former chamberlain, asked Cromwell to pass on 'certain remembrances of things to be provided against the Queen's taking her chamber' to Thomas, Lord Burgh, Anne's chamberlain.[1] The following month, the carpenters began work in Anne's suite of rooms where she would spend the duration of her confinement. The false roof inserted into the queen's bedchamber was lined with fine tapestries, and a cupboard of state was built specifically to display the queen's rich plate. A great bed of estate was also made for her presence chamber.[2] The floor in the queen's bedchamber was lined with thick carpets, and even the windows were hung with arras, to prevent too much light or air from infiltrating the room, as this was seen as potentially harmful to both the expectant mother and unborn child. Undoubtedly, the queen's spiritual needs were also catered for. David Starkey asserts that as customary, 'crucifixes, candlesticks and images for the altar' would have been at hand,[3] however, Amy Licence rightly questions whether Anne would have made use of such things, considering her reformist leanings, and concludes that, at the very least, there would have been an altar and some religious texts to comfort the queen.[4] In any case, the overall idea was to recreate the feel of the womb: 'warm, dark and comfortable, restricting entry to evil spirits.'[5] Anne's greatest terror must have been the prospect that she would never again find herself within its safe embrace.

At around the same time, two folding tables were made for Anne, one was a special 'breakfast table' and the other, 'for her Grace to play upon'.[6] Cards, dice, tables (backgammon) and chess were popular pastimes at court, and often involved gambling. Henry VIII, like his father, loved to gamble and wagered on the outcome of a variety of spectator sports and games, including tennis, dog races, bowling, cards and dice, often losing substantial amounts of money. Between November 1529 and December 1532, the amount paid out of the king's privy purse to cover his gambling losses amounted to a staggering £3,243. 5s. 10d., equivalent to approximately £1.5 million today.[7] In January 1530 alone, the king's losses cost him £1,340. 7s. 6d.[8]

Like her husband, Anne also played a variety of sports and games, and regularly gambled. During their courting years, the king often provided Anne with 'playing money' and, on at least one occasion, paid off Anne's gambling debts.[9] On 22 May 1532, £12. 7s. 6d. was paid to Richard Hill, the sergeant of the king's cellar, 'for that he won of my lady Anne at bowls'.[10] Hill enjoyed Henry's personal favour, and evidently Anne's too, and was a frequent gambling companion of the king. On one occasion at York Place (later Whitehall Palace), he even partnered the king during a game of cards.[11] The sergeant's position involved overseeing the cellar, buttery and pitcher house (ewery). As such, he was in charge of the wine, beer and ale served at court, and, among his many duties, he, or one of his staff, was required to taste all the alcohol to ensure that it was of the very best quality.[12] While this was an important job and required almost daily attendance at court, it formed part of the household below stairs. But despite the sergeant's relatively low social rank, especially when compared to those whom normally surrounded the king and queen, it wasn't beneath them to socialise with him.

Anne was very fond of playing cards and dice, and according to one sixteenth-century French chronicler, 'was well skilled at all games fashionable at courts'.[13] So skilled in fact, that she often beat the king. On 20 November 1532, £9. 6s. 8d. was delivered to the king at Stone Castle in Kent to pay for the losses he had incurred during a card game known as Pope Julius. On this occasion, Anne, Francis Weston and Francis Bryan all triumphed against their royal master. Five days later, Henry lost 20 crowns, playing the same game with Anne and Bryan, and the following day at Greenwich, the king suffered another huge loss to the tune of 80 crowns, £18. 13s. 4d., at the hands of his wife-to-be and aforementioned courtiers. On 28 November 1532, Anne once again beat her royal lover at cards, this time pocketing £11. 13s. 4d. (around £5,000).[15] Of the popular card game Pope Julius, little is known. It appears to have been one of Anne and Henry's favourite games and may have been a predecessor to the one later known as Pope Joan. The latter was popular in Victorian times and involved a circular and revolving board that contained labelled compartments, including king, queen, pope, matrimony and intrigue. In George Cavendish's biography of Thomas Wolsey, written in the 1550s, he recalled an incident that occurred involving a card game, although he does not specify which, when Anne was still a lady-in-waiting to Katherine of Aragon. According to Cavendish – who served as a gentleman usher in the household of Thomas Wolsey and definitely knew Anne – once, when Henry was playing cards with the two women, Anne, who was winning the hand, stopped at a king. The queen noticed and remarked, 'My Lady Anne, you have good hap to stop at a king, but you are not like others, you will have all or none'.[16] It's possible that the trio were playing Pope Julius at the time of the awkward exchange.

Making certain that the king and queen were suitably entertained was a priority for those who served them. In preparation for the court's arrival at Greenwich in December 1534, James Nedeham, the clerk of the king's works, had been asked to dig holes in which to set boughs 'for the making of a forest in the said court for the lord of misrule and his company to hunt the wild boar with his hounds to show the king and the queen pastime.'[17]

Anne's general comfort was also of paramount importance, and not only during her confinement. In the same year, Nedeham was tasked with building timber coops at Greenwich to house a pelican and a peacock 'that were brought to the king out of the new found land', out of earshot of the queen's apartments, 'by cause the Queen's grace could not take her rest in the mornings for the noise of the same'.[18]

In mid-April, Francis I wrote to his ambassador in Rome, Charles de Hémard de Denonville, Bishop of Mascon, of his desire 'to see the sentence of the late Pope against the king of England declared null.'[19] If this news reached Anne, then it must have been heartening and given her some hope that the forthcoming English embassy to France, which would hopefully settle the matter of a French marriage for the Princess Elizabeth, would be a success. Henry kept to his earlier promise, and prepared to send his deputies to Calais to negotiate the details of the alliance. On 25 April 1535, John Husee informed Lord Lisle that the Duke of Norfolk, Cromwell and the king's almoner, Edward Fox, would be at Calais before Whitsuntide.[20] In the end, George Boleyn went to Calais in place of Cromwell. This may have been as a result of Cromwell's recurring illness, which had once again forced the king's secretary to absent himself from court since Palm Sunday, and retreat to the Rolls House on Chancery Lane – a grand residence, and just one of the many perks of his position as Master of the Rolls. Or perhaps, as Chapuys suspected, Cromwell 'excused himself in despair of the issue'.[21] The latter appears to be the more likely scenario, as Chapuys later informed the emperor that Cromwell had 'got himself exempted from the Commission', as he was confident 'that nothing would be concluded at all'. In fact, Cromwell secretly hoped that a marriage might be arranged between the

Princess Elizabeth, whom Chapuys refers to as 'the little bastard', and Philip, the Prince of Spain, and assured Chapuys that they would not do business with the French.[22] As we shall shortly see, Cromwell's predictions were correct. The embassy was another dismal failure, and hinted at cracks in Anne's relationship with the king's chief minister.

Yet on the surface, things appeared normal. Earlier in the month, George Boleyn had been granted the manor of South in Kent, previously in the hands of Thomas More, who was still languishing in the Tower.[23] On St George's Day 1535, a chapter of the Order of the Garter, the most senior and prestigious order of knighthood at the English court, was held at Greenwich 'at which were present the King, the marquis of Exeter, the earls of Arundel, Essex, Rutland, Oxford, Wiltshire, and Sir Wm. Fitzwilliam'.[24] Details of Garter elections and ceremonies from 1534 to 1551 are recorded in the richly illuminated Liber Niger, more commonly known as the Black Book because of its black velvet binding. The entry for the year 1535 records that the chapter was held at vespers, where it was ordered that 'the Feast of that saint [St George the Martyr] should as usual be kept at Windsor on the ninth of May following, and that the renowned Duke of Suffolk, who was not then present, should supply the Sovereign's Place, having the Earl of Arundel, Earl of Sussex, Lord Burgavenny, and Lord Sandys for his Associates.' As illness prevented Lord Burgavenny from attending the feast, 'the Illustrious Earl of Wiltshire', Anne's father, presided in his place.[25]

When a vacancy occurred in the Order, it was common practice for new members to be elected and announced at the annual meeting on St George's Day. However, there was no new appointment in April 1535, because the vacancy left by the death of Lord Mountjoy in November 1534 had been filled at a meeting held at Westminster on 20 January 1535.[26] On this occasion, the Dukes of Richmond, Norfolk and Suffolk, the Earl of Northumberland and William Fitzwilliam were with the king. Each Knight of the Garter present at the chapter meetings voted for nine men in three different categories: 'princes', which included the rank of earl and above; 'barons', which could also include viscounts; and 'knights'. The sovereign took the votes into consideration, but could ultimately choose whomever they desired. George Boleyn was nominated by the Earl of Northumberland, his uncle the Duke of Norfolk and the Duke of Richmond, but Henry VIII's nephew, James V, was elected by the king. He received five votes, compared to George's three.[27] This was not, however, the first time that Lord Rochford had been nominated. In 1532, Francis I voted for him at a meeting held in Calais, and, curiously, Sir Henry Guildford – an outspoken opponent of Anne Boleyn – voted for the young courtier in 1531.[28]

Disappointingly, for a palace that witnessed so many important events and ceremonies throughout the sixteenth century, including births, deaths and endless festivities, Greenwich's exact plan and appearance, and architectural evolution under the Tudor monarchs, remains something of a mystery. However, two sketches by the sixteenth-century artist, Antony van den Wyngaerde, convey its obvious appeal and grandeur.

Like Hampton Court and Richmond, Greenwich was one of only a handful of royal houses that could comfortably accommodate the whole court, which could number 'up to twelve hundred people in the winter and about eight hundred in the summer'.[29] In 1526, Cardinal Wolsey attempted to curb the rising influence of Henry's courtiers by introducing the Eltham Ordinances, a strict set of rules, devised 'for the establishment of good order, and reformation of sundry errors and misuses in his [the king's] most honourable household and chamber'.[30] The ordinances specified that, among other things, 'at all times when his highness shall lie in his castle of Windsor, his manors of Beaulieu, Richmond and Hampton Court, Greenwich, Eltham or Woodstock, his hall shall be ordinarily kept and continued; unless than for any reasonable cause by his Grace to be approved, it shall be thought otherwise expedient.' It also stated that 'the king's noble chapel [was] to be kept in the same place, for the administration of divine service.'[31]

There would be no mercy, however, for those who continued to preach the Pope's superiority. Towards the end of the month, the king penned a letter from Greenwich to John Lord Mordaunt, which reveals his darkened mood:

Trusty and well-beloved we greet you well. And, whereas it has come to our knowledge, that sundry persons, as well religious as secular priests, and curates in their parishes, and other places of this our realm, do daily as much as in them is set forth and extol the jurisdiction and authority of the bishop of Rome, otherwise called the pope, sowing their seditious false doctrine, and pestilent deceits with relics, praying for him in the pulpit, and making of him a God, to the great deceit, illuding, and seducing of our people and subjects, bringing them into error, sedition, and evil opinions; more preferring the said laws, jurisdiction, and authority of the said bishop of Rome than the most holy laws and precepts of Almighty God: we, therefore, minding not only to provide an unity and quietness to be had and continued amongst our people and subjects, but also greatly coveting and desiring them to be brought to a perfection and knowledge of the mere verity and truth, and no longer to be seduced nor blinded with any such superstitious and false doctrine of an earthly usurper of God's law: we will, therefore, and command you, that where and whensoever you shall find, apperceive, know, and hear tell of any such seditious persons, that do spread, teach, preach, and set forth any such pernicious doctrine, to the exaltation of the bishop of Rome; bringing thereby our people into error, grudge, and murmuration, that ye, without delay, do apprehend and take them, or cause them to be apprehended and taken; and so committed to ward, there to remain without bail or mainprise, until, upon your advertisement thereof to us or our council, ye shall receive answer of our further pleasure in that behalf.[32]

At around the same time, Henry instructed Cromwell to 'studiously... examine' John Mores, the receiver of Syon Abbey.[33] The king had already personally questioned Mores about his recent communication with Stephen Gardiner, the Bishop of Winchester, but he was unsatisfied by some of his responses or lack thereof. Henry expressed some doubts over Gardiner's loyalty and felt that perhaps he wasn't as committed to Henry's cause, as he had professed to be. The king was confident that Cromwell would uncover the truth of the matter.

Syon Abbey was a wealthy Bridgettine monastery, which housed both monks and nuns. It was situated across the river from Richmond Palace, and, up until Henry's break from Rome, had basked in the light of royal favour. But despite significant royal pressure, the monastery had held firm to their beliefs and continued to oppose the king's supremacy. Apart from interrogating its receiver, one of its monks, Richard Reynolds, whom we've already met, along with three Carthusian priors and a secular priest, were tried at the end of April. The men were found guilty of high treason and sentenced to be hung, drawn and quartered at Tyburn.[34] Their grisly executions sent a potent message to all of Henry's subjects – regardless of your rank or position, opposition to the king would be paid for in blood.

Chapter 5

The Cost of Courage

On 4 May 1535, the citizens of London gathered to watch five prisoners suffer one of the most barbarous punishments of the day and one reserved solely for men found guilty of what in the Crown's eyes was the most heinous crime of all – high treason. John Houghton, Augustine Webster and Robert Lawrence, priors of the charterhouses of London, Axholme and Bevall respectively, along with Richard Reynolds and John Hale, were drawn from the Tower of London to Tyburn, where they were hung 'with great ropes'.[1] The sight of the men dressed in their religious habits, being dragged on hurdles through the crowded streets, must have shocked even the most hardened onlookers.[2] Once at the place of execution, they were hung until near death, and while still conscious, cut down and their hearts and bowels removed and burned. While it was also customary for the victim to be castrated, this is not mentioned in any of the contemporary accounts. What we do hear, however, is that after the hangman cut out the victim's heart, it was 'rubbed upon their mouths and faces'.[3] According to the same commentator, despite the fact that the men were executed one at a time, so that each was forced to witness the full horrors of the punishment before he died, 'it is long since persons have been known to die with greater constancy'. He elaborated: 'no change was noticed in their colour or tone of speech, and while the execution was going on they preached and exhorted the bystanders with the greatest boldness to do well and obey the King in everything that was not against the honour of God and the Church'.[4] The men were then beheaded and quartered, and their parts displayed 'in public places on long spikes', as a deterrent to would-be traitors.[5]

Among the spectators were Anne's father and brother, the Dukes of Richmond and Norfolk, and many other courtiers. According to Chapuys, who wrote to his master of Henry's mounting bloodlust, the king's Groom of the Stool, Henry Norris, was also in attendance with forty of the king's bodyguard. The latter was one of five men, 'who went to the place of execution, accoutred and mounted as if he were going on an expedition to the Scotch borders'.[6] This unusual spectacle, and the fact that the men were secretly armed and their faces hidden behind vizors, aroused the suspicion of some of those in the crowd, who promptly departed the macabre scene.

What Anne thought of all of this, we do not know. Within a week of the executions, George had left for Calais, and Anne turned her attention to other important matters. During a sojourn at Whitehall Palace, the queen wrote to William Thornton, the Abbot of St Mary's in York, to essentially reprimand him for not having obeyed her instructions concerning the education of one of his monks, John Eldmer. At the time of the abbot's election in 1530, Anne had petitioned the new incumbent to allow Eldmer, who had also 'stood in election', to continue his studies at Cambridge, a request to which Thornton had obviously agreed at the time. However, as you shall shortly read, Anne discovered that the abbot had not only recalled Eldmer, but had also appointed him to a number of offices at the abbey, which she was certain would interrupt his studies. The queen was less than impressed and made her feelings perfectly clear:

> Trusty and well-beloved in God, we greet you well. And albeit at the time of your preferment to be head and governor of that my lord's monastery of Saint Mary beside his city of York, we then made request unto you for one dompne [sic] John Eldmer, bachelor of divinity, a man, as we [be] credibly informed, of good learning, sad demeanour, and virtuous governance, who then for the same his elect qualities stood in election (as you did) to be abbot, like as we doubt not but you remember right well, that the same dompne John Eldmer should apply and continue his study and learning at my lord's university of Cambridge for the increase of virtue and learning: wherewith at that time you were well content. Yet notwithstanding the same, you, contrary to our said request (as we be credibly informed), have not only called him from his learning at the said university, but also have intricate and charged him with sundry rooms and offices in your said monastery, to the no little disturbance and inquietation of his mind, and to alienate him as much as may be from his said study and learning: to our no little marvel. We, considering the good affection and desire the said dompne John Eldmer hath to the increase of virtue and learning, desire and heartily pray you, that you will permit and suffer him to repair again to the university for the intent aforesaid giving unto him sufficient exhibition to the maintenance of his study there, or else to signify unto us in writing, by this bearer, a cause reasonable why you defer to accomplish our said request made unto you in that behalf.
>
> Given under our signet, at my lord's manor of Westminster, the 13th day of May.[7]

This was not the only student that Anne generously patronised. One William Barker also studied at Cambridge at Anne's expense, and the queen likewise supported scholars studying in Europe.[8] William Latymer recalled how Anne 'maintained also one Mr Beckynsall in the universities beyond the seas, giving him towards his exhibition forty pounds by year'.[9] This is almost certainly John Beckynsaw, who studied in Paris with Thomas Wynter, Wolsey's illegitimate son. Maria Dowling has also suggested that this is the same 'Bekensall' that makes an appearance in the king's privy purse expenses in February 1530.[10] In the account book, he is described as 'a scholar of Paris' and received £4. 13s. 4d.[11] Interestingly, when a lack of funds forced Wynter to return home from his studies in Italy, he turned to Cromwell for help, and was promptly advised to speak with Henry and Anne. The young man did as the chief minister suggested, but found that while the king 'showed me much kindness', he was too busy shooting with his nobles to pay him much attention. Anne, on the other hand, warmly assured him of her support: 'I am aware, my dear Winter that you are beloved by the King and have many friends who wish you well. Reckon me among them'.[12]

According to Latymer, it wasn't only individual scholars who benefited from Anne's patronage; the queen also supported educational institutions, including Oxford and Cambridge. The chronicler recalled how 'she sent great sums of money to the maintenance of the poor scholars there; for the first year of her reign she gave to each university forty pounds and every year after to each of the said universities four score pounds [£80]'.[13] He also writes of how Anne, on being 'informed that the said universities were charged with the payments to tenths and subsidies she made earnest petition to the king's majesty in [sic] their behalf and obtained pardon for the same.'[14] While there are no extant records to corroborate the claim of an annual subvention, a letter from Cambridge University to the queen, dated 23 February 1536, does survive, in which they thank her for interceding with the king to secure the university's exemption from the payment of first fruit and tenths.[15] The university also thanked her for her 'gentle and loving acceptance' of the letters they had sent her while she was on progress in the West Country in the summer of 1535. An Act of Parliament, passed in early February 1536, exonerated the Universities of Oxford and Cambridge, as well as the colleges of Eton and Winchester, from the payment of the clerical tax.[16] These examples are not only evidence of Anne's genuine interest in education and scholarship, they also demonstrate that her contemporaries, not just later Elizabethan writers, considered her to be a generous patron of students and educational institutions.

The queen's influence and patronage, however, was not only limited to the secular sphere. On Whitsunday, John Smith, a canon and prebendary of St Paul's Cathedral, sought Anne's help to solve a dispute that had arisen between himself and a fellow prebendary, John Incent, who, in 1540, became dean of St Paul's Cathedral. Smith wrote to Anne's vice-chamberlain, Sir Edward Baynton, to ask that he inform the queen that 'my unkind brother, Mr Incent' was trying to remove him from his position in the deanery house, which Dr Sampson, dean of the King's Chapel, had helped him secure. He implored: 'I beg you will enterprise in this matter with the Queen for me, considering the diligent love and service I showed her at her coronation, and at the birth of my lady Princess. I have always furthered the promotion of her chaplains against Incent's opposition, who used such odious words as I am ashamed to write'.[17] Evidently, Incent did not sympathise with Anne's evangelical leanings or her choice of preachers.

Despite not belonging to this year, there's another example of Anne's religious patronage worth noting for the insights it provides into Anne's faith and character, potentially shedding light on her state of mind in 1535, as all around her, blood was spilled in the name of her husband's bid for supremacy. On 20 May 1534, Anne penned a stinging letter to Dr Edward Crome, admonishing the London cleric for not having yet accepted a promotion that she had secured for him. Archbishop Cranmer, at Anne's insistence, had installed Dr Crome at St Mary Aldermary, but he was yet to commence in his new role.

> Trusty and well-beloved, we greet you well, marvelling not a little that, albeit heretofore we have signified unto you at sundry times our pleasure concerning your promotion unto the parsonage of Aldermary, within the city of London, which we have obtained for you, yet you hitherto have deferred the taking on you of the same; by which your refusal, we think that you right little regard or esteem your own weal or advancement. We, minding nothing more than the furtherance of virtue, truth and godly doctrine, which we trust shall be not a little increased, and right much the better advanced and established, by your better relief and residence there, signify therefore unto you, that our express mind and pleasure is that you shall use no farther delays in this matter, but take on you the cure and charge of the said benefice of Aldermary, as you tender our pleasure in any behalf. Given under our signet, at my lord's manor of Richmond, the 20th of May.[18]

Educated at Cambridge, the former parson of St Anthony's in London, had found himself in trouble with the law in 1531, after 'preaching against purgatory, the cult of saints, pilgrimage, images, fasting and papal authority'.[19] He was examined in the presence of the king and forced to recant some of his opinions. The king, however, took no issue with Dr Crome's belief that the Pope was not head of the Christian Church; instead, he affirmed that it was 'quite certain and true'.[20] According to Chapuys, the preacher, whom the Duke of Norfolk considered one of the finest and most learned in the country, was 'in danger of being burned', but was spared through the intercession of Anne and her father, Thomas Boleyn. Chapuys noted, 'The general opinion is that he has been delivered by desire of the lady and her father, who are more Lutheran than Luther himself, seconded by the King's inclination because he had spoken in his favor [sic] against the Pope'.[21] This is not the last time Dr Crome would be called to recant; in fact, he would be required to do so on another three occasions before his death in 1562.[22] That Anne hand-picked this man for promotion in 1534 speaks volumes of her religious beliefs, but as Eric Ives wisely reminded us, 'the labelling of Anne Boleyn by her enemies as a Lutheran can be dismissed as an attempt to give a dog a bad name'.[23] Anne was deeply interested in religious reform, but she did not subscribe to radical ideas, like those which denied the sacrifice of the mass. What positions, then, did she adopt? As we've already noted, she rejected papal authority and championed quality education. She also supported and promoted promising scholars and reformers, and, as we shall soon see, took an active interest in monastic reform. There's one other crucial aspect of Anne's faith that we've not yet mentioned: her profound commitment to the Bible.

William Latymer describes the 'constant and fervent affection which she had to the setting forth of the lively word of God' and notes that whenever Anne dined with the king, it was her wont to debate scriptural matters.[24] Anne's lord chamberlain and vice-chamberlain, Thomas Burgh and Edward Baynton, shared their mistress's penchant for debate, 'and gave themselves wholly in all their dinners and suppers to the discussing of some one doubt or other in scripture'.[25] Towards the end of her reign, Anne encouraged her ladies to read a copy of the Bible in English, which she kept 'on a common desk' in her chamber, but 'her highness was very expert in the French tongue, exercising herself continually in reading the French bible and other French books of like effect and conceived great pleasure in the same, whereof her highness charged her chaplains to be furnished of all kind of French books that reverently treated of the whole scriptures'.[26] According to Latymer, Anne lamented her ignorance of Latin, and vowed that if God permitted her to live long enough to oversee Princess Elizabeth's education, she would ensure that her daughter was taught a number of languages, including Hebrew, Greek, Latin, Italian, Spanish and French.

Anne's preference for French texts was also observed by Louis (or Loys) de Brun, a French teacher resident in England. At New Year in 1530, he dedicated a French treatise on letter-writing to the then Madame de Rochford, and highly praised Anne's erudition and piety:

When I consider the great affection and real passion which you have for the French tongue, I am not surprised that you are never found, if circumstances permit, without your having some book in French in your hand which is of use and value in pointing out and finding the true and narrow way to all virtues, as, for example translations of the Holy Scriptures, reliable and full of all sound doctrines, or, equally of other good books by learned men who give healthy advice for this mortal life and consolation for the immortal soul.[27]

He also mentioned seeing Anne reading the Pauline Epistles during Lent in 1528 and 1529, 'those helpful letters of St. Paul which contain all the fashion and rule to live righteously… which you know well and practise'.[28] As we've already noted, while Anne was clearly fond of French texts, she was also keen to promote the vernacular bible. Her personal copy of William Tyndale's 1534 edition of the New Testament still survives and is now housed in the British Library. Anne was, however, not the only member of the Boleyn family eager to bring the Scripture to the people in the English language. George Boleyn was just as passionate as his sister in this regard.[29]

On 25 May 1535, the siblings were reunited at Greenwich Palace. According to Chapuys, 'before speaking to the King he went to the Lady, his sister, and conversed with her a long time'.[30] The news was not favourable and George wanted to be the one to break it to Anne, again suggesting a close bond between the pair. While the Imperial ambassador was not privy to the details of their conversation, he assumed that the tidings were not what the Boleyns had hoped for. Sir Nicholas Carew informed Chapuys that since George's return, Anne 'has been in a bad humour, and said a thousand shameful words of the king of France, and generally of the whole nation'.[31] The cause of Anne's antipathy towards the French is revealed in a letter that William Fitzwilliam penned to Cromwell from Dover, on the evening of George's return to court. He relates how he had come by George in Dover, probably early that morning, and had spoken with him of his recent mission. Fitzwilliam was shocked to discover that 'the Admiral arrived at Calais on Saturday, and was ready to leave upon Monday, making so light of the matter'.[32]

In trying to make sense of Chabot's behaviour, Fitzwilliam concluded that 'when Frenchmen are aloft, they are the highest men in the world, and the soonest forget their benefactors: when they are a little under foot they are the humblest'.[33] Although George had asked Fitzwilliam to remain in Dover until his return from court, presumably with further instructions from the king as to how to proceed, Fitzwilliam sailed for Calais the following day. He confessed that he was unable to resist the fair weather and the opportunity 'to take to sea at the tail of a storm', something he evidently loved. Cleverly, he added that his chief reason for disregarding Rochford's request was that the king had commanded him to take a message to Norfolk, who had been left behind in Calais to conclude the negotiations.

George was undoubtedly furious about the admiral's behaviour. His honour and reputation, and perhaps, more importantly, that of his sister's, were at stake. He had been charged with arranging a marriage alliance for his niece, but had been met with cool disdain. It's little wonder that the queen's devoted brother made the roughly 60-mile journey from Dover to Greenwich Palace in just one day, no doubt spurred on by his anger and frustration, and his desire to quash the rumours that would inevitably emerge and inform his sister first-hand of the latest developments. It wasn't long before whispers reached the ears of the Lady Mary. The French, it was said, had again insisted on her hand for the French Dauphin.[34]

Albeit a long and hard ride, a skilled horseman like George could have managed it, especially in late spring when the roads were less treacherous and the days long. Undoubtedly, it would have taken at least ten hours and involved a number of changes of horse.[35] While the details of his journey are unknown, the fact that George was on the king's business meant that he could have made use of the royal post network, and obtained a fresh horse at each postal town. These were located at regular intervals, of roughly 8 to 20 miles, along the country's main arterial roads, including the Dover Road.[36] Furthermore, as Lord Warden of the Cinque Ports and Constable of Dover Castle, he was intimately familiar with this particular thoroughfare and landscape.

Chapuys writes that on 25 and 27 May, the Council sat at Greenwich and were 'exceedingly busy', no doubt deliberating on the news brought by Rochford. But there were other events unfolding both at home and abroad, worthy of the Council's attention. Out of Rome came word that the Bishop of Rochester, who was presently languishing in the Tower, had been named a cardinal, along with eight others.[37] If Pope Paul III thought this gesture would soften Henry's resolve and offer some protection for the 65-year-old bishop, he was very mistaken. Henry saw the act as one of defiance and provocation, and declared that the Bishop of Rochester would have to wear the red cardinal's hat on his shoulders, 'for a head he will have none'.[38] While Henry debated matters of importance with his Council at Greenwich, a group of religious refugees from Flanders, known as Anabaptists, were examined by Archbishop Cranmer and others at St Paul's Cathedral. Anthony Waite summarised their religious beliefs in a letter to Lady Lisle on 27 May:

There are hither comen some of the country of Flanders, what with those that be from thence comen and other here dwellers, to the number of xxiii persons, and three be women. They hold these no less strange than damnable opinions (as by report I do hear); first, that Christ hath not the nature of God and man: Secondly, that Christ born of the Virgin Mary took no part of the substance of her body: thirdly, that the bread consecrate by the priest is not the Incarnate body of Christ: fourthly, that Baptism given in the state of innocency (that is, to children) doth not profit: fifthly, that if a man sin deadly after he be once baptised, that he shall never be forgiven... they be so stiff that as yet there is small hope of their conversion. And as tomorrow they shall be examined again, and take their Judgement, if they be obstinate. But if judgement be given it is doubted whether the King's Grace will suffer execution of them here, or else send them to the country there to suffer according to their laws and their deserts.[39]

Writing on the matter of the Anabaptists to Ambrogio Ricalcato, the Pope's secretary, the Bishop of Faenza, papal nuncio in France, noted that there were 'about 25 Anabaptists' in custody.[40] Cranmer and the others debated with them but in the end, they were found guilty of heresy. Eleven chose to recant their beliefs and so were spared the death penalty; instead, they were expelled from England. Stow records the fates of the others in his *Annales*: 'fourteen of them were condemned, a man and a woman of them were burned in Smithfield, the other twelve were sent to the other towns there to be brent [burnt]'.[41]

If, as Chapuys reported, the king's Council sat on the day of George's return, then discussions must have stretched late into the night. This was not uncommon it seems, as Chapuys also noted that the French ambassador – who had now become the target of Henry and Anne's fury – was disgruntled because he had not been invited to court, and that on Corpus Christi Day (27 May), he went to Cromwell's lodgings and waited for the chief minister to return from court until 10 at night, eventually leaving, 'greatly dissatisfied'.[42]

Within weeks, George was back in his saddle, armed with new instructions for the Duke of Norfolk and his colleagues in Calais.[43] According to Chapuys, Cromwell had tried to delay Rochford's departure, hoping instead for a renewal of amity with the emperor. He confessed that 'although they always wished to preserve the friendship of the French... he would take care that Rochford did not return so soon to Calais, and especially that nothing was treated to the disadvantage of your Majesty or to the hindrance of the new alliance'.[44]

Outwardly, all appeared well between the king's right-hand-man and his queen, but just beneath the surface of the courtly facade lurked a deep-seated rivalry that threatened to tear their world apart.

Part II

Summer 1535

Chapter 6

The King's Pleasure

I t's been widely assumed that because Anne Boleyn and Thomas Cromwell shared a deep interest in religious reform, that they were close allies, friends even. Chapuys certainly believed it. In May 1535, he told Nicolas Perrenot de Granvelle, one of the emperor's trusted advisers, that even if Henry wanted to give up his 'abominable obstinacy', referring to the king's break with Rome, 'the Lady and Cromwell, who are omnipotent with him, would prevent it, knowing that it would be their ruin'.[1] Eric Ives refers to the chief minister as 'her [Anne's] man', and argues that theirs was a close relationship, until he became 'a cuckoo in the Boleyn nest'.[2] However, as Diarmaid MacCulloch points out, the evidence to support anything more than a formal relationship is scant.[3] What is irrefutable, though, is that Cromwell was the king's man. He worked tirelessly to do the king's bidding, not Anne's. Furthermore, unlike Thomas Cranmer, Cromwell did not owe his rise into royal service to the Boleyns. He owed it to the associates of his former master, Thomas Wolsey, a man to whom Cromwell remained loyal until the very end. He even incorporated themes from Wolsey's heraldry into his own – a calculated gesture of fealty to the fallen cardinal which did not go unnoticed by the Boleyns. Likewise, Cromwell never forgot the role that Anne played in Wolsey's disgrace and downfall. This tension shaped and complicated their relationship. Cromwell's remembrances, a to-do list of sorts, reflect the wide range of business that occupied the minister's days, and often contain the expression 'to know the king's pleasure'.[4] While the king's pleasure was for Anne to remain his wife, Cromwell patiently bided his time. For now, they both continued to bask in the light of Henry's favour, and their hostility remained largely in the shadows. Occasionally, however, it became too difficult to mask.

In early June 1535, Chapuys informed the emperor of a possible rift between Anne and the king's chief minister:

Cremuel said lately to me that were the Lady to know the familiar terms on which he and I are, she would surely try to cause us both some annoyance, and that only three days ago she and he had had words together, the Lady telling him, among other things, that she would like to see his head off his shoulders. 'But', added Cromwell, 'I trust so much on my master, that I fancy she cannot do me any harm.' I cannot tell whether this is an invention of Cromwell in order to enhance his merchandise. All I can say is, that everyone here considers him Anne's right hand, as I myself told him some time ago. Indeed, I hear from a reliable source that day and night is the Lady working to bring about the duke of Norfolk's disgrace with the King; whether it be owing to his having spoken too freely about her, or because Cromwell wishes to bring down the aristocracy of this kingdom, and is about to begin by him, I cannot say.[5]

The ambassador's confusion is understandable. To an outsider, Cromwell may well have appeared to be Anne's 'right hand', but on closer inspection, the evidence put forward to support a close alliance is at the very least ambiguous. For example, he was appointed high steward of her lands, a position which carried a salary of £20 per year, however, he had paid to obtain the honour.[6] During the preparations for Anne's coronation, he had personally overseen the refurbishment of the royal apartments and other buildings at the Tower of London, but this was at the king's behest.[7] While it's true that from time to time, individuals petitioned the queen through Cromwell, this was part and parcel of his position; after all, he was the king's principal secretary and chief minister, and as such, wielded extensive influence at court.[8] The overall picture painted by the evidence is of a queen and minister who, despite occasionally working together, put up with each other because, for the time being, they had no other choice.[9] It's very likely that in public they maintained a decorous facade, as any open quarrelling would have reflected badly on the king. Most tellingly, perhaps, in terms of their relationship, is that Cromwell does not appear among the long list of men, eighty-one according to one source, who were knighted in honour of Anne's coronation in 1533.[10] 'A calculated snub', according to Diarmaid MacCulloch.[11] It certainly appears that way, especially considering that Cromwell was not knighted or raised to the peerage until after Anne's death.

The Imperial ambassador's assertion that Anne was working 'day and night' to bring about the Duke of Norfolk's downfall may bear some semblance of truth, especially considering that, as we've already noted, the queen's relationship with her uncle was becoming increasingly tense. However, it's also likely that Chapuys' 'reliable source' employed exaggeration in his or her account. Interestingly, the ambassador assumed that Cromwell was also involved or that he may have even been the instigator of the plot, however, judging by Norfolk's letter to Cromwell written from his country residence in

Kenninghall, in May 1535, the two men had become temporary allies: 'I have been advertised that since I saw you last you have most lovingly handled me. You will always find me a faithful friend, grudge who will'.[12]

We should not be surprised by Chapuys' sceptical attitude towards Cromwell's confession about his fall-out with Anne. Although he had always purported to be a friend of Mary and Katherine's, Cromwell's behaviour often left Chapuys puzzled. For example, in October 1534, while Anne and Henry were actively pursuing an alliance with France, Cromwell confided 'a fact which very few…were cognisant of' to Chapuys, namely that the king loved Mary a hundred times more than his last born. 'He had no doubt (Cromwell said) that in time everything would be set to rights'.[13] Even though he suspected that Cromwell was merely telling him what he wanted to hear, in order to allay the emperor's fears about the Lady Mary's treatment, he did 'praise and commend the affection and esteem which he seemed to entertain for the Princess'.[14] But less than six months later, in April 1535, Cromwell allegedly threatened to end the life of a man who had spoken kindly of the Lady Mary:

> Cromwell has always given me to understand that he is much devoted to the Princess; nevertheless, I have found no evidence of it, except words; and today a notable personage has informed me that the King, the day he went to visit Cromwell, told him that he had that day heard many good things of the Princess his daughter, of which he had not been so well informed before; and on coming to the particulars of what had been told him, Cromwell ventured to say they were all lies, and afterwards sent for a gentleman who had so informed the King, commanding him, if he did not wish to be destroyed and possibly lose his life, that he should go and unsay to the King what he had said in favour of the Princess; but the gentleman refused to obey.[15]

Unfortunately, the identity of this 'notable personage' is unknown, therefore, it's difficult to assess the veracity of the story.

While Cromwell felt secure in his master's protection, Anne still ruled the king's heart. On 16 June 1535, Chapuys informed his master that the king was 'extremely indignant at the bishop of Rochester having been created cardinal', but that he was likewise aggrieved by Jean du Bellay and Girolamo Ghinucci's nominations.[16] To soothe the king's anger, Chapuys writes that Anne threw Henry a lavish feast at one of her residences, yet somehow forgot to invite the French ambassador. But given the disappointing outcome of the recent embassy to Calais, this appears more like a deliberate affront to the ambassador, who, needless to say, was greatly displeased by the queen's neglect.

Chapuys confided in Charles V that 'she [Anne] has…so well managed to banquet and amuse her guests that, as the Princess [Lady Mary] sends me word this very day, the King loves his concubine now more than ever he did.'[17]

The evening's entertainments included a series of fine mummeries or masques, indicating that the queen invested a significant amount of time and money into organising this event. As Amy Livingstone reminds us, 'banquets served as an expression of power, wealth and position' and took a considerable amount of planning and skill, especially when royal guests were involved.[18] Frustratingly, we don't know which of Anne's residences served as the backdrop to the revelry. It's perhaps worth noting that in September 1532, Anne hosted a dinner for Henry and other notable guests at her house in Hanworth, so it's possible that this was once again the setting for Anne's banquet.[19] She did, though, own other properties in the vicinity of London, including Baynard's Castle.

The queen's vast estate comprised of 'castles, lordships, manors, lands and tenements' across divers English counties.[20] Even prior to becoming queen, Henry granted her the manors of Hanworth and Cold Kennington, and following her elevation to the peerage in September 1532, as Marquess of Pembroke, Anne received additional lands in England and Wales, including the manor of Hunsdon.[21] Following her marriage to Henry, Anne was granted 'certain lands and rents, the same as enjoyed by the princess Katharine, late wife of Arthur prince of Wales, the King's brother', which were confirmed as her dower and jointure by Act of Parliament in March 1534.[22] This same act legally empowered the queen to dispose of the income from her property as she pleased, 'as if she was a Woman Sole', or a femme sole. As customary, Anne was also granted the goods and chattels of felons and fugitives who resided on any of the lands granted to her.[23]

Anne's extensive property portfolio was managed by her Council, which, by 1534, consisted of her receiver general, George Taylor; a surveyor by the name of John Smith; a clerk of the Council named John Gregbyte; a keeper of the Council chamber listed as Hugh Carre; as well as an unnamed auditor, possibly Thomas Combe; an attorney and a solicitor.[24] The men met regularly in a room at Westminster next to the Exchequer. Also on the queen's payroll were 'six learned men retained of counsel', who did not attend all Council meetings but who could be called upon to give advice as required, and three court attorneys, including Robert Joynor, who served as an attorney in the Common Pleas.[25] The queen's Council was headed by her chancellor, who, according to William Latymer, was Anne's paternal uncle, Sir James Boleyn.[26] An account of bonds held by the late queen corroborates this assertion.[27] It is worth recording, however, that in March 1534, a payment of £54 was made to one Sir Robert Dymmoke, who is identified as the queen's chancellor.[28] Dymmoke had served Katherine of Aragon in the same capacity, from at least 1527, although he is also described as her almoner.[29]

Interestingly, a letter penned by the queen's cooks and dated 8 July 1535, addresses Dymmoke as 'the Queen's Chamberlain'.[30] It's unclear as to whether Dymmoke shared the role of chancellor with Sir James Boleyn or whether Anne's uncle took over from Dymmoke sometime in 1535, at which point he transferred to the role of chamberlain. However, as we've already noted, Lord Burgh also served Anne in this particular role. Professor Retha M. Warnicke offers us a possible solution to this conundrum in her study of Tudor queenship. She notes that some councillors and household officials worked 'three-month shifts'.[31] These part-time positions offered flexibility and allowed the chamber appointees to simultaneously function in multiple roles.[32] Dymmoke also served the queen as steward of her manors of Dedham, Stratford, Langham and Clare.[33]

It was also not uncommon for councillors and other household officials to transfer from one consort to the next. John Smith, Hugh Carre and Robert Joynor had all previously served Anne's predecessor.[34] This continuity of the consorts' staff also existed among the keepers, stewards and bailiffs of the queen's jointure lands.[35]

The chancellor was the chief financial officer of the queen's household and the link between the Council and Anne's household establishment.[36] In addition to Anne's lord chamberlain and vice-chamberlain, Lord Burgh and Sir Edward Baynton respectively, other members of the queen's household included her secretary, John Uvedale (or Udall); her master of the horse, William Coffin; and her avener and clerk of the stable, Denys Coppes.[37] Income from Anne's estate paid for her household expenses, including entertainments such as the grand feast she held for the king. But how else did the queen spend her immense wealth? The only account of her finances to survive was compiled by George Taylor for the period September 1534 to September 1535.[38] While only a summary of the queen's expenditure, not an itemised account, the document offers a tantalising glimpse into Anne, the shrewd businesswoman. During this period, Taylor received £4,423. 3s. 1¾d. from Anne's English estates, and £633. 13s. 10d. from her property in Wales – a total of £5,056. 16s. ¾d. from her lands. Dakota L. Hamilton argues that 'Anne was the most successful of Henry VIII's wives in maximizing the revenue from her properties'.[39] Katherine of Aragon, for example, was granted £4,129. 2s. 4d. for her jointure in 1515, about the same as what Jane Seymour enjoyed after certain fees were deducted.[40] Anne of Cleves, on the other hand, received just under £3,000.[41] In addition to income from Anne's lands, Taylor also received £1,324. 11s. 10d. from the queen's coffer to pay for day-to-day expenses, therefore in this one year he had to account for £6,381. 8s. 9¾d.[42]

In terms of expenditure, the following payments are recorded: £976. 13s. 4¼d. was expended on fees, wages and annuities. The Wardrobe of the Robes and the Wardrobes of the Beds cost £68. 17s. 6d. and £44. 7s. 8d. respectively. The sum of £186. 8s. 7d. went on gifts and rewards, £96. 10s. 3d. on riding expenses, and £593. 4s. 9¼d. to the Stables. Payment for lodgings amounted to £35. 13s. 8d., rewards for New Year's gifts cost £254. 16s. 8d., offerings in chapel came to £16. 9s. 2d., and outward offerings, £19. 3s. 1d. The royal barge cost the queen £22. 6s. 6d. and 'Divers Necessary Emptions' came to £1,525. 9s. 8¼d. This latter category may have included payments to mercers, drapers, tailors, embroiderers and other craftspeople to whom Anne owed money at the time of her death.[43] At the end of the accounting period, Taylor returned £2,508. 14s. 1½d. to the queen's coffers. The fact that the queen carried over surplus funds at the end of this financial year suggests that her income adequately covered all of her household expenses. This did not, however, preclude the king from rewarding her servants or presenting the queen with fine gifts. For example, at the end of June 1535, Henry paid for satin to be delivered to Anne.[44]

While the king revelled in his wife's hospitality, Fisher and More languished in the Tower. Lady Alice More, Thomas's wife, confessed to Cromwell that she had sold her clothing to pay for her husband's weekly board and the wages of his servant, which cost 15s.[45] It was common in the sixteenth century for prisoners, especially those from the upper echelons of society, to contribute to the cost of their upkeep. Lady More begged Cromwell 'to show your most favourable help to the comforting of my poor husband and me in this our great heaviness, extreme age, and necessity.' Despite her advancing years – she was in her early sixties at the time – she also requested permission to attend on the king. Perhaps she felt that her presence might soften the king's resolve?

It wasn't long, however, before the man Lady More described as 'her husband's greatest comfort' was back at the Tower interrogating the former Lord Chancellor. On 3 June, Thomas Cromwell, Thomas Cranmer, Thomas Audley, Thomas Boleyn and Charles Brandon questioned More about whether he believed the Act of Supremacy to be lawful.[46] More recorded the Council's visit in a letter to his daughter Margaret Roper, penned the same day.[47] He recounted how he had refused the oath offered to him, adamantly retorting that 'he never purposed to swear any book oath while he lived'. When asked if he had seen the statute and whether he considered it lawful or not, he answered that 'he had already confessed the first and would not answer the second'. Needless to say, his obstinacy angered the king's Council. More ends his letter to his daughter by describing how, at the conclusion of the interrogation, 'Mr Secretary said he liked him worse than the last time, for then he pitied him, but now he thought he meant not well'. It seems Lady More's pleas to Cromwell fell on deaf ears. More faced further questioning on 14 June, as did John Fisher. They were not, however, the only men under interrogation in the Tower. Humphrey Middlemore, William Exmewe and Sebastian Nudygate, monks of the Charterhouse London, had all been detained for declaring that they 'cannot nor will consent to be obedient to the King's Highness as a true, lawful, and obedient subject, to take and repute him to be Supreme Head in [*sic*] Earth of the Church of England under Christ.'[48] If the Bishop of Faenza's sources are correct, the king had gone to great lengths to obtain their obedience, including visiting the Charterhouse in disguise and urging them in person to accept his supremacy. But still they refused to waver, and instead replied unanimously, 'that he might do with their persons what he would, but they would never consent to what they considered unjust'.[49] The king took them at their word.

As Edward Hall reports, the churchmen were hung, drawn and quartered at Tyburn on 19 June and 'their quarters set up about London'.[50] A few days later, on 22 June, it was Bishop Fisher's turn. Spared the full horrors of a traitor's death, he was beheaded before a stunned crowd on Tower Hill and his head set upon a spike on London Bridge. Hall prudently observed that while many men lamented his death, because 'he was reported to be a man of very great learning, and a man of very good life', he was nonetheless, 'wonderfully deceived, for he maintained the Pope to be supreme head of the church, and very maliciously refused the king's title of supreme head.'[51] As far as Henry was concerned, there was no head too learned, devout or beloved that it could not be removed.

To drive his point home, on St John's Eve, the day after Fisher's execution, the king went to great lengths to attend a pageant based on the Book of Revelation. One particular scene depicted the decapitation of a number of clergymen, which Henry is said to have greatly enjoyed. So convivial was the king's mood, that 'in order to laugh more at his ease', and to 'encourage his people to persevere in such amusements' he set aside his crown and watched the entertainments bareheaded.[52] The following day, he sent word to Anne urging her to watch the play when it was next performed a week later, on St Peter's Eve.

And so the month ended as the previous one had begun – drenched in the blood of holy men. But the violence was far from over. One of the greatest shocks of Henry VIII's reign was yet to come.

Chapter 7

Pastime With Friends

On the day of Fisher's execution, the Bishop of Faenza informed Ambrogio, the Pope's secretary, that negotiations between the French and English ambassadors at Calais had come to naught 'on account of his [the admiral's] refusal to allow the duke of Angoulême to go to England until the girl [Princess Elizabeth] was old enough to be married, and because he would not declare in any way against the Church, or in favour of the King's second wife.'[1] He noted that while the alliance had not been concluded, 'both sides affirm the friendship to be firmer than ever'. He also reported that, 'the brother of the new Queen, came here for eight days, but, as far as could be seen, did nothing. It is only from his relation to the Queen that he is employed, for the King has very few to trust in. All business passes through the hands of people who depend on the new Queen, and must therefore be settled according to her purpose.'[2] This does appear to be a fairly harsh assessment of Lord Rochford's diplomatic skills. While he was less experienced than his colleagues, the papal nuncio was drawing his information from Philippe de Chabot, the Admiral of France, who earlier in the month had complained to Cardinal du Bellay that he was sick of his mission and tired of the 'haggling and carping of the English'.[3] Even a seasoned envoy would have found such an attitude challenging. Furthermore, as we've already noted, Cromwell, who now favoured an Imperial alliance, admitted to having delayed George's return to Calais, suggesting that he was, in fact, skilled at his job. Cromwell obviously feared that George might successfully conclude negotiations with the French and thwart his own plans.

By the end of June, Lord Rochford was back at Dover while the court prepared for their annual royal progress at Windsor Castle.[4] Originally built by William the Conqueror to guard the western approach to London, the fortress had undergone a number of refurbishments over the centuries. By the beginning of the Tudor reign, the royal apartments were essentially those built by Edward III, and later modified and embellished by Henry VII. In early 1500, work began on a new tower and gallery, which formed part of the monarch's private suite of rooms. This new building probably contained the king's private study and library, and functioned as a private space for the king, a retreat away from the public eye.[5]

While the royal apartments were undoubtedly spacious and luxurious, the castle's setting greatly enhanced its appeal and popularity with the Tudor monarchs. Windsor Castle was surrounded by a hunting forest and two royal parks, which meant that Henry could partake in one of his favourite sports and one long associated with English kings – hunting. The king was an avid and skilled sportsman and an accomplished horseman, obsessed by the thrill of the chase.

In 1519, the Venetian ambassador, Sebastian Giustinian, gushed that 'His Majesty is twenty-nine years old and extremely handsome; nature could not have done more for him... He is very fond of hunting, and never takes his diversion without tiring eight or ten horses, which he causes to be stationed beforehand along the line of country he means to take; and when one is tired he mounts another, and before he gets home they are all exhausted.'[6] The following year, a weary Richard Pace wrote that 'The King rises daily, except on holy days, at 4 or 5 o'clock, and hunts till 9 or 10 at night. He spares no pains to convert the sport of hunting into a martyrdom.'[7]

Anne Boleyn shared her husband's passion for the hunt. In July 1531, Chapuys observed that Anne 'always accompanies the King at his hunting parties', a role previously filled by Katherine.[8] The following summer, Jean du Bellay, Bishop of Bayonne, informed the French statesman Anne de Montmorency that Henry sometimes placed he and Anne together 'with their crossbows to shoot the deer as they pass, and in other places to see the coursing'.[9] The latter involved the pursuit of game, such as hares, by dogs, usually greyhounds. Du Bellay also reported that Anne had given him 'a hunting frock and hat, horn and greyhound', which the ambassador believed was a sign of Henry's affection for Francis I.

Henry, too, lavished his wife-to-be with expensive riding accoutrements. On 27 May 1530, a warrant was issued to Sir Andrew Windsor, Keeper of the Great Wardrobe, for a number of saddles, harnesses and other fine accessories to be delivered to Anne, including 'a saddle of the French fashion, with a pillow of down, covered with black velvet, fringed with silk and gold, the head of copper and gilt, graven with antique works'.[10] Henry also presented Anne with a footstool, 'covered with black velvet, and fringed with black silk, garnished with gilt nails, with two buckles of copper and gilt', as well as saddles of black leather and harness for the mules which carried her litter. Several of the saddles are recorded as being 'of the French fashion', which, once again, demonstrates Anne's fondness for all things French.

We find further evidence of Anne's interest in riding, hunting and archery in the king's privy purse expenses, which survive for the years 1529–1532. Not only do they demonstrate how inseparable the couple were during this period, they also attest to Anne's many and varied talents. At least four entries link Anne specifically to hunting and archery. In May 1530, Henry paid 23s. 4d. for 'bows, arrows, shafts, broad heads, bracer, and shooting glove for lady Anne'.[11] The following month, the king's bowyer was paid 13s. 4d. for four additional bows for Anne.[12] In September 1530, the king paid 10s. as compensation for a cow that had been killed by Anne and Urian Brereton's greyhounds while they were out hunting in Waltham Forest.[13] Brereton, whose first name was sometimes spelled Uryan, was a groom of the king's privy chamber and a younger brother of Sir William Brereton. In order to cement bonds or curry favour, dogs and other hunting paraphernalia were often given as gifts at court. In August 1532, Lady Russell's servant was rewarded for bringing a stag and a greyhound to Anne, who subsequently passed both on to the king.[14] Thomas Cromwell also received many such gifts. In late June 1535, Henry Parker, Lord Morley – the father of Anne's sister-in-law, Jane – gave Cromwell a greyhound 'as you will spend this summer in sporting'.[15]

In addition to providing recreation, the royal parks, as Jane Roberts reminds us, also served a more practical purpose by supplying food for the royal table.[16] They provided venison for the royal household and, like at Hampton Court, they were home to ponds where fish were kept and bred. This was an essential part of the Tudor diet and not just during Lent and Advent. Fridays and Saturdays were also fast days and meant that fish dishes replaced those with meat.[17] On one such day in the mid-1520s, the king and queen were served a variety of dishes, including herring, ling, eels or lampreys, pike, salmon, whiting, plaice, sea bream, porpoise or seal, carp, trout, crab and lobster.[18] The parks were also an important source of income, generated from offices, fines and dues.[19]

Lord Morley was correct when he stated that the summer would involve 'sporting', however, the royal progress of 1535 was designed to be much more than simply pastime with friends. As we shall shortly see, it would prove to be one of the longest and most politically significant progresses of Henry VIII's reign. It was a plum opportunity for Henry and Anne to show themselves to their people and to reinforce their authority in the different localities. Importantly, the royal couple were presented to their subjects 'against a background of ceremony and ritualised splendour', which left a dazzling impression on those who witnessed it.[20]

The importance of the progress should not be underestimated, but neither should the huge amount of planning and work required to move the cumbersome court from place to place. Royal progresses customarily took place in the 'grass season', between July and October, when the hay had been cut and the hunting was optimal.[21] The itinerary, however, was planned months in advance, although it could be altered, as Simon Thurley has pointed out, in response to 'adverse weather conditions, food shortages and disease'.[22] For example, before the court had even departed from Windsor, changes were made to the published itinerary. On 30 June 1535, Roger Coke, the Mayor of Bristol, wrote to the Privy Council to acknowledge their letter informing him of the 'doleful news' that the king would not visit Bristol as planned, on account of the 'sickness'.[23] The lists summarising the king's itinerary were known as 'giests'. They outlined the king and courts' intended movements over the summer, specifying the locations where the king would stay, the duration of each visit, as well as the number of miles between each of the staging posts.[24] While the king would often stay at royal residences and religious houses, he also enjoyed lodging with courtiers and noblemen. A visit from the king was indeed a sign of royal favour, but it often came at great personal cost and inconvenience. To give the intended hosts, and those accompanying the progress, time to prepare, the 'giests' were published and disseminated in around June each year. The 'giests' for 1535 survive, albeit in a damaged state.[25] [See Appendix 1]

The exact number of people who accompanied Anne and Henry on progress is unknown, but there's a clue in Edward Seymour's accounts for a three-day visit by the king and court in August 1539. The Earl of Hertford's household accounts testify to the vast amount of food required to cater for the royal entourage. On the day of their arrival at Wolfhall, 200 messes were provided, which suggests that there were around 800 people present, as a 'mess' was usually intended for four people.[26] As Neil Samman observed, there was a substantial increase in messes served over the succeeding two days: 470 and 440 respectively, which he concludes was 'the result of local families paying homage to their monarch'.[27] This also illustrates how numbers could fluctuate quite significantly from day to day.

As soon as the 'giests' were finalised, the officers of the King's Works rode out to survey the residences where the king intended on staying. If repairs were required, it was their job to ensure the work was completed in advance of the court's arrival. Royal officers also went ahead of the royal entourage to ensure that there was accommodation and provisions for the large number of people accompanying the king and queen. As most residences could not house the whole court, it was common for the court to be split among multiple locations. The king's harbingers pre-arranged accommodation for members of the royal party in local inns or private houses, within close proximity to the monarch and their immediate retinue. In May 1520, as the court made its way to the Field of Cloth of Gold, even the Lord High Chancellor, Cardinal Thomas Wolsey, had to rely on the harbingers to find him 'good and convenient' lodgings along the way, close to where the king was staying. 'To induce them to be more active', Wolsey offered them a bribe of 20 shillings.[28]

When it came to ensuring the court was properly fed while on the move, this responsibility lay with the officers of the Greencloth. According to Edward IV's household ordinances of 1471–2, known more commonly as the Black Book, the Clerk of the Market should ride ahead of the king 'to warn the people to bake, to brew, and to make ready other vittle [victuals] and stuff into their lodgings'.[29]

Although many of the greater houses had basic furniture and a skeleton staff, the king and queen's personal belongings, including plate, bed, tapestries and clothes travelled with them. The officers of the Wardrobe were primarily in charge of packing and of transporting the goods by cart, mule or boat, a process known as 'removing', and the Grooms of the Chamber or Privy Chamber were responsible for setting up and furnishing the royal lodgings at each new destination. This was no easy task, as the following extract from Cavendish's *Life of Wolsey* illustrates. In 1527, Wolsey entertained a French delegation at Hampton Court Palace and George Cavendish recalls how he along with other grooms were tasked with setting up the chambers:

> The yeomen and grooms of the wardrobes were busied in hanging of the chambers costly hangings, and furnishing the same with beds of silk, and other furniture apt for the same in every degree... Our pains were not small or light, but travailing daily from chamber to chamber. Then the carpenters, the joiners, the masons, the painters, and all the artificers necessary to glorify the house and feast were set at work. There was carriage and recarriage of plate, stuff, and other rich implements; so that there was nothing lacking or to be imagined or devised for the purpose.[30]

Moving this colossal entourage and their accompanying belongings required significant manpower, as well as many horses, coffers, chests and carts. When Henry VIII travelled to York in 1541, in the hope of meeting his nephew James V of Scotland, he is reported to have taken 4,000 to 5,000 horses along. The French ambassador, Charles de Marillac, noted that this was significantly more than the usual 1,000 taken on a 'normal' progress.[31]

There must have been an air of excitement at court, as the final preparations were made for Anne and Henry's imminent departure. No doubt they relished the prospect of a few months away from the capital – a much-needed respite from the tribulations and bloodshed of the last few trying months. A change of scenery is what their relationship desperately needed. For Thomas More, however, there was no promise of better times to cling to.

On 5 July, the very day that the court was scheduled to leave Windsor, he wrote his last letter to his daughter Margaret from his cell in the Tower of London. As his writing tools had been confiscated, he painstakingly scratched his farewell note using a bit of coal.[32] The following day, Henry's former friend and Lord Chancellor was beheaded on Tower Hill. Before the axe fell, he professed that he died the king's faithful servant, but God's first.[33]

Chapter 8

The Royal Progress

A little later than scheduled, on Friday, 9 July, Anne and Henry departed Windsor Castle and made their way to Reading Abbey, the first stop on their progress to the West Country and Hampshire.[1] The twelfth-century monastery, founded by William the Conqueror's youngest son, Henry I, was one of the wealthiest monasteries in England and featured regularly on Henry's summer itinerary. It was so highly regarded by the king, that in October and November 1525, the court resided there for twenty-seven days.[2]

Outwardly, the king's buoyancy appeared unmarred by the recent spate of executions. In fact, on 11 July, Chapuys marvelled that Henry 'is more given to matters of dancing and of ladies than he ever was'.[3] However, this jovial facade hid the king's deep frustration with those subjects who continued to defy him. On Midsummer Day, one Christopher Mitchell, parish priest of Winestead in Yorkshire, spoke out in favour of the Pope and urged his parishioners to pray for him, 'for he had made his testament and was bowne [bound?] to such a journey that he trowed never to see them again. And it is said there is no Pope, but I say there was one Pope'.[4] Not long before Mitchell had taken to his pulpit, the king sent out a circular letter which outlined the measures taken for the abolition of the Pope's authority. The bishops were instructed to enforce conformity in their dioceses, to erase the Bishop of Rome's name from all mass books, and to order preaching of the royal supremacy.[5] Nevertheless, when the authorities examined Mitchell's mass book, they found that he had not erased the Pope's name as instructed, he had simply 'covered it with bits of paper fixed with wax'.[6]

It wasn't, however, only the clerics who were voicing their dissatisfaction at the religious changes taking place. On the very same day that Sir John Constable and others penned a letter to Cromwell informing him of Mitchell's treasonous behaviour, the parish priest at Gisburn in Yorkshire had a violent confrontation with a disgruntled member of his congregation. As he was 'declaring the articles directed by the King to the archbishop of York', one John Atkinson, alias Brotton, violently ripped the book from the priest's hands and 'pulled it to pieces'.[7] Unlike the parish priest of Winestead, who was incarcerated for his defiance, Atkinson made a hasty escape. The king's demand for conformity had sparked a wave of dissension throughout his northern counties.

On 12 July, Anne and Henry left Reading and rode approximately 12 miles to the manor of Ewelme in Oxfordshire, formerly in the possession of Charles Brandon, Duke of Suffolk, and his wife Mary, the king's sister. On the same day, Sir Francis Bigod wrote to Cromwell from Jervaulx Abbey, near Middleham, to report that one of the monks, George Lazenby, had been taken into custody at Middleham Castle for contradicting Thomas Gerrard during his sermon. When Gerrard, whom the king had licensed to preach, declared that every bishop and priest had as much authority to remit sin as the Pope had previously had, Lazenby interrupted and stated that 'the bishop of Rome had the authority over all other bishops'.[8] He was executed in August 1535, following a series of lengthy examinations in which he vehemently maintained the authority of the Pope.[9] Curiously, Francis Bigod, an ardent evangelical, would later be executed for taking up arms against the king during the Pilgrimage of Grace. The preacher Thomas Gerrard would not fare any better. He was burned for heresy at Smithfield, along with Robert Barnes and William Jerome, just two days after Thomas Cromwell's execution for high treason in July 1540. On the same day as Gerrard and his fellow religious reformers were put to death, three Catholics – Edward Powell, Richard Fetherston and Thomas Abell – were hung, drawn and quartered at Smithfield, for denying the king's supremacy.[10] Walking the religious tightrope of Henry's England was a treacherous balancing act. To lean too far in any one direction meant certain death.

Presumably, Cromwell, who was still in London, was keeping the king apprised of the latest developments. Prior to Anne and Henry's departure from Windsor, temporary postal routes were established to ensure that the royal couple were able to maintain communication with their officials in London.[11] The king and queen spent two days at Ewelme, but they were not particularly impressed with the state of the house.[12] Henry had granted the estate to Charles Brandon in 1525, but following the duke's lukewarm enthusiasm for Henry's marriage to Anne, he had claimed it back in exchange for lands elsewhere.[13] While the duke insisted he had spent £1,000 on Ewelme, the couple had found the manor 'in great decay'.[14] While the court was in Oxfordshire, John Husee informed Lady Lisle that people were dying around Lincoln's Inn, presumably of the plague, which is why her son John Bassett would spend the summer away from London.[15] Unfortunately for the Tudors, the plague, of which there were various types, was only one of a number of epidemic diseases that frequently afflicted the population. The following day, Cromwell received a letter from William, Lord Sandys, lord chamberlain of the king's household, informing him that he was unable to wait upon the king, as he and other members of his family were unwell.

> Please to remember that whereas I have advertised you of the state of myself and my wife during the last week, I have been attacked anew with the sweat. I am grieved I cannot wait upon the King to execute his office. I beg therefore you will excuse me. As the King will shortly repair to East Hampstead, I dare not come near him unless I am signified of his pleasure. My son's wife is also very sick, on whose account I have sent this bearer, Master Augustine, to whom, as I hear, you have been special good master.[16]

'The sweat' or sweating sickness was one of the most feared and deadly diseases of the Tudor period. It was highly contagious and could kill its victims within a few hours of contracting the disease. As Edward Hall put it, one could be 'merry at dinner and dead at supper'.[17] During the first outbreak in England, in the summer of 1485, one eyewitness, the physician Thomas Forrestier, wrote of the suddenness of the attack: 'We saw two priests standing together and speaking together, and we saw both of them die suddenly. Also... we see [sic] the wife of a tailor taken and suddenly dead. Another young man walking by the street fell down suddenly'.[18] There was another good reason to fear this deadly disease; unlike the bubonic plague, which 'was distinctively a disease of the poorer classes', the sweat did not discriminate.[19] 'Gentlemen and gentlewomen, priests, righteous men, merchants, rich and poor, were among the victims', warned Forrestier.[20] It's no wonder that Lord Sandys would not venture near the king. The disease could strike with little or no warning. Victims would usually feel a sudden sense of apprehension, followed by headaches, cold shivers, muscle aches, dehydration and an overwhelming exhaustion. This was followed by a hot and sweating stage that was accompanied by delirium. The patient might also experience chest pains and difficulty breathing.

While many of those who contracted the disease perished within a day, those who survived the first 24 hours, usually made a full recovery. In 1528, during one of the most virulent epidemics of Henry VIII's reign, Anne, George and Thomas Boleyn contracted the disease, but all miraculously survived.[21] Anne's brother-in-law, William Carey, was not so lucky.[22] He perished along with many others, including two other prominent courtiers, Sir William Compton and Francis Poyntz.[23] It's also possible that the sweating sickness was the cause of death of Thomas Cromwell's wife, Elizabeth, and his two daughters, Anne and Grace, in the spring and summer of 1529.[24] One has to wonder whether this planted a seed of hostility in the minister. Why had the Boleyns been spared while his family were so cruelly taken?

Tragically, during the summer of 1551, the sweating sickness carried off his only son Gregory too, and also left the Duchess of Suffolk bereft, robbing her of her two teenage boys within hours of each other.[25] This was the last major outbreak of the mysterious 'sweat' in England.

From Ewelme, the court travelled in a north-westerly direction to another great monastic house, Abingdon Abbey.[26] They arrived on Wednesday, 14 July and lodged there for two nights as guests of the abbot, Thomas Rowland. While details of Anne and Henry's reception do not survive, we can be certain that Abbot Rowland would have received his royal guests with great pomp and ceremony. This was the case whenever the king and queen arrived at a new location, regardless of whether the host was a nobleman, courtier, city corporation or cleric. As customary, the royal couple and their immediate entourage were probably lodged in the abbot's house, which was the only building sufficiently spacious and sumptous to house such distinguished guests.

From Abingdon, the court travelled to the manor of Langley, a favoured royal residence sited in the royal forest of Wychwood that stretched from Woodstock in the east to Burford and beyond in the west. While the word 'forest' today conjures images of an area of land densely covered with trees and undergrowth, the word had a different meaning in the sixteenth century. In *Lawes of the Forrest,* a treatise written by John Manwood, published in 1598, he describes a forest as 'a certain territory of woody grounds and fruitful pastures, privileged for wild beasts and fowls of forest, chase, and warren, to rest and abide in, in the safe protection of the king, for his princely delight and pleasure'.[27] However, as John Cox points out, as well as woodland and pastures, forests consisted of 'extensive waste lands'.[28] Importantly, as Manwood alludes to in his description, royal forests like Wychwood were under forest law, which meant, among other things, that only the royal family and their guests could hunt within its boundaries.

Henry and Anne would have certainly made time for such pastimes, however, there were other matters requiring their attention. While Catholic Europe reeled in shock as news of More's execution spread, the king closeted himself with the Duke of Norfolk and Lord Rochford to arrange the details of an upcoming embassy to Germany.[29] Meanwhile, Anne wrote to Thomas Cromwell on Sunday, 18 July from 'my lord's manor of Langley', requesting that he bestow the abbacy of a monastery in Lincolnshire on the friend of one Robert Power.

Master Secretary, whereas heretofore, at our instance and for our sake, you have been good master unto Robert Power, whom we put to you in

service, insomuch, beside others, you granted him afore this time, as
we be informed, the nomination and preferment of an abbacy or house
of religion for his friend, through the which he might be the more able
to maintain himself in your service; and now, as we be informed, the
abbot of Wallryale [Vale Royal] in Lincolnshire[30] is lately deceased
and departed this world, wherefore the said monastery is now void
and without head: wherefore we desire and heartily pray you, at the
contemplation of these our letters and at our request, in preservation of
your said grants to be fulfilled, to help his said friend to the preferment
of the said house or monastery. And in so doing we shall hereafter have
you in our remembrance, with condign thanks &c. to be showed unto
you. Given under our signet, at my lord's manor of Langley, the 18th day
of July, in the twenty-seventh year of my said lord's reign.[31]

While this particular letter was dictated to a secretary, it is superscribed in
Anne's own hand, 'Anne the quene'. Despite Anne's obvious interest in the
matter, she failed to secure the appointment for the unnamed candidate.
In the end, the abbacy went to John Harwood or Harware, formerly the
Abbot of Hulton in Staffordshire.[32] He had been put forward by Dr Adam
Becansaw, whom Cromwell had hand-picked to undertake a series of
ecclesiastical visitations in Wales.[33] However, the two men had been acquainted
since at least the autumn of 1531, when Gregory Cromwell penned a letter
to his father from Toppesfield in Essex, where he had been undertaking his
studies. He acknowledged that he had received his token from Dr Becansaw
and added cheerily that 'when the latter was at Topsfylde he made the writer
and all his fellows great cheer, and gave him a crown to spend'.[34] Perhaps
unsurprisingly, the following year, Cromwell was appointed steward of the
lands of Vale Royal, a position which he used to secure advantageous leases.[35]
Closeness to the wily minister was certainly beneficial, but evidently the
queen was not considered part of his inner circle.

Perhaps in a bid to test his loyalty, Anne continued to press Cromwell for
favours. At around the same time, she penned a second letter to him about a
wardship that the king had granted her.

Master Secretary, I pray you despatch with speed this matter, for mine
honour lies much on it, and what should the King's attorney do with
Poynz obligation, since I have the child by the King's grace's gift, but
only to trouble him hereafter, which by no means I will suffer, and
thus fare you as well as I would ye did. Your loving mistress, Anne the
Queen.[36]

Unlike the previous letter, this one is written in the queen's own hand, demonstrating the importance and personal nature of the matter. The child in question, named 'Poynz', was a member of the Poyntz family from Iron Acton, however, his or her identity remains unknown. The letter implies that the king's attorney, possibly Sir Christopher Hales, was interfering with a wardship that the king had granted Anne. The queen looked to Cromwell for assistance because, as the late Professor Joel Hurstfield noted, 'Cromwell had long been interested in wardships... though there is no evidence whatsoever to show, as some of his correspondents believed, that he was ever master of the wards'.[37]

While we do not know for certain when this grant, or 'gift' as Anne refers to it, was made, we do know that sometime before December 1529, Anne was granted the wardship and marriage of her nephew Henry Carey, as well as custody of his lands during his minority. It's likely that the grant, which is undated, was made shortly after William Carey's death in June 1528. The wording places it before Thomas Boleyn's elevation to the earldom of Wiltshire and the Irish earldom of Ormond in December 1529, as Anne is identified as 'one of the daughters of Viscount Rochford'.[38]

As to the outcome of the queen's petition, the sources are frustratingly silent. But there is one more thing to note in regards to this letter – it offers us a rare glimpse into what Anne might have actually sounded like. As there was no standardised spelling at the time, people spelled phonetically, which provides a window into pronunciation. For example, Anne spells the word 'obligation' as 'hoblygassion', suggesting that the queen may have spoken with a faint but recognisable French lilt.

On Wednesday, 21 July, the day that Henry and Anne removed to Winchcombe in Gloucestershire, John Husee penned a letter to Lady Lisle from London, in which he addressed a number of matters, including Lady Lisle's 'mucky' or monkey. It's unclear as to whether Husee's patroness desired to present the queen with a pet monkey or whether she had already despatched the animal, but Husee made it perfectly clear that such a gift would not appeal to Anne: 'touching your monkey, of a truth, madam, the Queen loveth no such beasts nor can scant abide the sight of them'.[39] Not everyone, however, shared Anne's dislike of these exotic creatures. Jehan de Moucheau, a member of the French embassy that met with the English envoys in Calais, wrote to Lady Lisle in November 1534, noting that 'there hath been brought to him out of France certain small beasts, the which are come from Brazil... and the said beasts are called two marmosets, the smaller ones; and the larger is a long-tailed monkey, which is a pretty beast and gentle.'[40] These three animals, he sent to Lady Lisle, along with instructions regarding their diet and care:

And you must understand that the said beasts eat only apples and little nuts, or almonds, and you should instruct those who have the charge of them that they give them only milk to drink, but it should be a little warmed. The larger beast should be kept near the fire, and the two other small ones should always be hung up for the night close to the chimney in their *boite de nuit*, but during the day one may keep them caged out of doors.[41]

The French secretary also noted that the Admiral of France had given Lady Lisle's nephew, Sir Richard Grenville, a little marmoset for his wife, 'of the which gift, I ensure you, he is not a little proud'. It's possible that this is what inspired Lady Lisle to consider the gift of a monkey for Anne. Later that same year, William Kendal gave Henry a marmoset as a New Year's gift.[42] It's commonly reported that Anne's dislike of these animals stemmed from Katherine of Aragon's fondness for them, but this is too simplistic an argument, as Anne embraced many of the same things that Katherine loved. To get to the source of Anne's antipathy, we must delve deeper.

In about 1525, the Flemish artist Lucas Horenbout painted a miniature of Katherine holding a monkey.[43] Interestingly, another version of this portrait was made in around 1531. It, too, shows Katherine holding a monkey, but subtle alterations have been made to the iconography. In the later version, the queen offers the animal a coin, but he ignores it, reaching out instead for the bejewelled crucifix at her breast. The message is clear: the monkey is obedient to the church above all worldly goods – a comment, of course, on Katherine's unwavering piety and steadfastness, and the situation in which the queen found herself in, in the latter years of her marriage to the king. Furthermore, the art historian Bendor Grosvenor observed that the coin being proffered is an English groat, which has the royal arms on one side and a portrait of the king on the other. Thus, he concluded that the painting is not only a rejection 'of riches in favour of faith', but a rejection of Henry VIII himself, 'making it one of the most daring images of the Tudor period'.[44] These controversial elements are absent from the original miniature, which was made before Katherine's marital troubles had begun, proving beyond doubt that the later portrait was a calculated piece of pro-Katherine propaganda. It was designed to circulate a youthful likeness of the queen and keep her at the forefront of the minds of her subjects, but perhaps more importantly, it was also a way of assuring her adherents of her unshakeable resolution.

It has even been suggested that the monkey depicted is a marmoset, a very deliberate choice as it's a near-anagram of one of Katherine's most fervent supporters, Thomas More.[45] This is a plausible and thought-provoking proposition, especially considering how skilled the Tudors were at decoding allegory. If we accept that it was not shallow or puerile jealousies that bred Anne's repulsion, it was the fact that in her mind the creatures symbolised her predecessor's persistent and dangerous defiance. If allusions to Katherine's piety and righteousness were high on the list of what stoked Anne's fury, the dirty business of false relics came a close second.

In the itinerary published in early July 1535, Sudeley Castle in Winchcombe is one of the locations earmarked by Henry and Anne for a five-night stay. However, in Sir William Paulet's account books – one of the main sources for reconstructing the movements of the court during this time – we find only Winchcombe mentioned. This does not mean that the court did not lodge at the royal residence. In fact, it seems very likely that the king and queen and their immediate retinue stayed at Sudeley, while the rest of their entourage were accommodated at nearby Winchcombe Abbey. It's worth reiterating that it was common for the court to be split among various locations while on progress.

What is absolutely certain is that it was here that Thomas Cromwell joined the court. He left London on 21 July and was at Winchcombe Abbey by 23 July.[46] Within a week of his arrival, the visitations of monasteries and other ecclesiastical institutions began. This responsibility had in the past largely fallen to the diocesan bishop or his appointed commissioner. A handful of religious orders, though, were exempt from investigation by the diocesan bishop, so they relied on their own internal visitational process, which was overseen by their provincial chapters.[47] As Henry gained more control over church affairs, foreign chapters were removed from the process, and the Crown was given the authority to visit monasteries and other religious institutions that had previously been exempt from the bishop's jurisdiction. Planning and conducting these visitations was a mammoth task, and one that Henry entrusted to his right-hand man.

In early 1535, Cromwell was appointed 'Vice-Gerent in Spirituals', which, as Diarmaid MacCulloch explains, was a translation of the Latin for 'exercising in place of'.[48] In other words, Cromwell could now exercise power in place of Henry VIII, who was, of course, Supreme Head of the Church of England. Among other things, this title gave Cromwell the power to undertake all religious visitations and to collect information pertaining to the spiritual, moral and temporal state of all of England's ecclesiastical establishments, whether they be monasteries, secular colleges or hospitals. It also gave him the authority to delegate his power to subordinates. Therefore, Royal Commissioners were appointed to undertake the Royal Visitations, including Adam Becansaw, whom we've already met, Richard Layton, Thomas Legh and John Tregonwall.[49]

Dr Layton was, after Cromwell, the leading commissioner and the only priest involved in the Royal Visitations. He was in London on 18 July, so it's possible that he travelled with Cromwell to court and that he was responsible for undertaking the Visitation of Winchcombe Abbey.[50] After some initial teething problems,[51] each commissioner was required to administer a long list of questions, or 'Articles of Enquiry', at each location, and issue a list of 'General Injunctions' at the end of each visit. [52] One of these prohibited the use of 'relics or feigned miracles for increase of lucre' and required that 'pilgrims be exhorted to give to the poor', instead of making donations at shrines.[53]

According to Anne's chaplain, William Latymer, the queen fully supported this particular reform. While staying at Winchcombe, she sent her chaplains to nearby Hailes Abbey to investigate a renowned relic known as the Holy Blood, 'commanding them truly and faithfully to view, search and examine by all possible means the truth of this abominable abuse'.[54] This prized relic, which was said to cure the sick and even raise the dead, was widely believed to be a portion of the blood shed by Christ on the cross. Following its arrival in 1270, the monastery was transformed into one of the most popular pilgrimage sites in the country. 'I dwell within half a mile of the Fossway [Fosse Way],' wrote Hugh Latimer in 1533, 'and you would wonder to see how they come by flocks out of the West country to many images, but chiefly to the blood of Hailes.'[55] According to popular belief, just the sight of the Holy Blood relic could put you 'in a state of salvation'.[56] In 1535, it was estimated that offerings to this one shrine alone amounted to around £10 annually, a significant sum for the time.[57]

Anne's chaplains did as they were instructed, but what they found in the venerated crystal container 'was nothing else than the blood of some duck, or as some say, red wax'.[58] This was immediately reported to Anne, who, in turn, informed the king of this 'idolatrous abuse', and requested that the relic be removed. Latymer asserts that it was. However, this might have only been a temporary removal, as it was still on display at Hailes in October 1538, when it was investigated by Hugh Latimer, Richard Tracy and others. After pronouncing it to be nothing more than a gum-like substance, the relic was locked away.[59] With Cromwell's approval, it was later confiscated and taken to London where it was tested before the king and his Council. On 24 November 1538, John Hilsey denounced the relic in a sermon at St Paul's Cross, declaring that it was nothing but 'honey clarified and coloured with saffron'.[60] Interestingly, he also apologised for previously declaring that it was 'duck's blood', and 'showed plainly that it was no blood'. This suggests that this was not the first time the relic had been investigated and lends credence to

Latymer's account of Anne's intervention at Hailes in 1535, as 'duck's blood' is exactly what Anne's chaplains are said to have found there. Furthermore, Henry and Anne intended on visiting Hailes Abbey.[61] Whether the visit ever took place, though, is unknown.

Towards the end of the month, we find the court in Tewkesbury. They arrived on Monday, 26 July and remained for five nights. Some members of the court were housed at Tewkesbury Abbey, as a letter written by Thomas Cromwell on 29 July indicates.[62] Whether or not Anne and Henry were accommodated within the abbey precincts is uncertain. Like in Winchcombe, it's feasible that they stayed in a separate residence, possibly Forthampton Court, the country home of the abbots of Tewkesbury, situated just a few miles away from the abbey.[63]

From his London base, Eustace Chapuys kept a close eye on the court's perambulations, reporting anything of interest to the emperor. In late July, he wrote to Charles regarding the recent embassy to Calais and the upcoming deputations to Lubeck and Denmark. He also expressed horror at the news of the executions of John Fisher and Thomas More, and apprised his master of his latest efforts to reunite Katherine and Mary.[64] Unsurprisingly, he also informed the emperor that the lives of mother and daughter remained in peril as Anne, whom he refers to as 'le concubine', works tirelessly to convince the king to put them to death: 'she is continually telling the King that he does not act rightly or prudently in allowing the Queen and the Princess to live, for they deserve death (she says) much more than those who have lately been executed, since, after all, they were and are still the cause of all the mischief.'[65] But, as is so often the case, Chapuys does not reveal his sources.

On the Feast of St James, another scandalous story reached the ambassador's ears.

> He [Henry] the other day nearly murdered his own fool, a simple and innocent man, because he happened to speak well in his presence of the Queen and Princess, and called the concubine 'ribaude' and her daughter 'bastard.' He has now been banished from Court, and has gone to the Grand Esquire [Sir Nicholas Carew], who has sheltered and hidden him.[66]

Some historians have asserted that the 'fool' was Master Sexton, more commonly known by his nickname 'Patch', who began his career in the household of Cardinal Wolsey,[67] while others claim the story relates to William Somer, who went on to serve Edward VI and Mary I.[68] Both these men were 'natural fools' or innocents, and required keepers to take care of them. What is unquestionable is that Somer was in the king's service by 28 June 1535, when the Keeper of the Great Wardrobe was issued a royal mandate for new clothes for the king and members of his household, including 'William Somer, our foole'. He was provided with a doublet of worsted, lined with canvas and cotton; a coat and a cap of green cloth, fringed with red crewel, and lined with frieze; a doublet of fustian, lined with cotton and canvas; a coat of green cloth, with a hood to the same, fringed with white crewel lined with frieze and buckram; a coat with a hood of green cloth, fringed with crewel of red and white colours, and lined with buckram; and two pairs of hose of blue cloth, guarded with red and black cloth.[69] The same mandate sheds a revealing light on the many artisans employed at the Tudor court. Andrew Windsor was authorised to make payments to John Malt, the king's tailor; William Crofton, his hosier; Thomas Addington, the king's skinner; Lettice Worsop, his silk woman; as well as to Henry Cornelius and Henry Johnson, the king's cordwainers. William, the king's spurrier, was also paid for providing the king with twenty-four pairs of spurs, half of which were made from velvet and the other half from leather. This army of artisans produced the props of magnificence integral to Henry and Anne's rule.

The other members of the household whom the king provided for were Culpeper, 'our page', three officers of the wardrobe of the robes, two royal barbers, five grooms of the privy chamber, sixty-seven yeomen of the guard, and Mark Philip and Culpeper 'of our privy chamber'. Anne, who is referred to as 'our dearest wife the queen', received yards of green satin and green cloth of gold.

This account appears to clarify the matter of whom Chapuys was referring to in his letter. We can infer that Somer was employed to replace Sexton, whose remarks had so infuriated the king. It's worth noting, though, that Sexton's banishment may have been temporary, as one of Cromwell's correspondents claimed that he was still in the king's service in early 1536. On 26 January, Thomas Bedyll wrote to Cromwell about Henry's 'one old fool, Sexten...[sic] which by reason of age is not like to continue'.[70] Bedyll, who was recruited as a royal commissioner in around December 1535, suggested a 'young fool at Croyland' as a suitable replacement. However, in light of the fact that Bedyll had been away from court for the latter half of 1535, it appears that he was simply mistaken and completely unaware of what had transpired the previous year.

Both Sexton and Somer were known for being witty and verbally inventive. Their gift for repartee made them exceptional entertainers. Writing in the early sixteenth century, the Renaissance humanist, Erasmus of Rotterdam, noted that while a wise man has two tongues, 'one to speak the truth with, the other for saying what he thinks fits the occasion', fools speak frankly: 'They can speak the truth and even open insults and be heard with positive pleasure; indeed, the words which would cost a wise man his life are surprisingly enjoyable when uttered by a clown. For the truth has a genuine power to please if it manages not to give offence, but this is something the Gods have granted only to fools.'[71]

However, in 1535, not even 'a simple and innocent man' could get away with insulting the king. In Henry's eyes, you were either with him or against him. The truth was always on his side.

Chapter 9

Queen of the Cotswolds

In the late nineteenth century, records of the Corporation of Gloucester, that had long been thought lost, were discovered and thankfully preserved. Among the valuable collection is an often-overlooked account of Anne and Henry's visit to Gloucester, including a detailed account of their reception.[1] Not only do these records furnish us with a wealth of information about this particular visit, they also provide an unparalleled window into the ritual and elaborate ceremony that accompanied all royal entries. As such, they are worth studying closely.

On Saturday, 31 July, the king and 'his most entirely beloved and lawful wife Queen Anne' were received by Gloucester's mayor, John Falconer; the town's aldermen; and sheriffs Thomas Payne and Richard Edwardes; all clad in their 'scarlet gowns and velvet tippets'. As customary, the mayor and other dignitaries, which also included around one hundred burgesses, met the royal couple outside the town 'where they did their obeisance all on horseback'. While still mounted, Thomas Payne then approached the king and declared, 'Thanks be to God of your Grace's health and good prosperity, which God long continue!' He kissed the town mace, a symbol of his authority and power, and handed it over to the king. This ritual was accompanied by the following address:

> All such liberties, privileges, customs, and grants as your Grace and other your noble progenitors heretofore have given unto the Mayor and Burgesses of this your town of Gloucester, we deliver up unto your Grace, trusting that your Grace will be as good and gracious Lord unto us now as ye have been heretofore. And furthermore, I here present myself unto your Grace as Mayor of your said town of Gloucester, certifying you that all your burgesses there be in readiness and obedient at your Grace's commandment, and heartily thanks your Grace for such liberties, privileges, and grants that your Grace hath given unto us, beseeching you of your gracious aide and assistance hereafter in the execution thereof in doing justice.

The king accepted the mace, before immediately returning it to the mayor. The two parties then merged to form a procession, headed by the burgesses, aldermen and sheriffs. Then came all the 'gentlemen, esquires, knights, lords, and other great men', followed by the mayor, with the mace still in his hand, accompanied by the 'King of Arrodes', or King of Arms. The latter was the title given to the three chief heralds of the College of Arms.[2] Finally, the royal couple themselves, preceded by the Sword of State, encircled by sergeant-at-arms. Trailing behind the king and queen were Anne's ladies and gentlewomen, the royal guard and 'other sundry persons following the court'.

The vast entourage then snaked its way towards the abbey church. The royal couple brought their horses to a halt at the White Friars, located outside the north gate of the town, where they were met by the clergy, all dressed in their fine ceremonial copes, and 'lord Suffragan', mitred and holding a cross. Without dismounting, they lovingly kissed the cross, before riding on through the town – the streets lined with jostling onlookers, all eager to catch a glimpse of the magnificent procession.

The royal party entered the abbey precinct via Saint Edward's Lane and were greeted by Abbot William Parker and his brethren in the porch of the church, which was adorned with splendid carpets and cushions. Once again, a cross was on hand, but this time the king and queen alighted from their horses and knelt on the cushions before kissing the cross 'with great reverence'. After a visit to the high altar, the mayor led the couple to their lodgings, at which time gifts were traditionally exchanged. These 'clearly established patterns of actions and behaviour' were followed at all royal entries.[3]

At around 10 in the morning, on Monday, 2 August, the mayor and a number of his brethren met Anne and Henry in the abbey churchyard and presented the king with ten fat oxen, for which he gave 'his loving thanks'. The royal couple were preparing for a day of riding and hunting in and around the village of Painswick, known today as the 'Queen of the Cotswolds' on account of its fine architecture and abundant charm.

At some stage during the day, the king had an audience with Sir John Dudley (later Duke of Northumberland) about a matter involving his late mother's second husband, Lord Lisle.[4] The setting for this discussion was almost certainly a residence known as Painswick Lodge, situated to the northeast of the town. It was surrounded by picturesque parklands and boasted unsurpassed views over the undulating valley. The lodge was part of the manor of Painswick, which at the time of the royal visit was held by Lord Lisle, with reversion to John Dudley.[5] The king was greatly perturbed by news he had heard from Anthony Kingston, son of Sir William Kingston, who was the Constable of the Tower of London, about a proposed sale of wood.[6] The bailiff confirmed that Lord Lisle had sold 400 trees from within the park to one Mr Button, but while the deal had been brokered in May 1534, the trees had not yet been felled. The king forbade the sale from going ahead, insisting that 'Button should not have them [the trees], for the lordship were utterly destroyed if should so be spoiled, which were too much pity.'[7] This undoubtedly pleased the young Kingston, who had an interest in the property. In the end, however, it was his father who acquired the manor in 1540.

The bucolic setting agreed with the king and queen, who did not return to Gloucester until nightfall. They were met at the abbey's east gate, 'for which they gave hearty thanks', and travelled by torchlight back to their lodgings. Anne rewarded the fifteen torchbearers with four 'angellett nobles', gold coins worth half the value of an angel.[8]

The queen's visit to the area captured the imaginations of local residents. Writing in the early twentieth century, the amateur archaeologist and historian Welbore St Claire Baddeley, proudly recalled how 'Anne Boleyn... smiled through our green woodlands while hunting in the (former) Park and Longridge Wood.'[9] He also noted that a portion of Longridge, a wooded area located across the valley from Painswick, was known as 'the Queen's Wood', and that a parcel of land there had been named the 'Queen's Acre'.[10]

According to local tradition, the royal couple also visited Prinknash (pronounced locally Prinnish or Prinidge), one of the country residences of the Abbot of Gloucester.[11] Considering that it was within easy reach of Gloucester and that breaks from the saddle would have been welcomed, a visit would not have been out of the question. However, there is no evidence to prove or disprove the local tale.

The following morning, the mayor and all his brethren met the queen in the abbey churchyard, where they presented her with a purse of gold containing £11. 5s., 'for which her grace gave loving thanks'.[12] As another full day of riding and hunting was on the agenda, Anne would have been appropriately attired for outdoor activities. While it's generally assumed that the riding habit originated in the seventeenth century, Professor Maria Hayward asserts that it was in fact a much earlier invention.[13] She notes that the earliest discovered reference to one dates from 26 November 1502, when Robert Johnson was paid to make a riding gown for Elizabeth of York. This particular gown was made of black satin and trimmed with black velvet 'for an edge and cuffs'.[14] It was lined with black buckram and canvas, while sarsenet, a lightweight silk, was used to line the vents.[15] We can imagine Anne dressed in something just as sumptuous. If a full riding gown was deemed unnecessary, a safeguard might have been worn to protect the queen's gown and kirtle.[16]

Anne and Henry spent the day exploring Coberley and the surrounding area. We also hear that the same day, the king hunted at Miserden Park, around 10 miles southeast of Gloucester.[17] Given Anne's penchant for the sport, and the fact that Miserden was one of the queen's properties, there's no reason to suppose that she wasn't by the king's side.[18] The manor and park of Miserden were settled on each of Henry's successive consorts and, following Katherine Parr's death, passed into the hands of Sir Anthony Kingston, who had received a reversionary grant of the said manor in November 1546.[19] Clearly enamoured by the sport and countryside, the royal couple once again returned to the abbey after dark, where they were met at the abbey's east gate by eleven burgesses, all dressed 'in their best apparel'. The torchlit procession made its way through the streets of the ancient town, described by the antiquary John Leland as 'well builded of timber, and large, and strongly defended with walls, where it is not fortified with a deep stream of Severn water.'[20] When they reached the abbey precincts, the king gave the men his sincere thanks, as well as a reward of five marks in gold.

The fact that the queen was able to spend consecutive days in the saddle, participating in such strenuous activity alongside her husband, speaks volumes of her physical stamina and high level of fitness. Anne was an accomplished horsewoman, of that there can be no doubt, but it also reveals a great deal about her character. The picture that emerges is of a woman who was courageous, competitive and driven, and one accustomed to venturing to the edge of her limits.

Frustratingly, the corporation records then fall silent and we hear nothing else of the royal couple's visit until their departure on Friday, 6 August. From letters written to the king and Cromwell, however, we can piece together a peripheral drama that unfolded at Gloucester. Not long after arriving at Winchcombe Abbey, Cromwell received a letter from a disgruntled monk at the monastery of Worcester, named John Musarde (also known as Johannes Musard).[21] In the letter, Musarde accused a fellow monk, Richard Clyve, of treason, specifically for 'railing against the King and queen Anne, and upholding queen Catharine and the authority of the Pope'.[22] Cromwell immediately despatched his commissioners, Thomas Legh and John ap Rice, to investigate.

Unfortunately for Musarde, stories emerged of his questionable past. In 1531, Worcester's beadle and others were paid a reward for 'fetching and conveying Dan John Musard home from Overbury after he robbed his master of certain plate and other things'.[23] Furthermore, the commissioners were given reason to believe that his accusation against Clyve was solely fuelled by a desire for revenge. The details were recorded in a letter penned to Cromwell a few weeks after the visitation. John Russell, MP for Worcestershire and Justice of the Peace, noted that the previous Lent, 'one monk had accused another of buggery' and 'that monk so accused afterwards charged the other monk, his accuser, with certain words against the king's highness or the Queen's grace'.[24] Yet Musarde maintained his innocence and implored Cromwell not to 'accept their false accusations'.[25] Dr Legh, no doubt at Cromwell's behest, commanded William Moore, the Prior of Worcester, to report to Cromwell at Gloucester on the night of Monday, 2 August, and to take with him three of his brethren.[26] These men were John Musarde, Richard Clyve and one Thomas Blockley, whom Musarde claimed had stolen evidence from his cell.[27] The men were examined before the king, and Musarde was imprisoned on returning to Worcester, from where he wrote an impassioned appeal to the king. He noted how his father and three of his brethren had loyally served Henry VII and 'promised their lives in defence of his title', and added that one of the men had even comforted 'your Grace's mother', Elizabeth of York.[28] He continued:

> As a religious man I felt bound to send the words of treason, and the cloaking of them by my master [Prior Moore], to master Secretary at Winchcomb; for which certain of my brethren conspired against me, and they have procured master Secretary as under visitor to put me in prison at Worcester, where I have been ever since I was before you at Gloucester. I desire your pardon that I may continue to be your true beadsman, and that gracious lady queen Anne's, the which hath the name to be as mediatrix betwixt your Grace and high justice.[29]

Whether Anne interceded for this monk – or even what she made of this snafu – is unknown. He was still in prison on 31 January 1536, when he begged Cromwell to agree to his transfer to Westminster Abbey, where he hoped to live out his days.[30] The transfer does not appear to have taken place and at some point before May 1538, Musarde was permitted to leave the community.[31]

On the day of Anne and Henry's departure from Gloucester, the mayor, brethren and other dignitaries assembled in the churchyard to await the royal couple's arrival. Among the servants rewarded by the mayor and other burgesses during the visit were the king's and queen's footmen, the king's trumpeters, servants of the king's buttery and pantry, the Herald of Arms, a servant of the king's almoner, and 'the blacke garde'. The latter were the most low-status servants of the royal household.[32] While money was the most common gift, Master Secretary received a gift of geese, capons and chicken.

Once the whole party was gathered, they rode out in procession and exited the town via the south gate. The king and queen were escorted as far as 'Quoddesleys Grene', the present-day Quedgeley Green, located around 3 miles south of Gloucester, where they said their farewells. Before departing,

Anne and Henry rode by the mounted townsmen and gave them all their heartfelt thanks. The corporation records indicate that the royal party departed Gloucester on Saturday, 7 August and overnighted in Leonard Stanley, before continuing onto Berkeley Castle.[33] However, this does not agree with the household accounts, which have the court overnighting in Leonard Stanley on Friday, 6 August and arriving at Berkeley on Saturday, 7 August. Either way, they travelled via the village of Leonard Stanley, home to a small priory dedicated to St Leonard, where the royal party rested for the night, before moving on to the castle in Berkeley. Despite spending a full week at the royal residence, no records pertaining to the visit survive. Two extant letters, though, confirm Cromwell's continued presence at court.[34] He and his Welsh nephew, Richard Cromwell, had only recently been granted a number of offices related to the castle and its surrounding parks and woods, including the position of constable.[35]

It was during this particular visit that Cromwell met with Richard Layton to draft a set of injunctions that would be issued to all future monastic houses visited.[36] Layton had been with Cromwell earlier in the week, but left the court on Tuesday, 10 August, apparently without Cromwell's permission, because he thought his master wanted him to forge ahead with the visitations. In a letter written at midnight from Cirencester Abbey the following day, a panicked Layton, who had obviously received a scolding missive from Cromwell, further justified his actions: 'I was the more willing to do so [leave court] because my horses were all that day in an old barn without meat and litter and I not then assured of any lodging in the town, neither could be by the provision of any [of] the harbingers.'[37]

The real source of Cromwell's irritation, however, was not Layton's hasty departure from court, it was the sting of the dressing down he had received from Henry about the lack of general injunctions. The king's principal secretary in turn blamed the oversight on Layton, hence his defensive tone. Layton, though, assured Cromwell that he could explain his position, but, understanding the seriousness of the matter, added 'that rather I may be buried quick than to be the occasion why the king's highness should diminish any part of the affiance, confidence or the expectation of your [Cromwell's] assured and proved mind towards his grace.'[38]

Layton was back at Berkeley the following morning, for what must have been a tense and lengthy reunion with his master. What the royal commissioner's letter also reveals is just how challenging it was to accommodate the peripatetic court. Not even an official engaged in the king's urgent business was guaranteed a place to lay his head. The huge stress that royal progresses imposed on the host town should also not be underestimated. All available buildings were commandeered for accommodation or stabling, and the strain on the town's food supply was enormous.

Nevertheless, it was a necessary and important instrument of Tudor government and one which, as we've already seen, utterly captivated the local people. On 10 August, Chapuys informed the emperor of the latest developments at court:

> This King is still on the borders of Wales, hunting and visiting that principality with a view to gain popularity with his subjects. This he attempts by all possible means and ways, and it is reported that a large number of peasants in the villages through which he has passed, after hearing the preachers who follow the Court, have been so deceived as to believe that God inspired the King to repudiate his legitimate Queen owing to her having once been married to his brother. But those who believe in such things are only idiots and ignorant people, who would be soon converted to the truth, were there only an appearance that the remedy was at hand.[39]

While Anne and Henry relied on public displays of magnificence and munificence to win over their subjects and reinforce their legitimate authority, the former queen used her pen and powerful familial ties to try to remedy her situation. From her chamber at Kimbolton Castle, Katherine of Aragon wrote to her niece, Mary of Hungary, who governed as regent of the Netherlands, imploring her to act on her behalf. After hearing of a planned meeting between Mary and her sister, Queen Eleanor of France, Katherine begged Mary for two things: 'first, to inform the Emperor of the extreme urgency of the matters of this kingdom; and, secondly, when she sees the Queen her sister, to beg of her, with Katharine's recommendations, to use her influence with the King her husband [Francis I] to be a good friend to Henry in getting him to abandon the sin in which he stands.'[40] Katherine explained that while she did not want to trouble Mary, she felt compelled to write because of the 'offence given here to God, the danger of her husband's conscience, and the scandal to Christendom.'[41]

Katherine's daughter Mary, who was once again troubled by illness, followed suit, penning her own letter to her cousin in which she thanked her for her kind letters, which she assured her were the source of great joy and comfort, and allowed her to live in hope. In a bid to convince her cousin of her 'melancholy circumstances', Mary signed off, 'written in haste and fear'.[42] In the end, the meeting of the two sister queens took place in Cambrai, however, nothing of great importance was achieved, as the emperor had categorically forbidden the conclusion of any business. 'Showing her [Eleanor] good cheer', however, was permitted.[43]

While the court was at Berkeley (or possibly at Thornbury, their next destination), Henry received news of the emperor's 'glorious and most important storming of the Goulette of Tunis' from Richard Pate, the resident English ambassador with Charles V.[44] Chapuys immediately sent his own man to court with the happy tidings, which, according to the ambassador, brought Henry so much pleasure that he gave the messenger a handsome reward, including a buck that he had taken in the hunt that day.[45] Never one to be outdone, the French ambassador, Antoine de Castelnau, also intended on joining the court to inform the king of the meeting of the two queens and of other matters. His plans were foiled when a member of his entourage died suddenly on the road of a suspected case of plague. The French merchant, Alain, was just one of hundreds of souls who would succumb to the disease over the summer.

On 7 August, Thomas Audley informed Cromwell that he was retreating to his house at Colchester, 'as they are dying of the plague in divers parishes in London.'[46] The following day, one of Cromwell's servants, Richard Pollard, requested permission to depart London for Devonshire and noted that 'the sickness is very sore'.[47] Another servant and friend of Cromwell's, Stephen Vaughan, warned the minister that if he returned to London, he must avoid large gatherings of people, as he feared 'these great humidities will engender pestilence.'[48] The end of the month brought no relief. The king was informed that there was 'great death in London'; 157 of his subjects had perished in one week and pestilence had claimed 140 of them.[49] While the plague continued to ravage the city and other parts of the country, including Bristol, Anne and Henry and their army of attendants retreated to Thornbury Castle, where they arrived on Saturday, 14 August.[50] The large double-courtyard mansion had once harboured the hopes and aspirations of the king's cousin once removed, Edward Stafford, third Duke of Buckingham, who was executed for alleged treason in 1521. It had been the jewel in Stafford's property crown and one of the most magnificent building projects of the time. Had the duke's ambitious plans been realised, Thornbury would have comfortably rivalled Wolsey's Hampton Court Palace in size and splendour. But now it belonged to Henry, and it stood unfinished – a symbol of the duke's untimely end and the danger of reaching too high.

Chapter 10

A Jewel in the Crown

The royal party entered the former ducal palace via the spacious base court, which, among other things, contained the great stable, storehouses and the foundations of two ranges, originally intended to provide accommodation for servants and men-at-arms. The unfinished west range connected the inner and outer wards and contained the porter's lodge and additional accommodation. It also once housed the duke and duchess's lavish wardrobes.[1] While it had been more than fourteen years since Buckingham's execution, his memory remained etched into the very fabric of the building, as did hints of his royal ancestry. Above the inner gateway, which led into the castle's inner ward, were Buckingham's heraldic badges displayed on shields, including the Stafford knot and Bohun swan, and a scrolled inscription declaring that the gate was begun in 1511 by 'me, Edward, Duke of Buckingham, Earl of Hertford, Stafford and Northampton'.[2] No doubt as Henry and Anne passed under the gate, they noticed the duke's motto, 'Dorenesavant', also adorning the gatehouse.[3] This was Old French for 'from now on, henceforth or hereafter', and was interpreted by some as evidence of the duke's ambition for the English throne.[4]

The magnificent inner court – enclosed on all four sides by buildings made of fine ashlar from the Cotswolds, as opposed to local stone used in the construction of the outer ward – contained all the usual features and amenities. Opposite the inner gateway stood the east range, which housed a large great hall, with a scullery, buttery and pantry. This area stood unrenovated at the time of Buckingham's death, hence when the king's officials, William Walweyn and Thomas Magnus, were sent to survey the property, they described it as 'of the old building, and of a homely fashion'.[5] The east side was also home to a chapel (accessed from the lower end of the great hall) and a set of chambers known as the Earl of Stafford's lodging, as well as a series of thirteen rooms probably constructed by Henry's great-uncle, Jasper Tudor, Duke of Bedford and Earl of Pembroke. This range of lodgings was referred to as 'the Earl of Bedford's lodgings' in a survey of 1583, but as A.D.K. Hawkyard explains, this was 'probably because the royal duchy had ceased to exist by that date and the surveyors confused it with the contemporary Russell earldom.'[6] In the final years of his life, Jasper Tudor spent time at Thornbury with his wife Katherine Woodville (or Wydville), who was a younger sister of Edward IV's queen consort, Elizabeth Woodville. In fact, he made his will and died there in December 1495. Katherine's first marriage to Henry Stafford, second Duke of Buckingham, produced four children, including Edward Stafford, third Duke of Buckingham, who was, as such, a first cousin of Henry's mother, Elizabeth of York, not to mention descended via his father from Edward III. Although the evidence against Buckingham was flimsy, it was his royal blood and arrogance that ultimately condemned him.

As for the all-important domestic buildings, the larders, boiling house, bakehouse and kitchens were situated on the ground floor of the northern range, with additional accommodation and a long room known as the 'cook's loft' situated directly above. To the south were the principal apartments, where Anne and Henry were accommodated during their visit. Known as the 'new building', this range originally housed the Duke and Duchess of Buckingham's sumptuous lodgings, described in 1521 as 'stately' and 'fully furnished with curious works'.[7] Anne's rooms were on the ground floor, once the domain of Eleanor Percy, Duchess of Buckingham. These consisted of three interconnecting chambers in the main body of the range, culminating in an octagonal bedchamber in the south-west tower. The king's apartments were situated on the floor directly above, and could be accessed via a private staircase in the tower, as well as one at the opposite end of the suite of rooms. They contained the same arrangement as the floor below, with the exception of two additional rooms, one being an ante-room to the great chamber and the other a jewel house. Both suites were lit by exquisite oriel windows, which overlooked the stunning privy garden. As was to be expected, the windows in the king's rooms were more intricate than the ones below. Should the weather turn wintry, a fireplace in each of the chambers ensured the occupants' comfort.

From Anne's great chamber, a gallery paved with brick led to the privy garden, which was enclosed by a cloister and a covered gallery. While the castle had its own chapel, the king and queen could, if they chose, access the parish church of Thornbury, which stood adjacent to the castle, from the king's great chamber via an extension of the above gallery. 'At the end whereof', noted Elizabeth I's surveyors in 1582, 'is a fair room with a chimney and a window into the said church, where the Duke sometimes used to hear service.'[8]

During their visit, the royal couple also had access to a more expansive garden to the east. It, too, was enclosed by high crenellated walls and accessed via the gallery and other 'privy ways'. The orchard, situated beside the chapel, was also home to many delights, with its maze of covered alleys, planted with a variety of fruit and ornamental trees and plants, including hazel and whitethorn.

As always, the court required access to good hunting grounds, and the manor of Thornbury did not disappoint. From the orchard, several postern gates led into the 'New Park', which, in 1521, was over 4 miles in circumference and contained around 700 deer, and 'many hedgerows of thorn and great elms'.[9] Nearby was another smaller park called Marlwood, home to 300 deer, and within 2 miles of the castle was Eastwood, a large park of 7 miles circumference which, in Buckingham's day, contained 500 fallow deer and fifty red deer.[10] New Park also contained several hunting lodges; a rabbit warren, which supplied the household with rabbits and coneys; and twelve fishponds that by 1583 were 'utterly decayed'.[11]

The royal lovers had originally planned to remain at Thornbury for a week before visiting Bristol, but an outbreak of the plague resulted in a change of plans. In the end, a delegation of townsmen, including Thomas White, Nicholas Thorne, and the chamberlain of Bristol, travelled to Thornbury instead, arriving on Friday, 20 August.[12] During their stay, they presented the king with ten fat oxen and forty sheep 'towards his most honourable household', and 'to the right excellent Queen Anne', they gave 'one cup with a cover of silver overgilt, weighing twenty-seven ounces, with a hundred marks of gold within the same cup'.[13] It has been suggested that Anne's gift may have been Queen's Gold, 'an ancient revenue accruing to every Queen Consort'.[14] As Retha M. Warnicke explains, this was another source of income for queen consorts, 'a traditional payment of 10%... for example, from voluntary licenses for the alienation of lands or from voluntary pardons for enclosures.'[15] Unfortunately, records detailing payments of Queen's Gold to the Tudor consorts either do not survive or remain undiscovered. Either way, after receiving her gift from 'his majesty's town and her chamber of Bristol', the queen responded by promising to visit Bristol in the future.

Within a few days of the visit, Roger Coke, the Mayor of Bristol, wrote to Cromwell to thank him for his 'zeal towards our town, and especially for your kindness to our brethren, Mr. White, Mr. Thorn, and the chamberlain of Bristol, at their last being at the King's manor of Thornbury'.[16] There appears to be no truth to a story that claims that Henry VIII slipped away from Thornbury and visited Bristol in disguise, vowing to transform the town of Bristol into 'the city of Bristol'.[17] In fact, there is evidence to suggest that the king was not at Thornbury on the day of the delegation's arrival. On 24 August, William Burton, the Abbot of St Augustine's Abbey in Bristol, wrote to Cromwell to acknowledge that he had received the king's 'most honourable letters', dated 'Beawdley' [Bewdley] the 20th of August, 'commanding him to pluck up the weirs in the Severn that the king may be advertised of it before his departure from Thornbury.'[18] It seems that Henry left Anne and Cromwell to receive their guests while he, and presumably a small entourage, travelled to Bewdley. It would explain why the Mayor of Bristol wrote to Cromwell to thank him for his hospitality and not, as far as we know, to the king. Thornbury lay just a mile from the Severn. According to Leland, an armlet or creek flowed into the New Park, and Buckingham had begun to construct a canal across the park to link it to the castle.[19] This would have allowed him to travel directly by barge to his properties in Wales. While it's unlikely that the canal was ever completed, Henry could nonetheless have easily accessed the river and travelled by barge to Bewdley, which lay on the banks of the River Severn. Once again, it's to Leland we turn for a description of the town and the inland port as it appeared in around 1539. He describes the fair stone bridge of five arches, which had only recently been rebuilt, crossing the river at Bewdley, noting that it was the only bridge between Bewdley and Worcester. The river was a hive of activity with the 'many flat long vessels' that sailed up and down carrying 'all manner of merchandise'.[20] As for the town itself, Leland waxed lyrical about its splendour:

> The town self of Bewdley is set on the side of a hill, so comely, a man cannot wish to see a Town better. It riseth from Severn bank by East upon the hill by west; so that a man standing upon a hill *trans potem* by East may discern almost every house in the town, and at the rising of the sun from East the whole town glittereth (being all of new building) as it were of gold.[21]

If the king overnighted at Bewdley, it's likely that he stayed at Tickenhill House, a splendid royal residence located on a hill to the south-west of the town, and set within a 'goodly park'. At the time of Leland's visit, the buildings were largely those erected by Henry VII for his son, Arthur, Prince of Wales, whose Council resided chiefly at Tickenhill and at nearby Ludlow Castle. The manor house boasted a great court and a garden with several outbuildings. It also contained a chapel where, on 19 May 1499, Prince Arthur was married by proxy to Katherine of Aragon, and where less than three years later, his lifeless body rested the night before being taken to Worcester for burial.[22]

While there's no record of how the king spent his time in Bewdley, it's possible that he met with Roland Lee, Bishop of Coventry and Lichfield, who also served as the president of the Council in the Marches of Wales, and discussed the matter of the monks of Worcester.[23]

It wasn't long before the king was back at Thornbury and preparing to travel once again. While the household accounts do not mention Acton

Court, the home of Nicholas Poyntz, it had been singled out for a visit in the original itinerary. Anne and Henry had planned to spend a weekend at 'Mr Poyntz's place' following their stay in Bristol, before moving onto Little Sodbury Manor, the home of Poyntz's aunt and uncle, Sir John and Lady Anne Walshe.[24] The court, however, had departed Windsor later than scheduled and had made changes to their plans to avoid the outbreak of plague in Bristol, so the weekend visit never came about. In fact, a letter dictated by Cromwell and penned by the Lord Chancellor, Thomas Wriothesley, is signed 'Thornbury, 23 August', the very day the court had planned to depart Acton Court for Little Sodbury.[25] This does, however, not preclude the possibility of a visit having taken place at a later date, possibly on 23 and 24 August. Perhaps, while the majority of the court remained at Thornbury, Henry and Anne and a small party of attendants rode the 6 or 7 miles across the Gloucestershire countryside to the outskirts of the village of Iron Acton. By all accounts, Poyntz had gone to a great deal of trouble and spent a vast amount of money adding a lavish new east wing to the existing moated house, all to impress his sovereigns.[26] Despite coming from a staunchly Catholic family, Poyntz favoured reform. His grandfather, Sir Robert Poyntz, was with Henry Tudor, Earl of Richmond, during his exile in Brittany and fought by his side at the Battle of Bosworth, where he was allegedly knighted on the field by the new Tudor king.[27] His loyalty was duly rewarded with lucrative and prestigious offices, including positions in Katherine of Aragon's household, where he served successively as her vice-chamberlain and chancellor until his death.[28]

Poyntz's grandson, the young Nicholas, was around 25 years old at the time of the royal progress. He, too, demonstrated his loyalty through active service. In 1534–1535, he was one of a number of Gloucestershire men who served in Ireland, for which service he was knighted.[29] Many have conjectured that the ceremony may have taken place during Anne and Henry's visit to Acton Court, possibly even falling on the fiftieth anniversary of the Battle of Bosworth. While there's no contemporary record to support this, it would have been an especially felicitous date to honour the grandson of a man who risked his life for the Tudor dynasty.

Speculation aside, what is undebatable is that in January 1535, Nicholas is referred to as 'Nicholas Poynes', then in July he is 'Mr Poyntz', but in a grant made to him in November 1535, he is styled Sir Nicholas Poyntz.[30] Furthermore, his elevation is recorded in a portrait drawing by Hans Holbein the Younger, which survives in the Royal Collection, in which he wears a chain of knighthood and a stylish feathered cap with badges. Unfortunately, the exact date of the drawing is unknown, but it's thought to date from the mid-1530s.

Holbein's portrait not only records Poyntz's knighthood, it also reflects his love of the latest Renaissance fashions, which extended beyond his own attire to the furnishings and decorations of his house at Iron Acton. While no building records survive, recent archaeological evidence has proved that the timber used to build the magnificent new east range was felled in the spring of 1535.[31] Poyntz tore down the medieval kitchens and replaced them with a two-storeyed range of luxury state apartments, containing three interconnecting chambers on the first floor, boasting decorative ceilings, a fireplace and an adjacent garderobe. The suite comprised of a spacious presence chamber, privy chamber and bedchamber. The latter contained a vast rectangular window that overlooked the walled garden, which, as at Thornbury, was enclosed by a gallery. Amazingly, this range survives, as do some of the original interior decorations, including softwood panelling and plaster-impressed motifs depicting Tudor roses. The most striking, however, is a painted frieze on the south wall of the central room, where Anne and Henry probably dined. It was almost certainly painted by a French or Italian artist and is executed in a classical style known as *antike* work. Its exceptional quality suggests the work of a royal artist.[32] Holbein may have even been involved in its design.

Poyntz spared no expense furnishing the new apartments. Fine tapestries lined the walls and the rooms were well stocked with expensive tableware, including sets of Spanish and Italian ceramic plates and superb Venetian glass goblets.[33] Fragments of such treasures were discovered in the backfilled moat during excavations. Time has, though, completely robbed us of the layout of the rooms at ground-floor level. Perhaps, as with Sudeley and Thornbury, they mirrored those on the floor above. If this was not the case, then it's likely that Anne would have been housed in the great chamber located in the south range and connected to the new building by a pentice. Robert Bell concluded that 'the combination of the tree-ring date and the internal decoration leaves little room for doubt that the range was built quite specifically for the king's benefit'.[34] Furthermore, when many of the buildings were taken down in the seventeenth century, the east range was preserved. The layout of the ground floor was altered, but the first floor remained virtually unchanged, which suggests that it was conserved as a shrine because of its royal association.

After likely indulging in Poyntz's extravagant hospitality, Anne and Henry moved to Little Sodbury Manor, the home of Poyntz's aunt and uncle, Sir John and Lady Anne Walshe. As was often the case with private residences, the royal couple only made a fleeting visit, arriving on Wednesday, 25 August and departing on Friday, 27 August. On the day of their arrival, Chapuys wrote to the emperor to inform him that on the previous day, James V of Scotland had been inducted into the Order of the Garter.[35] The ceremony had taken place at Windsor Castle in the presence of several Knights of the Garter and the Scottish ambassadors. King James did not attend in person, as he was in the midst of negotiating a possible marriage to Mary of Bourbon, while still attempting to maintain friendly relations with the emperor. Earlier in the month, he had penned a letter to Charles V from Stirling Castle, professing that 'no alliance that he may make [with the French] ... will impair the good will he bears to the Emperor'.[36] To affirm his loyalty, he added that he 'prays that God may restore his aunt and her daughter to their former splendour and freedom.' He was, of course, referring to Katherine and Mary. Despite this, or perhaps because of James's fluctuating loyalties, Henry and Anne wrote to James's mother, Margaret, the former Queen of Scotland and Henry's elder sister. Accompanying the letters were fine gifts, including £200 and a selection of splendid fabrics, including cloth of gold and silver, crimson and purple satin, and black velvet.[36] Anne also sent Margaret a piece of cloth of tissue from her own wardrobe, as a mark of her sisterly affection. Tissue, as Herbert Norris explains, was 'a particularly rich material in gold or silver, of thinner substance than cloth of gold'.[37] It's likely that this luxurious fabric was of Italian origin because it was generally acquired from Italian merchants.[38] The 1533 Act for Reformation of Excess in Apparel forbade anyone other than the king and his immediate family from wearing purple silk or cloth made of gold tissue.[39] The only exception was for dukes and marquesses, who were permitted to wear cloth of gold tissue in their doublets and sleeveless coats, as long as it did not exceed £5 the yard.

John Gostwick, another of Cromwell's employees, delivered the king's and queen's letters to the Scottish delegation headed by John Erskine, along with gifts of silver plate and cash.[40] Lord Erskine was the father of Margaret Erskine, who was reputedly James's favourite mistress and the mother of the king's illegitimate son, James Stewart, the future Earl of Moray. The latter was born in around 1531 and would later serve as Regent of Scotland for his half-nephew, the infant James VI. Interestingly, there is evidence to suggest that Lady Margaret accompanied her father to England and was received by Henry and Anne at Thornbury. In April 1536, Lord William Howard, Anne's maternal half-uncle, travelled to Scotland to, among other things, finalise the details of a proposed meeting between the two kings. He penned a lengthy letter to Henry from Edinburgh concerning the status of the negotiations and mentioned a rumour he had heard about the Scottish king's marriage to Mary of Bourbon.

Sire, I hear both by the Queen's Grace your sister, and divers other, that the marriage is broken betwixt the King's Grace your nephew and Monsieur de Vendome, and that he will marry a gentlewoman in Scotland the Lord of Erskine's daughter, who was with Your Grace the last summer at Thornbury; by whom he hath had a child, having a husband; and His Grace hath found the means to divorce then. And there is great lamentation made for it in this country, as far as men dare.[41]

In the end, James did not marry his mistress nor the Duke of Vendome's daughter; he took as his first wife, Francis I's daughter, Madeleine, despite Henry's protestations. At the time of the French princess's birth in August 1520, Anne was a member of her mother's household and so may have served Claude during her confinement. Unfortunately, nothing else is known about Lady Margaret Erskine's time at Thornbury Castle.

On the day of Anne and Henry's departure from Little Sodbury Manor, Thomas Poyntz penned an impassioned letter to his 'well-beloved brother', John Poyntz, from his home in Antwerp, in defence of William Tyndale who had been arrested there in the spring of 1535.[42] The religious reformer and bible translator, originally from Gloucestershire, had been living with Poyntz and his wife for about nine months in the English House in Antwerp, when he was tricked by an unscrupulous young Englishman named Henry Phillips into leaving the safety of the home, and was ensnared by Imperial officers in a nearby alley.

Coincidentally, as Thomas Poyntz furiously scratched his missive, Anne and Henry were lodged with his kin, in the very house where Tyndale probably began his translation of the Bible. In the early 1520s, he became a tutor to the children of Sir John and Lady Walshe at Little Sodbury Manor and translated for them Erasmus's *Enchiridion militis Christiani*, also known as *The Handbook (or Manual) of a Christian Knight*, into English. When not teaching, Tyndale devoted much of his time to studying, debating matters of religion with local churchmen and preaching in the neighbouring villages. It's also been speculated that it was during his sojourn with the Walshes, who were themselves connected to the reform movement, that Tyndale began translating into English, Erasmus's Greek *New Testament*.[43] This was, of course, a very risky endeavour, as the law at the time stipulated that the Bible should only be available in Latin.

An accusation of heresy and his failure to win the support of Cuthbert Tunstall, the Bishop of London, prompted Tyndale to flee to Germany where he continued his work. Eventually, in 1526, his English translation of the New Testament was finally printed in Worms, and, before long, it was smuggled into English ports in bales of cloth. For the first time ever in England, anyone could read, or have read to them, a faithful translation of the New Testament in their native tongue. The authorities responded by zealously hunting down and burning all the confiscated copies.

In October 1528, Tyndale's second most influential book was published, *The Obedience of a Christian Man*, a treatise which declared the 'two fundamental principles of the English reformers: the supreme authority of scripture in the church, and the supreme authority of the king in the state'.[44] This, too, was immediately banned, however, it did not stop Anne Boleyn from acquiring a copy shortly after its publication.

After reading the book, and marking certain passages to show the king, she lent it to her lady-in-waiting, Anne Gainsford, who, in turn, discussed it with her suitor, George Zouche. Believing the book to be hers, he took it from her, 'among other love tricks'.[45] Before long, the dean of the Chapel Royal, whom Wolsey had instructed to purge the court of any such heretical books, discovered him reading it and delivered it to the cardinal, who sent for Zouche and demanded to know how he had come by it. After discovering Anne Boleyn's involvement, Wolsey 'thought better to defer the matter till he had broken it to the king first'.[46] When news of what had transpired reached Anne, she asserted that 'it shall be the dearest book that ever dean or cardinal took away', and promptly went to see the king to discuss the matter, before Wolsey could make any complaint against her.[47] With the king's support, Anne recovered the book and showed him the marked passages. She 'besought his grace most tenderly' to read it, which he did.[48] While we don't know exactly which passages Anne highlighted, there are many that she must have known would strike a chord with the king, including the following passage: 'He that judgeth the king judgeth God, and he that layeth hands on the king, layeth hand on God, and he that resisteth the king resisteth God, and damneth God's law and ordinances. If the subjects sin they must be brought to the king's judgement.[49] And should the king sin, he was accountable to God alone: 'The king is in this world without law, and may at his lust do right or wrong, and shall give accounts, but to God only.' Tyndale also concluded that no person, regardless of their title, was exempt from this ordinance of God.[50] Henry delighted in Tyndale's work and declared that 'this book is for me and all kings to read.'[51]

Henry's enthusiasm for Tyndale's work, however, soon soured. In 1530, Tyndale published *The Practice of Prelates*, in which, among other things, he argued against the king's planned divorce from Katherine of Aragon. Needless to say, this greatly displeased Henry. Nevertheless, the following year, Stephen Vaughan attempted to convince Tyndale to renounce his radical views and return to his native country.[52] Negotiations, however, ceased abruptly in May 1531, when Vaughan sent the king a copy of Tyndale's *An Answer unto*

Sir Thomas More's Dialogue of 1531, which, as the title suggests, was a response to a book Thomas More had written in 1529. This work infuriated the king, who ordered Vaughan 'to desist from persuading Tyndale to come into England, for he has no hope of reconciliation in him'.[53] According to Henry, his realm was better off without him and 'his uncharitable, venomous, and pestilent books', and concluded that Tyndale's work was filled with 'seditious and slanderous lies and fantastical opinions, showing therein neither learning nor truth'.[54] Despite the king's express commandment, Vaughan forwarded another of Tyndale's books to Cromwell in November 1531, asking that he deliver it to the king.[55] It was Cromwell's response that finally made Vaughan cease from promoting Tyndale's work and prompted him to find other ways to advance religious reform in England.[56] The following year, Henry demanded Tyndale's apprehension and extradition, however, his agents were unable to locate him.

Despite their complicated history, according to Thomas Poyntz, following Tyndale's arrest, it was rumoured that Henry had written in his favour, but that the letters had been intercepted by Tyndale's enemies. In September 1535, Cromwell wrote two letters to his contacts in the Low Countries, attempting to secure Tyndale's release, but to no avail.[57] The Bible translator lingered in prison for more than a year, before being publicly executed in around October 1536. As he was being tied to the stake, he implored God to 'open the king of England's eyes!' He was then strangled by the executioner and his corpse burned.[58]

Regardless of Henry's lukewarm feelings towards Tyndale, he allowed Cromwell to intercede on his behalf. But why? In one of Cromwell's 'remembrances' from this period, he noted, 'to know the King's pleasure for Tyndalle [*sic*], and whether I shall write or not.' Not long after, he composed his two carefully written letters to his contacts abroad, suggesting that Henry had given his permission.[59] As Anne had been an early supporter of Tyndale's work and was passionate about disseminating the Bible in the vernacular, it's likely that she played a major role in the discussions that ultimately influenced the king's decision. Anne's personal copy of Tyndale's 1534 edition of the New Testament, which may have been a presentation copy, is still extant.[60] This was a book that was banned in England, yet Anne was so invested in the reform movement that she was prepared to defy the authorities, and not for the first time either. Even before becoming queen, one Thomas Alwaye hoped for Anne's intercession following his arrest and imprisonment for possessing a number of banned books, including an English New Testament.[61]

As the month drew to a close, the court moved to Bromham House in Wiltshire, the home of Anne's vice-chamberlain, Sir Edward Baynton.

Sometime before 1531, he had married Isabel, the daughter of Sir John Leigh and Joyce Leigh (née Culpeper). Following her father's death, Isabel's mother married Lord Edmund Howard, Anne Boleyn's maternal uncle. The couple had a number of children, including a daughter by the name of Catherine, who would in the future catch the king's wandering eye and become his fifth wife.

Virtually nothing is known of the appearance and layout of Baynton's house, but it was reputed to have been almost as large as the Palace of Whitehall. While this may be apocryphal, the fact that Henry and Anne stayed for a full week is a testament to its obvious size and grandeur.

While staying with the Bayntons, Anne received a letter from Hugh Latimer, soon-to-be Bishop of Worcester, about one of his parishioners, a man named Mr Ive. William Latimer provides the details in his *Chronicle*. As this gentleman had recently lost the most part of his cattle 'to his almost utter undoing', Hugh Latimer, concerned for his and his wife's welfare, turned to the queen for help. Anne at once invited the man's wife to Bromham House, where she spoke comforting words to her and gave her a purse of gold containing twenty pounds, assuring the woman that 'if this will not redress your lack, repair to me another time, and I will consider better of you'.[62] This was certainly not an isolated occurrence. In the aforementioned petition that Thomas Alwaye was preparing to send the queen, he noted Anne's goodness to 'strangers and aliens [foreigners]' alike.[63]

Furthermore, in 1535, William Marshall, a reformer, printer and translator with Boleyn connections, dedicated to Anne his study of poor relief in Flanders, *The Form and manner of subvention or helping for poor people, devised and practised in the city of Ypres in Flanders*. He hoped that Anne would be 'a mediatrix and mean unto our most dread sovereign lord' and encourage the king to establish similar provisions for the poor in England.[64] In light of this, and of the queen's obvious deep interest in poor relief, it's possible that she played some role in the poor law legislation enacted in 1536. The fact that Henry went in person to the Commons to support the poor law lends credence to this assertion, although this could just as easily be seen as evidence of Cromwell's influence.

Interestingly, the official legislation is based on a draft written in 1535 by an unidentified Englishman. Sir Geoffrey Elton referred to it as a 'remarkable document' on account of its highly original ideas, including a scheme of public labour, where those who were strong enough would be given work; a dedicated Council to oversee the scheme; and the introduction of an income tax to pay for it. The unknown author even proposed free medical care for the poor. In the end, many of its most revolutionary suggestions were overlooked, but it went on to form the basis of the official legislation of 1536. Elton concluded that while we cannot be certain of who wrote the draft, 'Marshall's name is the most likely one to attach to it'.[65] There is no doubt that Anne saw the urgent need for a national system of poor relief. It's even possible that the queen found opportunities to discuss these more radical ideas with Marshall and possibly even with the king himself, but a recent assertion that she was in fact wholly responsible for the draft is simply untenable.

On Friday, 3 September, the royal procession departed Bromham and rode east to the edge of the ancient Savernake Forest, where they would remain for almost a week as guests of Sir John Seymour and his wife Margery. Anne and Henry's visit to Wolfhall has over the centuries become shrouded in myth and legend, with hindsight leading many to believe that it's when Henry first fell in love with John and Margery's eldest daughter, Jane. The name Wolfhall has become almost synonymous with Anne's downfall. The truth, however, is far less momentous.

Part III

Autumn 1535

Chapter 11

The Centrepiece

Owing to a lack of contemporary descriptions or plans, it's difficult to determine what the Seymour house looked like in the sixteenth century. It was obviously sufficiently palatial to accommodate the royal party for an entire week and boasted a spectacular forest setting. Fragmentary building accounts also confirm that, like many grand houses of the day, it was a double-courtyard residence set amid formal gardens and expansive orchards, and contained a great hall, a chapel, a long gallery and a series of fine chambers, including ones reserved solely for the king.[1] Presumably such a grand establishment must have also contained accommodation for servants, service rooms to support the running of the household, various outbuildings, and lodgings for the family. As historian Graham Bathe notes, 'the scale of the house is inferred from the Longleat papers which describe that Edward Seymour, later Duke of Somerset, removed 30 beds from Wolfhall to Beauchamplace (later Somerset House) in London.'[2]

The assumption that it was at Wolfhall that the king first fell in love with Jane Seymour is not supported by any contemporary source. In fact, it's not even known if Jane was present during the visit. If she was in attendance, it was probably as a member of the queen's entourage, which had been travelling with the royal party since their departure from Windsor. Furthermore, Jane already had a long association with the court, having served Katherine of Aragon, before transferring to Anne's household, where she and others of Anne's ladies, including Anne Zouche (née Gainsford), Madge Shelton and Elizabeth Holland (commonly known as Bess), received New Year's gifts from the king in 1534.[3] If any member of the Seymour family grew in favour with the king during the visit, it was Jane's eldest brother, Edward. Following what must have been a successful visit to the family home, Henry considered overnighting at Edward's Hampshire house in Elvetham, instead of visiting Farnham where a number of people had died of the plague, although in the end he decided against it.[4]

As far as the records are concerned, the most significant thing that occurred during the visit was the finalisation of the paperwork required for the upcoming consecration of three new reformist bishops, Edward Fox, Hugh Latimer and John Hilsey.[5] Since leaving Windsor, the king had been so thoroughly enjoying himself that he had signed very few documents. In a letter to his master, John Husee marvelled that 'his Grace never signed so few as he hath done this progress.'[6] In the end, the elected bishops were in something of a panic and implored Cromwell to get the formalities completed.[7]

As Henry and Anne basked in the Seymour hospitality, Chapuys entreated his master to help execute the recent papal censures against the king, arguing that it was the only apt resolution, 'considering the great discontent prevailing among all classes of society here at this King's disorderly life and government'.[8] The ambassador also reported that owing to a poor harvest, famine was on the horizon. This is corroborated by Thomas Broke's letter to Cromwell in which he noted that the bread being sold in London is 'so musty and of so evil wheat' that it is more poisonous than nourishing.[9] While the bread being baked outside of the city was of better quality, there were only limited quantities available, which led to increases in food prices. 'What was sold for a halfpenny when you were here', revealed a concerned Broke, 'is now a penny', and the price of wheat and rye, according to Lord Chancellor Audley, had also risen significantly.[10] Broke exhorted Cromwell to redress the problem, lest the cost of bread 'be as dear this year as ever it was'. The scanty harvest was a result of unseasonably high rainfall. In the south-west of the country, there had been almost constant rain.[11] The severe hardship caused by food shortages and inflation were only exacerbated by the prevalence of the plague in the city and elsewhere.

Despite the numerous external pressures on their marriage, the king and queen were in good health and high spirits when they departed Wolfhall.[12] The next stop on the royal progress was hosted by one of the king's esquires of the body, or personal attendants, Thomas Lisle and his wife Mary. Anne and Henry spent two nights at their home in Thruxton.[13] While the household accounts confirm that the couple arrived on Thursday, 9 September, Cromwell was still at Wolfhall the following day, which suggests that once again the court was split.[14] On Saturday, 11 September, Anne and Henry travelled to Winchester. The original plan was to break up the journey with an overnight stay at the manor of Hurstbourne Priors, but Paulet's accounts make no record of the stop.[15] However, considering that the distance from Thruxton to Winchester was around double what the court was accustomed to travelling in a day while on progress, it's likely that they at least rested there en route.

Unfortunately, there is no record of where the court was lodged during their stay in Winchester, once the heart of Anglo-Saxon and Norman royal power. The most likely contender is the bishop's palace of Wolvesey, situated just a stone's throw from the cathedral. For hundreds of years, it had served as a palace for the exceptionally wealthy and powerful bishops of Winchester, and was at the time the official residence of Stephen Gardiner, who held the bishopric for two decades until 1551. The city had a long association with royalty and authority, and was even linked to the celebrated King Arthur. Winchester was believed to be the location of his fabled Camelot, and according to William Caxton, Arthur's round table was still visible there in 1485.[16] It was, thus, the perfect backdrop to the centrepiece of the progress – the consecration of Edward Fox, Hugh Latimer and John Hilsey as bishops of Hereford, Worcester and Rochester respectively, which took place on Sunday, 19 September.[17] Unlike Nicholas Shaxton and Thomas Cranmer's own consecrations, performed in the shadows of St Stephen's Chapel, this would be a public event and a grand slap in the face for those who opposed the king's religious reforms and his marriage to Anne. These were, after all, men whom the queen had championed. To add salt to the wound, Cranmer himself officiated, almost certainly in the presence of the king and queen, and 'the cream of the English episcopate'.[18] Anne, in fact, had ensured Latimer's elevation by lending him £200 towards the first fruit charges that all newly appointed bishops were required to pay the king.[19] As Latimer himself admitted, without help he would not be able to cover the charge.[20] Anne had done the same for Nicholas Shaxton, who had previously served as her almoner, when he was raised to the bishopric of Salisbury earlier in the year.[21]

In around mid-September, a French envoy arrived at Winchester, headed by Jean de Dinteville, bailly of Troyes. The diplomat was well acquainted with the king and Anne, as he had served as resident ambassador to England in 1533, and had played a prominent role in Anne's coronation. On 15 September, Dinteville, or a member of his entourage, wrote to Francis I's sister, Marguerite de Navarre, (also known as Marguerite de Angoulême), about their first audience with the royal couple, in which he conveyed Marguerite's compliments to the king and Anne. 'The Queen', reported the envoy, 'said that her greatest wish, next to having a son, is to see you again'.[22] Anne's remark is not necessarily evidence of a close friendship between the two queens, but it does suggest that they were, at the very least, on amicable terms. The two women had certainly met during Anne's time in the household of Queen Claude, Marguerite's sister-in-law, and appear to have maintained a cordial relationship throughout Anne's reign. In 1534, during an embassy to France, Lord Rochford was instructed to assure Marguerite that 'that there was nothing she [Anne] regretted at the last interview so much as not having an interview with the said queen of Navarre'.[23] The interview in question took place in Calais in 1532, when the newly created Marquess of Pembroke was officially presented to Francis I, as the king's intended wife. Not surprisingly, Francis's wife Eleanor refused to receive Anne, and Marguerite was either unable or unwilling. While this may be seen as evidence of Marguerite's hostility towards Anne, the following year, after two five-hour consultations with her, the Duke of Norfolk assured Henry that she is 'as affectionate to your Highness as if she were your own sister, and likewise to the Queen', and, in his opinion, Marguerite was 'a sure friend'.[24]

It's unclear whether or not Dinteville was present for the first royal audience, as the evidence is contradictory. On 25 September, Chapuys informed the emperor that the bailly of Troyes had reached Winchester 'six days ago'.[25] However, on 24 September, the Duke of Norfolk notified Cromwell that 'he [Dinteville] will probably be at Winchester tomorrow, where I intend to be'.[26] He also observed that even though the Frenchman, who was about twenty years his junior, had had a 30-minute head start, he 'rode so softly' that Norfolk could have overtaken him. The king of France, however, had ordered Dinteville to travel to court 'in all possible haste', so why was the ambassador dallying? The answer lies in his diplomatic bag. The news Dinteville was charged to deliver to Henry was not pleasant. Pope Paul III, who had succeeded Clement VII in 1534, was appalled by the English king's behaviour, and incensed by the beheading of John Fisher, whom he had elevated to the cardinalate just before his execution. The time for waiting for the king to repent was well and truly over. Pope Paul III was compelled by 'the unanimous solicitation of the cardinals, to declare Henry deprived of his kingdom and his royal dignity', and he wanted Francis, the Roman Catholic Church's 'most dear son', to help execute the sentence.[27] Henry received the news calmly. According to Chapuys' informants, 'he appeared sad and melancholy when he had read the letters the bailly presented'.[28] The king responded by calling an emergency meeting, attended by the leading bishops, including Cranmer and Stephen Gardiner, and, despite the looming threat, proceeded with the consecration of the three new bishops.[29] He also summoned the chief nobles, including the irascible Duke of Norfolk, who was disappointed about being called away from his home at Framlingham, where he had been hunting with friends, to attend on the king and his niece.[30] Personal preferences, however, were of little importance. It was critical that the king and queen and the cream of the English nobility present a united front. Charles Brandon, Duke of Suffolk, rushed to the king's side.[31] Unlike Norfolk, he must have been in higher spirits, as just days earlier, his young wife, Katherine Willoughby, had given birth to a healthy son and heir, which they named Henry.[32] While the king's relationship with Charles had become increasingly strained, he nevertheless rewarded the midwife and nurse with £4 at little Henry's christening.[33]

Another honoured guest at Winchester was Lord Leonard Grey. He had arrived on around 13 September with a most valuable gift for the king – Thomas Fitzgerald, Earl of Kildare, the leader of the Irish rebellion.[34] Silken Thomas, as he later became known, had surrendered the previous month and had requested that Lord Grey, who was his stepmother's brother, conduct him personally to England. It's clear that the latter had promised him something, probably his life, 'to allure him to yield'.[35] But according to the well-informed Imperial ambassador, Kildare 'attaches little importance to the promise made to him by lord Leonard', yet he was buoyed by the fact that the king had agreed to give him an audience. If this did take place, then it happened at Winchester, where, as Chapuys informed the emperor, the rebel 'goes about the Court at liberty'.[36] Just how much freedom the young man enjoyed though is uncertain. In a letter from John Atkinson to Lord Lisle, he described how Fitzgerald was brought to court manacled to William Pole, the Provost Marshal, and confessed that the rebel's fate was yet unknown.[37] Dr Ortiz in Rome, however, went as far as to report to the empress that Fitzgerald had been hunting with the king for a fortnight.[38] Given the scale of the rebellion, this seems highly unlikely. John Husee clarified the matter in the last paragraph of a letter to Lord Lisle. On 26 September he informed his master that Fitzgerald was at court, 'with the Lord Leonard, in keeping', which suggests that he was, as Muriel St. Clare Byrne concluded, 'under open arrest but closely guarded'.[39] Hopes of a pardon were soon dashed. By the end of the month, Thomas Fitzgerald was in the Tower, and Lord Leonard Grey returned to Ireland a much wealthier man.[40] His send-off was another opportunity for the king and Anne to display their munificence. The king rewarded him generously with money and lands, and even gifted him a new, fully equipped ship. Anne, too, played her part impeccably: she removed a chain worth a hundred marks from around her waist and presented it to the future Lord Deputy of Ireland, along with a purse containing 20 sovereigns. The queen understood that her performance during these public occasions was of great importance because it would be recorded and commented on by courtiers and diplomats alike. But even in her personal sphere, Anne was being constantly observed and scrutinised.

It had been a month of sunshine and storms, but the king and Anne remained merry and united, making the most of the hunting and hawking on offer in the area. They divided their time between the bishop's palace of Wolvesey and another grand residence of the bishops of Winchester, Bishop's Waltham.[41] The struggles of the past few months, and the much-needed change of scenery, brought the couple closer than ever, and onlookers noted an increased level of intimacy and happiness in the king and Anne's relationship.

But summer had faded, and nature was repainting the landscape in the rich colours of autumn, the bright green leaves giving way to shades of russet, red and gold, signs that soon it would be time for the court to return to Windsor. As Anne departed Winchester for the final time, perhaps she sensed that change was in the crisp air. While the queen could not have known it yet, new life was growing within her.

Chapter 12

The King and Queen are Merry

In the opening days of October, Henry and Anne left Winchester and rode the roughly 13 miles to Southampton, through countryside ablaze with colour.[1] They had been on progress for almost three months, yet were reluctant to return home. The break from the capital had reinvigorated their relationship and provided them with precious time to indulge in their many shared passions. Their love of riding, hunting and hawking is well known, but they were also ardent music lovers and accomplished instrumentalists and performers. Music played a role in every aspect of court life and was a vital part of religious worship. The Eltham Ordinances of 1526 decreed that a reduced Chapel Royal was to travel with the king and queen on progress to provide religious services.[2] The Master of the Children, who was essentially 'the Director of Church music', and six other men, as well as some officers of the vestry, were to give continual attendance at court.[3] They were required to conduct 'a mass of our Lady before noon, and on Sundays and Holydays, mass of the day, besides our Lady mass, and an anthem in the afternoon'.[4] In addition to the singing-men of the Chapel Royal, secular musicians also accompanied the court.

A talented young musician by the name of Mark Smeaton was with the court at Winchester. He was a groom of Henry's privy chamber and a favourite of the king, as evidenced by the fact that he makes no less than forty appearances in the king's privy purse expenses between November 1529 and December 1532. During this period, Henry paid for his hose, shirts, shoes and boots.[5] He also bought him Milan bonnets and gave him rewards of cash at Easter and Christmas, and at other times throughout the year.[6] In December 1529, he received 40 shillings from the king; during Easter 1531, he was gifted the substantial sum of £3; and on 6 October 1532, he was awarded £3. 6s. 8d.[7] Another young courtier by the name of Francis Weston enjoyed the same privileges and the two men must have been acquainted, however, unlike Weston, Smeaton was not a gentleman. His father, according to George Cavendish, was an English carpenter.[8] It's also been suggested that he may have been a Fleming, as many of the king's musicians were.[9] Despite his humble beginnings, from the privy purse accounts we can surmise that Smeaton's career was advancing steadily. He was certainly a skilled musician, as Anne sent for him to play the virginals for her in her chamber at Winchester.[10] Hindsight might lead some modern observers to raise an eyebrow at this, but there's nothing at all unusual about it. Smeaton was a favoured court entertainer and, as such, would have frequently sung and played for the king and queen in their private apartments.

No amount of music or revelry, however, could drown out the longings of Anne's heart. What she wished for more than anything was a son to fill the royal cradle and an heir to appease her capricious husband. Only the birth of a healthy boy would render her position unassailable and silence her opponents, and, after all, a son is what she had promised the king.[11] Given the fecundity of the women in Anne's family, there was no reason for her to think that she could not achieve this. Her mother had given birth to at least three sons, although two had died in infancy, and her maternal grandmother, Elizabeth Tilney, had given birth to eight. Her paternal grandmother, Lady Margaret Butler, had brought at least five boys into the world, so why should Anne be any different?

As the queen and her ladies settled themselves into their temporary accommodation, probably at Southampton Castle, Anne watched and waited for any sign that she was with child. No doubt her physician, Richard Bartlett, was on hand to confirm any suspicions. In an age when death and disease lurked around every corner, skilled physicians were greatly valued and favoured. Earlier in the month, Bartlett had been appointed bailiff of the lordship of Redmarley, which at the time fell in Worcestershire, and keeper of the park there.[12] As Dr Elizabeth T. Hurren explains, 'physicians were trained in all the intellectual refinements… astronomy, astrology, geometry, mathematics, music and philosophy', and provided what we might now refer to as holistic care.[13] Henry greatly admired them and took a keen interest in the medical world. For their everyday needs, though, the king and Anne would have turned to the court apothecaries, who were skilled herbalists. One of Henry's favourites was Cuthbert Blackeden, who had attended Anne at her coronation.[14] He performed a number of tasks at court, including preparing medical recipes for common ailments such as headaches, insomnia and constipation. In consultation with his physicians, the king was also known to prepare his own medical remedies, which, from 1536 onwards, were chiefly concerned with the treatment of his painful chronic leg ulcers. A manuscript containing more than 100 medical recipes survives today in the British Library, and over thirty of the treatments were devised by Henry himself.[15]

Interestingly, a number of the recipes were made outside of the main London palaces, which suggests that the apothecary equipment travelled with the king on progress. Considering the length of the 1535 progress, it's likely to have done so on this occasion. A surprising ingredient included in at least ten of Henry's recipes is unicorn horn, which was thought to have great curative powers. For this reason, it was considered precious and was highly sought after, as the following example demonstrates. On 25 September 1535, Chapuys informed Charles V that on the king's arrival at Winchester, he ordered an inventory to be made of the cathedral's 'treasures' and 'appropriated to himself certain very fine and rich *licornes* [unicorn horns], besides a large gold cross set with precious stones'.[16] The so-called unicorn horn was probably a narwhal tusk or possibly walrus ivory. Occasionally, the king shared his medical knowledge with others, but he was not the only member of the Tudor court to do so. Treatments were frequently passed around among family members, associates and friends, with varying degrees of success. In an undated letter, Anne's uncle, Lord Edmund Howard, wrote to thank Lady Lisle for sending him a remedy for his kidney stones. While the medicine helped to break up the stone, it did have an embarrassing side effect: 'But for all that [good], your said medicine hath done me little honesty, for it made me piss my bed this night, for the which my wife hath sore beaten me, and saying it's children's part to bepiss the bed. Ye have made me such a pisser that I dare not this day go abroad.'[17] To resolve the issue, he was told to eat a wing or leg of a stork.

Henry and Anne remained in Southampton for just a few days, the king using the time to attend to his correspondence, which he had been somewhat neglecting.[18] Cromwell, too, was still at court, although he was preparing to return to London.[19] The minister's in-tray was, as ever, overflowing with the usual missives from his contacts at home and abroad, including a steady stream of letters from his agents who had been visiting religious houses since July. The letters were often accompanied by gifts from grateful or hopeful petitioners. In the last week of October, Cromwell received cash, two geldings, a pair of gloves and seven pheasants. The following month, presents included swans, cranes, pheasants, herons and two does. Occasionally, Cromwell's agents also sent him confiscated relics. After assessing Maiden Bradley in Wiltshire, Richard Layton sent Cromwell a bag of relics, containing 'strange things', such as God's coat, Our Lady's smock and part of God's supper.[20] Bruton Abbey in Somerset was forced to part with 'Our Lady's girdle' of red silk, and 'Mary Magdalen's girdle', which was sent out to women 'travailing'.[21] It was common practice for monastic houses to loan out holy girdles and other relics, like belts and necklaces, to women who were pregnant or in labour.[22] Given Anne's feelings towards false relics, we can only imagine what she made of this bag of curiosities.

While up until Winchester the progress had largely followed the original 'giest', the visit to Southampton marked the first of a series of deviations, and appears to have been a fairly last-minute decision, because the first we hear of it is on 27 September, in a letter from one Walter Blackwell to Cromwell. The writer states that the king will shortly go to Southampton and then to 'Sarum' [Salisbury].[23] James Hawkysworthe provides us with further details in his letter to Lord Lisle penned the same day: 'On the 26th the King removed from Waltham to Winchester. On Tuesday next he comes to Hampton [Southampton], after which he goes to Portsmouth'.[24] The original plan was to travel from Winchester east to Alresford, and then via Alton to Farnham and Easthampstead, before returning to Windsor.[25] In total, the return journey was scheduled to take just over a week. However, the original plans were abandoned in favour of a much more leisurely and indirect route to Windsor, which included at least eight stops and took around four weeks. Why such significant changes were made to the original itinerary is unclear, although it's likely that it had something to do with the fact that the royal couple were so thoroughly enjoying themselves. On no fewer than four occasions throughout the month, they're reported as being 'merry'.[26] On Saturday, 2 October, Sir Richard Grenville reports that 'the King and Queen is [sic] merry and hawks daily, and likes Winchester and that quarter and praises it much'.[27] The following week, the Bishop of Exeter, who was with the king and Anne at Winchester, informed Sir Thomas Arundell that 'he [the king], the Queen, and all the other nobles of the Court were in good health and merry.'[28] Just a few days later, Sir Anthony Windsor, updated Lord Lisle on some business matters and echoed Grenville's words: 'The King's Grace and the Queen's Grace were very merry in Hampshire, thanking be our Lord'.[29] The king is still being referred to as 'merry' in the latter half of the month.[30] Notice that the word used to describe their joyful state is 'merry' and not 'happy'. In the sixteenth century, the word happy usually meant fortunate or lucky. In light of this, Anne's motto, 'The Most Happy', rather than being haughty or egotistical, is a humble acknowledgement of her privileged position. She was essentially 'the most lucky' because Henry had raised her to be his queen.

Reconstructing the route taken by the royal party on their unhurried return leg to Windsor is not without its challenges. The household accounts for this period do not survive and so we must rely on other sources, namely letters. From these accounts, we know that on Monday, 4 October, Henry and Anne sailed from Southampton to Portsmouth in one of Lord Lisle's ships to inspect the king's fleet, including the *Henry Grace à Dieu*, commonly known as 'the Great Harry', and then onto Portchester, where they lodged at the castle.[31] From there they travelled via Southampton to Salisbury in Wiltshire, where we find them on 9 October.[32] Just like at Gloucester, a magnificent reception awaited them. While the details do not survive, a brief account outlining the city's plan for receiving the royal couple does.[33] At a meeting held on 27 September, it was decided that the mayor and his brethren dressed in their scarlet robes, and other 'honest' men dressed in violet, would welcome the couple, and then the mayor would present the queen with a purse of gold containing £20. 3s. 4d. Should the royal party arrive after dark, torches and 'convenient bearers' would be at the ready to light the way to the royal lodgings. On account of a letter penned by John Lord Audley to Cromwell on 10 October, we know that they stayed in his house, probably the present-day Church House on Crane Street.[34]

During their sojourn in Salisbury, the king decided that the 2-year-old Princess Elizabeth, 'shall be weaned with all diligence', and ordered that the manor of Langley 'be put in readiness'.[35] No evidence survives to prove that Henry discussed the matter with his wife, but it's of course possible that he did. In any case, Anne made her wishes perfectly known by writing directly to Lady Bryan.[36] Unfortunately, like so much of the queen's personal correspondence, the letter does not survive. It's clear, though, that the welfare of her beloved daughter was never far from Anne's mind.

Once these important family matters were concluded, the couple moved to Clarendon, once home to a grand and much-loved medieval palace, which, by the time of Anne's visit, had fallen into disrepair. When Anne's daughter stayed there for the last time in 1574, all that remained of the former royal residence was a 'lodge'. Nevertheless, it was still surrounded by one of the finest hunting parks in the country, which is undoubtedly what lured Anne and Henry to the area. While the couple made the most of the picturesque setting, Cromwell was left to deal with one of the queen's disgruntled and fiery relatives.

Katherine Daubeney, née Howard, was Anne's mother's half-sister, and served as chief female mourner at Elizabeth Boleyn's funeral in 1538, which hints at a close relationship between the sisters. Following the execution of her first husband, Rhys ap Gruffydd, for treason in December 1531, Katherine married Henry Daubeney, the future Earl of Bridgewater. Theirs was not a happy marriage and, by 1535, both parties were actively seeking a divorce. In early October, Katherine appealed to Cromwell for support, and lamented that she has many kin 'and few that doth for me, unless then the queen's highness, which I am very much bound unto.' She noted, though, that her enemies were trying to 'set her grace to withdraw her favour from me'.[37] According to Lady Daubeney, her volatile husband 'hath paid well… to make friends against me. But I do trust that at length the truth what I do suffer will be known'. She asked Cromwell to speak to the king on her behalf, and ends her desperate plea on a chilling note: 'I pray you that it [her letter] be not seen; for though

I be fair spoken unto, yet am I not always in surety'. Despite the controversy that surrounded Katherine's marriages, Anne did not turn her back on her kinswoman like most of her Howard relatives had done. Remarkably for the time, the divorce was granted in the spring of 1536, as well as '£80 a year and her whole jointure at his death, as was appointed at their marriage'.[38] It's hard not to see Anne's influence behind this surprisingly favourable outcome, especially when we consider that within days of Cromwell receiving Lady Daubeney's moving note, penned in her own tidy hand, the king and Anne announced a visit to the Daubeney home, Bramshill House.

After a couple of days spent in the blissful seclusion of Clarendon, the court resumed its travels and wended their way back into Hampshire. Meanwhile, in London, Chapuys met with Cromwell to again plead for Katherine and Mary's case. He was disappointed but not surprised to learn that the king had not granted permission for him to visit 'the Princess', nor for her to be moved with her mother. Chapuys feared that unless 'God and Your Majesty [Charles V] interfere soon', some great tragedy would befall them.[39] From Kimbolton, Katherine too implored the emperor to act, even penning a forceful letter directly to the Pope, declaring that if 'a remedy be not applied with all speed, there will be no end to the loss of souls or to the making of martyrs'.[40] Regardless of the external pressures, Katherine would not back down. In fact, she confessed that if need be, she and Mary were prepared for death. Chapuys did his best to improve Katherine's living arrangements, petitioning Cromwell for some money that was owed to her. Cromwell assured the ambassador that if it was just a question of paying the arrears due to Katherine, he would waste no time in getting it done, but the issue wasn't as straightforward: 'the disposition of the King, his master, was such that if he [Cromwell] meddled with it he fell under suspicion of taking the Queen's part, which might cost him his head.'[41] During one of his candid exchanges with Chapuys, Cromwell also confessed that apart from bringing a copy of the papal brief, Dinteville had 'made a request for the marriage of the Princess [Mary] with the Dauphin.' The king, however, would never permit such a union, and the queen was undoubtedly opposed to it.

Eager to show off her own daughter, Anne instead insisted that the resident French ambassador, Antoine de Castelnau, Bishop of Tarbes, and Dinteville visit the Princess Elizabeth, before the latter departed for France. The diplomats reluctantly agreed because, unbeknownst to Anne, they hoped for a chance to see Mary, who still resided with her half-sister. In the end, however, they were disappointed because Mary remained behind closed doors for the duration of the visit. Chapuys paints a picture of flawless filial obedience: to not provoke her father's anger, 'the Princess, following my instructions… kept aloof and remained indoors, playing on the spinet'.[42] Another reference to this visit appears in a lengthy set of instructions, almost certainly given by the Bishop of Tarbes to the Bailly of Troyes before his return to France in October 1535.[43] It must be pointed out, though, that the original, which is six pages long, is undated and bears no salutation or signatures, resulting in it being variously interpreted by historians. A translation of the letter is printed in the appendix of James Anthony Froude's *The Pilgrim: A dialogue on the life and actions of King Henry VIII* published in 1861, but is attributed to Dinteville and dated October 1534.[44] The editors of *Letters and Papers, Foreign and Domestic, of the Reign of Henry VIII*, ascribe the letter to October 1535 on account of the context, and base their summary on a transcription of the French letter printed in Nicolas Camusat's *Meslanges Historiques*, published in 1619, and not on the original.[45] The importance of this final point will shortly be addressed. The fact that the memorandum refers to the terrible weather and small harvest, the general discontent of the English people, the rumoured union between Mary and the Dauphin, and the widespread opposition to the king's second marriage strongly suggests that it was written in early October 1535, before Dinteville returned to France.[46] Furthermore, the writer mentions a visit to the household of the Princess Elizabeth, although the details differ from Chapuys' account.

According to the Frenchmen, a great 'storm' broke out between Mary and her governess when they went to visit Elizabeth. The ambassadors were told that she had to be 'carried off by force to her room', and that she was only pacified once she was assured by the gentlemen who escorted them that it was her father's wish that she should not show herself while the visitors were in the house.[47] While this fits with Mary's wilful nature, Henry would have ensured that his instructions were known and communicated to his daughter well before the visit, so it appears that the ambassadors were misinformed. The fact that Chapuys had time to advise Mary on how to behave indicates that she was in fact pre-warned, and that after being informed of her father's wishes for her to remain secluded, she wrote to Chapuys to ask whether she should obey or not. Chapuys, well acquainted with Henry's anger, counselled acquiescence.

In his missive, the Bishop of Tarbes also mentions a most curious event: when Mary was removed from Greenwich, a large group of women, 'bourgeois and others', came out in support of her. They wept and called out that in spite of everything, she was still their princess. According to the French ambassador, the ringleaders were sent to the Tower.[48] In a marginal note, written in the same hand as the body of the text, are noted two names: 'My Lord Rochford and My Lord William'. This has led some historians to postulate that Anne's sister-in-law, Jane Boleyn, and one of her aunts, 'Lady William Howard', were involved in the incident and punished for their disloyalty with a spell in the Tower.[49] However, this is highly implausible. It must be stressed that Jane Boleyn is not mentioned by name and that as Julia Fox has pointed out, 'her involvement rests entirely on the handwritten marginal note, but that is too vague and inconclusive to be relied upon'.[50] Furthermore, neither Chapuys nor any other source make any mention of the so-called 'public demonstration'. Had Anne's close relatives been arrested and imprisoned for supporting Mary, at the very least the well-connected Imperial ambassador would have heard about it and gleefully reported the incident to the emperor. Mary herself, who was in regular communication with Chapuys, would have revelled in recounting the details to him. Additionally, it seems improbable that members of the nobility would be described as 'bourgeois and others'; surely the ambassador would have named such prominent women.

There is one final important point to make. The summary that appears in *Letters and Papers*, based on the translation by Camusat, states that 'a great troupe of citizens wives and others, unknown to their husbands', presented themselves before Mary.[51] This has lent credence to the story of Jane's involvement because it makes perfect sense that she would take part without her husband's knowledge. He was, after all, the queen's brother and her most devoted subject. However, not all historians agree with this translation. Froude's version reads 'at their husband's desire', which, after close examination of the original document, is a more accurate translation.[52] George Boleyn would never have encouraged his wife to take part in any public demonstration in support of Mary. Either the French ambassador was once again misinformed, or the incident was grossly exaggerated. The latter appears more likely, and a clue lies in a comment made by Chapuys soon after the Bishop of Tarbes arrived in England to take over from Charles de Solier. He was told that the new ambassador had been charged to 'speak very strongly on behalf of the Princess', and that he had been entrusted with the task of negotiating and promoting Mary's marriage to the Dauphin, even if it meant resorting to empty threats.[53] Evidently, exaggeration was just another diplomatic tool in his arsenal. There's little doubt that as Mary left Greenwich, the local citizens did turn out to watch. Royal appearances always attracted large crowds, but it's unlikely that any kind of formal demonstration or protest ever took place, let alone one spearheaded by Jane Boleyn.

For now, the king and Anne were still far from the intrigues of London. On Friday, 15 October, they arrived at The Vyne, the home of William, Lord Sandys, a leading courtier and Lord Chamberlain of the Royal Household.[54] It was one of the grandest houses in the area, and spacious enough to provide the

A carving of Anne Boleyn's falcon badge, discovered by Paul Fitzsimmons at an auction in 2019. It probably once formed part of the decoration of Anne's private apartments at Hampton Court Palace. (*Courtesy of Paul Fitzsimmons/ Marhamchurch Antiques*)

The Old Royal Naval College, Greenwich. Beneath the Old Royal Naval College in Greenwich lie the remains of Greenwich Palace, where Anne Boleyn gave birth to the future Elizabeth I on 7 September 1533. (*Author's collection*)

The Palace of Whitehall by Wenceslaus Hollar, c. 1647. This was a favoured Tudor residence and the backdrop to many momentous moments in Anne Boleyn's life, including her marriage to Henry VIII. (*The Metropolitan Museum of Art Open Access Policy*)

The Tower of London. This mighty fortress has stood sentinel over the City of London for 900 years. Anne Boleyn stayed here on at least two occasions – prior to her coronation in 1533 and again during her imprisonment in May 1536. (*Adobe Stock, 219408474*)

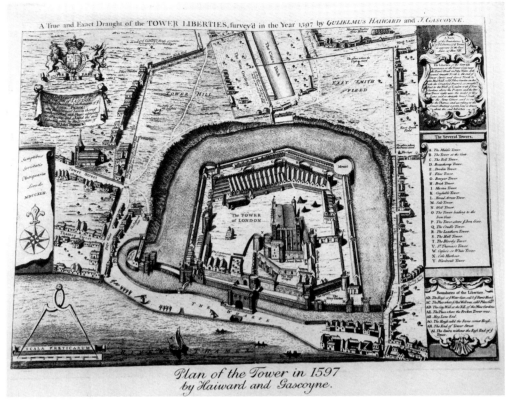

A plan of the Tower of London in 1597, by Gulielmus Haiward and J. Gascoyne. This is very much how the Tower would have appeared during Anne's imprisonment. Clearly visible are the Great Hall, where Anne and George Boleyn's sensational trials took place, and the now-lost Queen's Apartments, where the fallen queen spent her final days. (*Author's collection*)

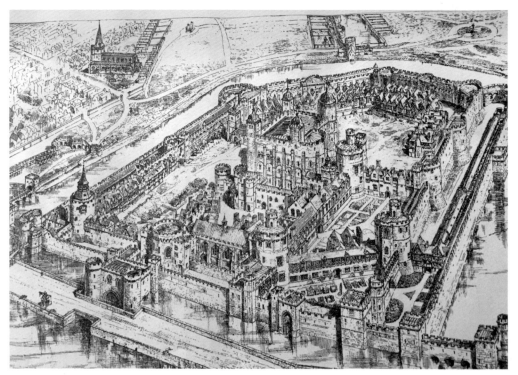

A reconstruction of the Tower of London, as it would have appeared during Anne Boleyn's lifetime. (*Author's collection*)

Early twentieth-century photograph of the interior of the Chapel of St Peter ad Vincula, Tower of London. Among those buried in the chapel are Anne Boleyn, her brother George and sister-in-law Jane, as well as Catherine Howard, Thomas Cromwell and Lady Jane Grey. (*Author's collection*)

Site of the scaffold on Tower Hill, c. 1900, where the five men accused alongside Anne Boleyn were publicly executed in May 1536. (*Author's collection*)

Hampton Court Palace, Surrey. This is a palace that Anne Boleyn knew well. She had her own apartments there from as early as 1529. (*Adobe Stock, 232848346*)

The sunken gardens, Hampton Court Palace. In the sixteenth century, this area was home to ponds where fish were kept and bred. (*Adobe Stock, 300008337*)

Westminster Abbey, London. Within its ancient walls, Anne Boleyn was crowned Queen of England on Sunday, 1 June 1533. (*Adobe Stock, 221375907*)

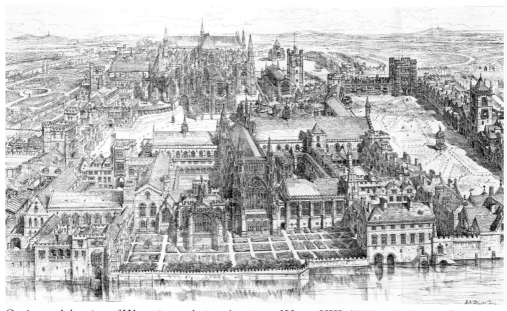

Conjectural drawing of Westminster during the reign of Henry VIII. (*Wikimedia Commons*)

Windsor Castle, Berkshire. In late June 1535, the court prepared for their annual royal progress at Windsor Castle. (*Adobe Stock, 358310439*)

The great hall at Eltham Palace. This is the only surviving part of the medieval palace that Anne Boleyn would have known. It was constructed by Edward IV in the 1470s. (*Adobe Stock, 400008566*)

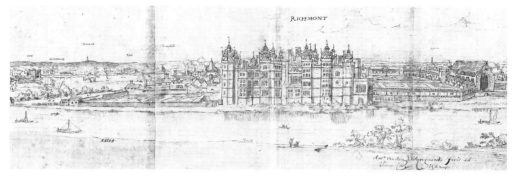

Richmond Palace by Anton van den Wyngaerde in c. 1558–1562. This is the view that greeted the royal party as they approached Richmond from the river. (*Wikimedia Commons*)

The restored gateway of Reading Abbey, Berkshire. (*Wikimedia Commons*)

Site of The Old Palace of Langley, Oxfordshire. The manor of Langley was a favourite royal residence. During the court's stay in July 1535, Anne penned at least one letter to Thomas Cromwell. (*Author's collection*)

Aerial view of Sudeley Castle. The ruined east range, where Henry VIII and Anne Boleyn almost certainly stayed, can be seen adjacent to the formal gardens. The church where Katherine Parr is buried is also visible. (*Wikimedia Commons*)

Ruins of Hailes Abbey, Gloucestershire. While staying at Sudeley Castle in July 1535, Anne Boleyn sent her chaplains to Hailes Abbey to investigate a renowned relic known as the Holy Blood. (*Adobe Stock, 299074217*)

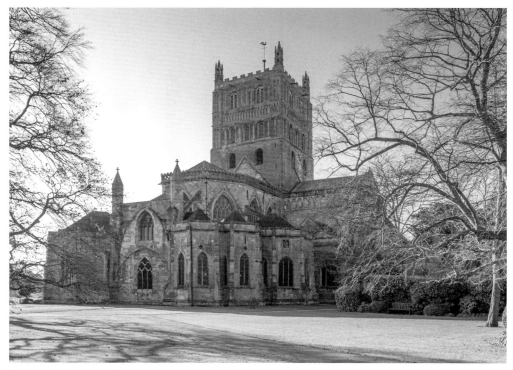

Tewkesbury Abbey, Gloucestershire. (*Adobe Stock, 308574208*)

Gloucester Cathedral, Gloucestershire. Abbot William Parker and his brethren received Anne Boleyn and Henry VIII at the south porch of the church, pictured here. (*Wikimedia Commons*)

Berkeley Castle, Gloucestershire. The royal party stayed at the castle for a week in early August 1535. (*Adobe Stock, 273303728*)

The west front of Thornbury Castle, south Gloucestershire. This was only partially completed at the time of Henry and Anne's visit in August 1535. The royal couple rode through the gateway visible in the centre of the range. (*Author's collection*)

The south range of the inner court at Thornbury Castle, overlooking the magnificent privy gardens. Anne Boleyn and Henry VIII were housed in these apartments during their stay in August 1535. Anne's bedchamber was on the ground floor of the south-west tower and Henry's was directly above. (*Courtesy of Sarah Morris*)

Acton Court, Gloucestershire. One of the surviving wings of Acton Court, where Henry VIII and Anne Boleyn probably stayed as guests of the young Nicholas Poyntz. (*Author's collection*)

Little Sodbury Manor, Gloucestershire. The royal couple lodged here as guests of Nicholas Poyntz's aunt and uncle, Sir John and Lady Anne Walshe, in late August 1535. (*Author's collection*)

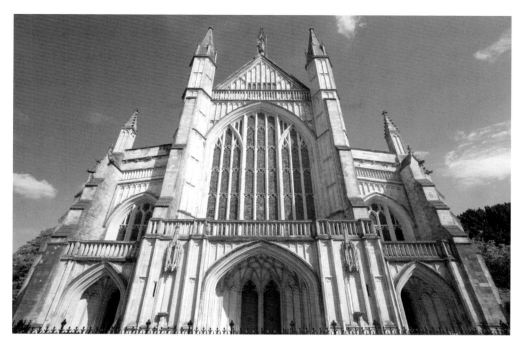

Winchester Cathedral, Hampshire. On 19 September 1535, Winchester Cathedral bore witness to the centrepiece of the 1535 royal progress – the consecration of three newly appointed reforming bishops: Edward Fox, Huge Latimer and John Hilsey. (*Adobe Stock, 175286137*)

Ruins of Portchester Castle, Hampshire. Anne and Henry lodged at the castle during their stay in October 1535. (*Adobe Stock, 144604351*)

Aerial view of Salisbury Cathedral, Wiltshire, where the royal party was received with great pomp and ceremony in October 1535. (*Adobe Stock, 265552502*)

Hever Castle, Kent. This was the childhood home of Anne Boleyn. Following Anne and George's executions, Elizabeth and Thomas Boleyn retreated to Hever to grieve their beloved children in private. (*Adobe Stock, 86797893*)

king and Anne with their own suite of first-floor rooms. An inventory taken in February 1541, after Lord Sandys' death, offers an intriguing insight into the level of luxury to which the royal couple were accustomed. While some of the contents may well have changed in the preceding years, the state rooms were almost certainly appointed for the king and queen's visit in 1535. The queen's apartments contained a series of three rooms: a 'great chamber', 'lying chamber', and 'pallet chamber'. The centrepiece of the queen's great chamber was 'a bed of green and crimson velvet, dressed in a valance fringed with silk and gold, and a red satin quilt'.[55] The walls were lined with tapestries and the windows hung with red and yellow satin curtains. The room contained an additional bed, presumably for one of the queen's ladies; a black velvet chair; and a gilded looking glass.[56] The bed in her lying-in chamber had a celure and tester of cloth of gold and russet velvet, with a matching valance fringed with silk and gold, and a quilt of russet and yellow satin. The two windows were hung with sarsenet curtains lined with buckram, and the walls were hung with five tapestries. Other pieces of furniture included a livery cupboard, a chair and a trussed bed.[57] The king's rooms were just as sumptuously appointed.

On Tuesday, 19 October, after four days spent in the comfort of Lord Sandys' mansion, the royal party moved to Basing House, the principal seat of Sir William Paulet, Comptroller of the Household. They were originally hoping to visit Farnham, but those plans were discarded when it was discovered that several locals had died of the plague.[58] From there the court had intended on lodging with Edward Seymour at Elvetham, but instead they decided on another last-minute change and overnighted at Bramshill House.[59] As previously mentioned, Bramshill was in the possession of Lord and Lady Daubeney.[60] It had not been singled out for a visit in the original itinerary and the first we hear of it comes in a letter penned by Sir Francis Bryan, who was travelling with the court, to Cromwell on 19 October. In light of this, we can surmise that while staying at The Vyne, the queen received word of her aunt's predicament and was sufficiently concerned to persuade Henry to visit their home instead of the Seymours'. Given the state of the Daubeney marriage at the time, we cannot be certain that both husband and wife were still living under the same roof. However, Lady Daubeney's unease and desire for secrecy implies that they were. Furthermore, on the same day that Katherine wrote to Cromwell, her husband did as well, although neither records their location.[61] Rather than coincidence, this strongly suggests that they were in close enough physical proximity to each know that the other was writing. One can only imagine that if all parties were present, it must have been a tense reunion.

Anne's compassion, however, was not solely reserved for family. According to William Latymer, whenever the queen was on progress, she would order large amounts of canvas and flannel to turn into clothing for the needy.[62] The queen and her ladies would make shirts, smocks, petticoats and sheets 'with their own hands', which would then be distributed to the poor of each parish, along with a donation of money. Anne was particularly generous towards destitute mothers with infants. They were given a pair of sheets and 2 shillings, 'such was the wonderful affection of this virtuous queen to all needy householders', extolled Latymer.

On Friday, 22 October, the king and Anne set out on the penultimate leg of the progress, riding 10 miles to Easthampstead, which stood on the south-western edge of Windsor Forest.[63] It's possible that they made a small diversion to Hartfordbridge on the way, although this is not confirmed.[64] On the same day, Dr Thomas Legh issued additional injunctions to the University of Cambridge, one of which required that all heads of houses, scholars and students be present at a mass to be 'publicly celebrated' at St Mary's Church, 'for the souls of the founders of the University, Colleges and Halls, and for the happy state of the King and the Lady Anne, his lawful wife, and Queen of the realm'.[65] While this tantalising mention of the couple's 'happy state' might simply have referred to their general state of contentment, it might equally have been an acknowledgement of the queen's longed-for third pregnancy.

After a few days, the court packed its bags one final time and prepared to travel the short distance to Windsor. Evidently, Cromwell was eager for the king's return as he had considered rejoining the court at Easthampstead, but in the end awaited their arrival at the ancient fortress.[66] For now, the storm clouds that had threatened to consume Anne had dissipated, and the future stretched brightly before her.

Chapter 13

Seeds of Doubt

While the court was at Windsor Castle, Henry and Anne received news that Francis I was dangerously ill with 'flux [dysentery] and tertian fever' and was 'more likely to die than be cured'.[1] This must have served as a sobering reminder for Henry of his own mortality, and of how swiftly illness and death could strike. If Francis died, he had a 17-year-old heir to succeed him, and two other boys to secure the dynasty, but Henry only had daughters and an illegitimate son. The latter was with the king and Anne at Windsor. In early November, 16-year-old Henry Fitzroy sought Cromwell's help to resolve an issue relating to the keepership of the park at the Palace of Collyweston, his principal home from 1531 to 1536. He had hoped to present the keepership to one of his servants, Anthony Driland, but complained to Cromwell that the king had intervened and 'desires that the Queen should have it'.[2] There was little that Cromwell could do to help the young duke, as Henry had already decided to grant the royal manor to his wife. In February 1536, Collyweston, as well as Haseley, was settled on Anne by Act of Parliament.[3]

In the end, the French king's condition improved, and on Friday, 12 November, a great procession was held at St Paul's Cathedral in London to give thanks for his recovery.[4] Chapuys observed that it was 'the most solemn procession that ever took place in this kingdom, at least in the memory of man'. He recorded the following details in a letter to the emperor:

> It was composed of three bishops and four mitred abbots, dressed in pontifical robes, besides innumerable friars, priests, and other ecclesiastics most richly accoutred. As to people of all classes attending it, their number was incalculable, and in addition to that there were several bands of musicians playing on all manner of harmonious instruments. The very precious and most Holy Sacrament of the Altar was taken by the bishop of London through the streets of this capital, almost the whole length of it; all this being intended as a thanksgiving and praise to God for king Francis' convalescence.[5]

Chapuys was, though, surprised that neither the French ambassador nor any of the 'lords of this court' attended the ceremony. The king and Anne were also notably absent, which suggests that the French were still out of favour. But, as Chapuys reports, Henry 'gladly seized the opportunity of gratifying the French nation...and at the same time making his subjects believe in the existence of a great friendship and brotherhood between the king of France and himself'.[6] This belief, he said, 'is necessary for him to inculcate if he is to raise, without scruple or difficulty, the heavy taxes he has imposed on his people.'

How Anne felt about increasing the taxes on an already struggling population is unknown, but given her deep concern for the needy, this must have caused some apprehension. It had been a challenging year; the country's food supply had been affected by the poor harvest, which yielded only about half the amount of corn of previous years.[7] Roland Lee noted that in Ludlow, the scarceness of grain had given rise to increased robberies, and one John Lambart observed that the price of corn was increasing rapidly.[8] In other parts of the country, the general discontent triggered by the recent religious and political changes compelled some citizens to publicly incite rebellion. Anne's servant, William Oxenbridge, was charged with investigating the treasonous utterances of the vicar of Rolvenden, who had told his parishioners to 'not follow the saying of evil princes, nor evil rulers, but rather put on your harness and fight against them'.[9] Similarly, the Earl of Northumberland was called to investigate claims made against William Thwaites, parson of Londesborough, who, among other things, was charged with saying that England had no allies but the Lutherans.[10] Much closer to home, at the Blackfriars in London, one Dr Maitland said that 'he trusted to see every man's head that was of the new learning...to stand upon a stake, and Cranmer's to be one of them'. He also hoped that the king might suffer a 'violent and shameful death', and that the queen, 'that mischievous whore', be burned at the stake.[11]

Englishmen and women all over the country were angry and looking for someone to blame. According to Chapuys, they attributed the 'dreadful scourge' to the 'bad administration and tyranny of the king', but, as Dr Maitland's rant clearly demonstrates, they also blamed Anne and her supporters.[12] The king and Anne responded by ordering the royal preachers to say that 'whom God loves, He chastises', but their subjects remained objurate.[13] They feared war and famine, and an end to profitable trade routes, which would cripple the country.

In the past, when harvests failed, the English imported grain from the Hanseatic merchants, but this source of supply was currently unavailable. The previous month, Henry had ordered that their ships and goods be sequestered, as he suspected that they had been involved in the capture of some English ships in Copenhagen in September 1535.[14] While most of their goods were later released, the damage had been done and they took their business elsewhere. This meant that the English were now dangerously reliant on imports of corn from France and the Low Countries. Both Chapuys and the French ambassadors believed that their masters should forbid the export of corn to England, until Henry could be persuaded to agree to their terms.[15] The Pope advised Charles V to cease all trade between his dominions and Henry's, as this would 'be the ruin of England' and greatly assist in future negotiations.[16] He assured Charles that the French would gladly cooperate.

In early November, Chapuys received a message from one of his informants, Gertrude Courtenay, Marchioness of Exeter, who was married to Henry Courtenay, Marquess of Exeter, the king's first cousin. Despite being selected to stand as godmother at Princess Elizabeth's christening, she was a close confidante of Katherine of Aragon and no friend to Anne. Her father had served as Katherine's chamberlain and her stepmother, Inez de Venegas, had come with Katherine from Spain.[17] The marchioness informed Chapuys that Henry planned to rid himself of Katherine and Mary:

> The king has lately said to some of his most confidential councillors that he would no longer remain in the trouble, fear, and suspense he had so long endured on account of the Queen and Princess, and that that they should see, at the coming of Parliament, to get him released therefrom, swearing most obstinately that he would wait no longer.[18]

A fortnight later, the marchioness entered London in disguise and went to Chapuys in person to beg him to warn the emperor of Henry's plans and to solicit his urgent help.[19] Unsurprisingly, the ambassador blamed Anne for the dangerous turn of events, as she is 'the person who governs everything, and whom the king is unable to contradict'.[20] If we are to believe Chapuys' informants, Anne, the '*diablesse*', was working day and night to convince Henry to execute Katherine and her daughter.[21] But the truth is that regardless of the considerable influence that Anne exerted over Henry, it was the king who was ultimately in charge, and where his former wife and daughter were concerned, he required no goading. Unaccustomed to being disobeyed, Katherine and Mary's behaviour infuriated and frustrated Henry in equal measure. His mood was not helped by the fact that, like his subjects, he too was preoccupied by the fear of invasion and war. Wherever the king looked, noted Paul Friedmann, he saw his enemies gathering:

> He saw his people utterly disaffected, the pope exasperated and striving to raise against him as many enemies as possible, the King of France negotiating with the emperor for the purpose of dethroning him, the

Protestant princes of Germany offended and deeply suspicious, and the fleets of Sweden, Denmark, and Prussia capturing and pillaging his ships.[22]

Henry responded by preparing his fleet for war and tightening security in London.[23] On Wednesday, 3 November, Thomas Megges, one of Cromwell's business associates, informed him that his 100 pikes were ready.[24] The king asserted openly that Katherine was the cause of all his problems and that he longed to be free of her.[25] But during quiet moments, doubt crept into his thoughts. As the pressure and challenges mounted all around him, Henry must have wondered whether freeing himself of Anne wasn't the only way out of his present predicament. After all, didn't his troubles stem from his union with her?

For now, though, the prospect of an heir in the royal cradle kept the king's doubts at bay and his fury directed towards his former wife. The birth of the king's son would prove to the world, and to Henry himself, that he had made the right decision in marrying Anne and that God stood firmly on their side.

Part IV

Winter 1535–1536

Chapter 14

Calm Before the Storm

In early December, the king and queen returned to Richmond Palace.[1] At some point during her stay, Anne paid a visit to the nuns of Syon Abbey, a monastic house of the Order of the Most Holy Saviour, founded by St Bridget of Sweden in the fourteenth century, and established in England in 1415 by Henry V. The abbey was originally built on a site in Twickenham, near the River Thames and virtually opposite the royal palace of Sheen (later renamed Richmond), but this position proved unsuitable. Therefore, in 1431, the Syon community moved a few miles downriver to a new site in Isleworth, where Syon House stands today.[2] Religious houses of this order accommodated both men and women, although they were strictly separated. Interestingly, the women took precedence over the men, and held all the principal offices within the monastery, including treasuress and cellaress.[3] At the top of the pecking order was the abbess, 'whose authority was final in every aspect of the monastery's governance', with the exception of some spiritual matters that were the remit of the confessor general.[4] Syon Abbey was the only Bridgettine monastery in the country and, by the time of Anne's visit, was renowned for its culture of learning and fine libraries. Surprisingly, in order to aid their study and learning, the sisters were permitted to collect as many books as they liked.

The abbey flourished under royal patronage, becoming one of the wealthiest and most influential in the country. However, in 1533, this ended abruptly when their involvement with the outspoken prophetess, Elizabeth Barton, was uncovered. The Nun of Kent, as she was also known, had prophesised that if Henry abandoned Katherine and married Anne, he would lose his kingdom and die 'a villain's death'.[5] In April 1534, she was executed for treason at Tyburn, alongside a number of her supporters. This association with a known traitor and enemy of the Crown marked the end of Syon's ascendancy and the beginning of an organised campaign to silence their opposition to Henry's second marriage and ecclesiastic supremacy. The queen's visit in December 1535 was part of this organised effort.

According to William Latymer, Anne arrived while the nuns were at their 'common prayer' in the choir, but was denied entry, as 'it was not lawful for any married person to enter into their oratory'.[6] Not one easily dissuaded, the queen waited with her attendants and was eventually allowed in, where she found all the nuns prostate, 'with their faces downward to the ground'. Latymer writes that the queen then 'made a brief exhortation' about the 'enormity of their cloaked liberty and wanton incontinence'. She also reprimanded them for continuing to pray with their Latin primers, which they could not understand, before distributing prayer books in English that Anne hoped would stir them 'to more devotion'. While Latymer is the only source for this event, the fact that he mentions that Anne was staying at Richmond at the time of the visit lends credence to his story, because we know that in December 1535, while the court was undoubtedly at Richmond, there was a concerted effort being made to persuade the community to accept Henry's supremacy. Richard Layton and Thomas Bedyll were at Syon that month, attempting to enforce 'the king's title and also in the king's graces matter of his succession and marriage'.[7] The king's physician, Dr William Butts, and Anne's own almoner, John Skipp, were there on Tuesday, 14 December.[8] The following day, the king sent four academics to Syon to argue his case, and earlier in the month, Cromwell himself had visited the community and personally examined the abbess, Agnes Jordan.[9] While Cromwell's agents concentrated their efforts on the brethren, the nuns were also in the firing line. The Bishop of London visited the women's chapterhouse on 16 December, and on Saturday, 18 December, Bedyll and Layton reported their findings directly to the king.[10] Despite the concentrated effort being made to persuade the Syon community to conform to the king's supremacy, the brothers, reported Bedyll, remained obstinate. The nuns, on the other hand, had shown themselves more amenable. In light of this, a visit by the queen seems entirely plausible. Considering the influence and power that the nuns of Syon possessed, perhaps the king and queen thought that a woman, in this case Anne herself, could persuade them to see sense and that they, in turn, might convince the brothers to follow suit. What is questionable, though, are some of the details that Latymer provides. For example, Latymer's assertion that the nuns of Syon, who were among the best Latinists in the country, were unable to understand their Latin primers seems totally absurd.[11] Surely Anne would have been well aware of their scholarly reputation. While we may never know exactly what went on during the queen's visit, we can be fairly confident that it did take place, probably just days after Bedyll's meeting with the king. Although, in the end, it did not have the desired effect – Syon would not respond 'to either threat or blandishment'.[12]

After spending most of Advent at Richmond Palace, the court moved to Eltham for Christmas.[13] It's possible that the Princess Elizabeth's household was also in residence, as during the 1530s, the palace primarily functioned as a royal nursery. It was common for a lord of misrule or 'master of merry disports' to oversee the Christmas entertainments at court, which ran from Christmas Day to Twelfth Night, 5 January. His duties involved organising 'fine and subtle disguisings, masks and mummeries', as well as various games, including card games.[14] In 1552–1553, George Ferrers was appointed master of the king's pastimes, a role that required him to create and perform traditional lord of misrule shows, many of which he described in a letter to Sir Thomas Cawarden, master of the revels.[15] This document shines an important light on the range of events organised at this time of year – from arriving at court 'on some strange beast' to sending 'an orator speaking in a strange language' to the king on Christmas Day.[16] Henry VIII appointed a lord of misrule in 1533 and 1534, but there is no record of one being present at court in 1535.[17] Nevertheless, there would have been lively entertainments and a great deal of revelry.

On Christmas Day, the court gathered in their finery to watch the king and Anne, resplendent in either purple or red velvet, process to the chapel under a cloth of estate.[18] The palace interiors, dressed in seasonal flowers and wreaths, and evergreens such as holly, laurel and ivy, provided a suitably magnificent backdrop to the day's events. Following the formalities, the fun and feasting would begin. Fanfare announced the arrival of the centrepiece of the Christmas Day meal, the boar's head, which was presented to diners by the steward or head of the household. Many other courses of meats, pies and delicacies followed. The leading members of the royal couple's households and the nobility were expected to join in the celebrations. If illness or some other misadventure prevented one from attending, it was prudent to advise the king, like Lord Sandys, Henry's Lord Chamberlain, did in November 1535.[19] The only member of the queen's immediate family that we know was present was her brother, Lord Rochford, although it's entirely possible that her mother and father were there too. Although Lady Lisle was unable to be there in person, she sent one of her agents to court to enquire as to what gift would best please the queen. According to Margery Horsman, 'the Queen's Grace setteth much store by a pretty dog, and her Grace delighted so much in little Purkoy that after he was dead of a fall there durst nobody tell her Grace of it, till it pleased the King's Highness to tell her Grace of it. But her Grace setteth more store by a dog than by a bitch'.[20] Whether Lady Lisle took Margery's advice and presented Anne with a dog is unknown, as the New Year's gift roll for 1536 does not survive.

On Wednesday, 29 December, Henry left Anne at Eltham and travelled to nearby Greenwich Palace to meet with Chapuys. While the king had solicited the meeting to discuss 'matters of great importance', the ambassador was anxious to speak with Henry about Katherine's failing health, which Henry had known about for several weeks. At first, her physician concluded that it was nothing serious and intimated that he expected her to make a full recovery.[21] Indeed, by 13 December, Katherine appeared to have turned the corner and was well enough to pen letters to Chapuys, Charles V and Dr Ortiz, containing news 'which would move a stone to compassion'.[22] But her condition soon worsened.[23]

While the court feasted and celebrated, Katherine lay dying in her bed at Kimbolton. She was unable to keep down any food or drink, and the pain in her stomach prevented her from sleeping more than an hour at a time.[24] Her apothecary, Philip Grenacre, scribbled a desperate letter to Chapuys' secretary, Montesse, begging him to tell the ambassador to visit Katherine as soon as possible. Eventually, Henry granted permission for him to do so, but not out of compassion for his former wife, whom he coolly assured Chapuys would not live long. Henry gloated that her death would mark the end of his troubles because the emperor would have no cause to concern himself with the affairs of his kingdom.[25] Chapuys retorted that Katherine's death 'could not profit anyone'.[26] How right he was. Ironically, the death of Henry's first wife would leave Anne more vulnerable than ever.

Chapter 15

Changing Tides

At the Tudor court, gifts were commonly exchanged on New Year's Day, rather than 25 December. As this was a significant social and political event, the process was recorded in minute detail in the yearly gift roll, which included information about presents that the monarch gave and received. The gifts, which usually included money, plate, jewels and clothing, were presented to the king and queen with great ceremony, as recorded in a series of regulations drawn up for Henry VII's household.[1] It was decreed that just as the king finished dressing on New Year's morning, an usher of the chamber should stand at the entrance to the room and say, 'There is a new year's gift come from the queen', to which the king should respond, 'Sir, let it come in'. The queen's messenger then entered carrying her gift, followed by the servants of other noblemen and courtiers carrying their master's presents. Each messenger would receive a monetary reward, ranging from 40 shillings to 10 marks, depending on the rank of their master or mistress. The queen would receive her gifts in her chamber in a similar fashion. Once the gifts had been presented, the king would 'prepare to go to service in what array it pleaseth him'. The queen, too, would go in procession to the chapel.

While the gift roll for 1536 does not survive, one of the thousands of items recorded in the inventory of Henry VIII's possessions, commissioned by Edward VI after his father's death, is a magnificent pair of silver-gilt bottles, adorned with the king's and Anne's arms, weighing an impressive 209 ounces (almost 6 kilograms).[2] They were made by Morgan Philip, alias Wolf, the king's goldsmith, as a gift for either Henry or Anne, for New Year's Day 1536.[3] These extraordinary objects are described as follows:

> a pair of gilt bottles, the feet and body chased in panes, with branches of two sundry works having the king's arms in a plate on the one side, and on the other side the king's arms and the arms of Queen Anne in a plate together, having on either side an angel with a great chain and a small [one] on either bottle, their necks graven with branches, the knops or stopples having double roses and thereupon the crowns imperial.[4]

Wolf was not the only royal goldsmith active at this time. Another of Henry and Anne's favourite craftsmen was Cornelius Hayes. In the latter half of

Anne's reign, he was commissioned to make an elaborate silver cradle for the royal couple.[5] It was decorated with Tudor roses and precious stones, and lined with white satin and cloth of gold. He even provided luxurious swaddling bands for the baby. Unfortunately, Hayes' bill is undated. However, the cradle was one of a number of items delivered to 'Mr Secretary', and therefore must post-date Cromwell's appointment as principal secretary, which took place in around April 1534. It's unlikely that the cradle was made for Edward VI's birth in 1537 because, following Anne's demise, Cromwell replaced her father as Lord Privy Seal and was addressed as such.[6] Therefore, it was either made for the expected birth in 1534 or 1536. Interestingly, the same bill records money owed to one 'Hance, the painter', almost certainly the artist Hans Holbein the Younger, for painting Adam and Eve. While there is no record of Holbein ever having painted Anne, the fact that we know he was active at court during her time as queen increases the likelihood of him having done so.

Returning to the royal gift-exchange, the gift rolls from 1532 and 1534 provide a tantalising insight into the range of presents given and received.[7] In 1532, Anne gave Henry 'an exotic set of richly decorated Pyrenean boar spears', and received in return from the king, a matching set of hangings for her room and bed, 'covered with gold and silver cloth, crimson satin, and embroidery richer than all the rest'.[8] From Anne's father, the king received 'a box of black velvet, with a steel glass set in gold', and from the Countess of Wiltshire, 'a coffer of needlework, containing 6 shirt collars, 3 in gold and 3 in silver'.[9] Lord and Lady Rochford presented the king with two gilt 'hyngers' (knives), with velvet girdles, and four caps, (two velvet and two satin), all trimmed with gold buttons, and Anne's sister, Mary, gave the king a black-collared shirt.[10] In 1534, Anne gifted her husband a lavish silver-gilt table fountain, described as follows:

> A goodly gilt bason, having a rail or board of gold in the midst of the brim, garnished with rubies and pearls, wherein standeth a fountain, also having a rail of gold about it garnished with diamonds; out thereof issueth water, at the teats of three naked women standing at the foot of the same fountain.[11]

This was almost certainly designed by Holbein, as two drawings in the Kunstmuseum Basel collection strongly suggest. If the king accepted a gift, then custom dictated he give one in return, usually of a higher value to demonstrate his generosity. More often than not, Henry gave gifts of plate; the weight of the item commensurate with the recipient's rank or relationship with the monarch. It was a very public way for Henry to display his favour. The political nature of gift-giving was tellingly illustrated in January 1532, when Henry rejected Katherine's gift of a gold cup and accepted Anne's boar spears. [12] Similarly, there's no record of the Lady Mary having received a gift at New Year 1534 and presumably she was once again left off the list in 1536. While this must have grated on Mary, she had more important things to concern herself with, namely her mother's rapidly deteriorating health.

Following his meeting with the king at Greenwich, Chapuys rode in haste to Kimbolton, where he arrived at around 10 or 11 in the morning on Sunday, 2 January, and remained for four days.[13] During his stay, the ambassador spent hours in conversation with Katherine, who was weary but greatly comforted by his company. Chapuys was, however, not Katherine's first visitor. On the evening of 1 January, her former lady-in-waiting and close confidante, Maria, Lady Willoughby de Eresby, arrived at the castle.[14] The king had not granted her permission to visit, so she devised another way to gain entry. When questioned by the king's men, she claimed to have fallen off her horse just a mile from the castle and requested permission to rest and recuperate by the fire. The crafty Lady Willoughby also promised to produce the proper paperwork authorising her visit in the morning. Convinced by her charade, the household officials granted her immediate access and took her directly to her ailing mistress, who was overjoyed to see her old Spanish friend. According to Sir Edmund Bedingfield, neither Lady Willoughby nor the paperwork were thereafter seen again.[15]

In the company of two of her most loyal supporters, Katherine rallied somewhat. She rested a little more and kept down some food. When Chapuys took leave of her on the Tuesday evening, Katherine was in good spirits, and even requested 'to have some pastime' with one of the ambassador's men. Confident that she was in no immediate danger, Chapuys departed the following day and made his way unhurriedly back to London. Ever Katherine's loyal champion, the moment he arrived he requested an audience with the king to ask that she be moved to better accommodation. His efforts were, however, in vain. Unbeknownst to Chapuys, at just before 2 o'clock in the afternoon on 7 January, 50-year-old Katherine of Aragon breathed her last.[16] The cause of death is unknown, but it has been suggested that she died of cancer.[17] Before long, rumours that she had been poisoned on Henry's orders began circulating at home and abroad, after it was discovered that the embalmer, whose job it was to prepare her body for burial, had found her heart 'black and hideous', with a strange growth attached to it.[18] It's important to note that there is absolutely no substantive evidence to support these allegations.

The ambassador was not informed of Katherine's death until Sunday, 9 January, when one of Cromwell's messengers delivered 'the most cruel news'.[19] It's likely that Henry and Anne received the news at Greenwich Palace on the day of Katherine's death or early the following morning. According to Chapuys' informants, it was met with absolute 'joy and delight', especially by Anne's brother and father, and by Henry who is said to have jubilantly declared,

> Thank God, we are now free from any fear of war, and the time has come for dealing with the French much more to our advantage than heretofore, for if they once suspect my becoming the Emperor's friend and ally now that the real cause of our enmity no longer exists I shall be able to do anything I like with them.[20]

Chapuys indignantly informed the emperor that on the Sunday, Henry 'dressed entirely in yellow from head to foot, with the single exception of a white feather in his cap', and travelled in triumphant procession to the chapel with the 2-year-old Princess Elizabeth by his side. After dinner, he went to the great hall where the ladies of the court were dancing and made a 'great demonstration of joy', before proudly carrying Elizabeth to his private apartments, showing her off 'first to one, then to another'. When the king tired of playing the role of doting father, he turned his attention to the tiltyard.[21] While the Tudor chronicler Edward Hall reported that Anne too 'wore yellow for the mourning', Chapuys makes no mention of her clothing.[22] He does, though, note that, like her husband, she showed great joy at Katherine's death and handsomely rewarded the messenger who brought the news.[23] For Anne, the real cause for celebration was that for the first time in her reign, she was England's only queen.

Once the jubilant performances were out of the way, the king threw himself into overseeing the arrangements for Katherine's funeral and ordered his solicitors to find a way of acquiring what remained of Katherine's property, even though he maintained that she had never been his wife.[24] He ordered that she be buried at the abbey at Peterborough, in a solemn funeral ceremony befitting her position as Dowager Princess of Wales. Henry was not interested in honouring his former wife, but rather in using her funeral to convince the people, once and for all, that Katherine had never been his true wife nor England's queen. On account of this fact, Chapuys refused to attend.[25] Among the principal mourners assigned to accompany Katherine's funeral cortege from Kimbolton to Peterborough was Lady Bedingfield.[26] According to Chapuys, 'the king's own niece… the daughter of the duke of Suffolk' was to act as chief mourner. It's not clear whether he was referring to Frances or Eleanor Brandon, who were both daughters of Charles Brandon and Henry's late sister, Mary, and thus, Henry's nieces. Confusingly, he also states that the 'duchess, her mother' will also attend, however, he could only have been referring to her stepmother and Suffolk's fourth wife, Katherine Willoughby. The Duke of Norfolk's wife, Elizabeth, was also present, as were 'several other ladies in great numbers'.[27] Unsurprisingly, Mary was not permitted to attend the funeral. This may not have sat well with Anne, who once again extended the hand of friendship to her stepdaughter, only to be completely rebuffed.[28] There would be no further olive branches offered. The queen responded by writing the following letter to Lady Shelton:

> Mrs. Shelton, my pleasure is that you do not further move the lady Mary to be towards the King's Grace otherwise than it pleases herself. What I have done has been more for charity than for anything the King or I care what road she takes, or whether she will change her purpose, for if I have a son, as I hope shortly, I know what will happen to her; and therefore, considering the Word of God, to do good to one's enemy, I wished to warn her beforehand, because I have daily experience that the King's wisdom is such as not to esteem her repentance of her rudeness and unnatural obstinacy when she has no choice. By the law of God and of the King, she ought clearly to acknowledge her error and evil conscience if her blind affection had not so blinded her eyes that she will see nothing but what pleases herself. Mrs. Shelton, I beg you not to think to do me any pleasure by turning her from any of her wilful courses, because she could not do me [good] or evil; and do your duty about her according to the King's command, as I am assured you do.[29]

Chapuys suspected that the letter was a ruse, as Lady Shelton left it seemingly forgotten in Mary's oratory, giving her the opportunity to transcribe it, before returning the original to where she had found it.[30] It seems unlikely that Lady Shelton would have been so careless with a missive from the queen, especially one containing such sensitive information, unless that is exactly what Anne had intended. There is, though, another possible explanation. On 21 January, Chapuys informed the emperor that Lady Shelton had permitted one of the ambassador's men to see Mary, even though the king had strictly forbidden anyone from seeing or speaking with his daughter, without his express permission.[31] This courtesy, observed Chapuys, was as a result of a few 'small presents' that he had lately sent her. Might the incident with Anne's letter have been another example of Lady Shelton bending the rules to please the ambassador and Mary?

What is certain is that the initial relief that Anne felt at being the only queen soon turned to despair, as it dawned on her that there was now nothing preventing Henry from discarding her and taking another wife.[32] Things became even more tense after the king suffered a fall from his horse while training in his tiltyard at Greenwich. According to Chapuys, 'on the eve of the Conversion of St. Paul [24 January], the king being mounted on a great horse to run at the lists, both fell so heavily that everyone thought it a miracle he was not killed, but he sustained no injury'.[33] However, Dr Pedro Ortiz, Charles V's ambassador in Rome, reported in early March that he had heard from the French ambassador, who presumably heard it from a source in England, that Henry had been 'for two hours without speaking'.[34] The fact that Ortiz was not in London at the time, often reported inaccuracies, and gleaned his information from third-hand sources, casts doubt on his version of events. Furthermore, Chapuys' testimony is corroborated by Charles Wriothesley, who was also in London; he recorded in his *Chronicle* that Henry had fallen from his horse, 'but he had no hurt'.[35] Early the following month, Cromwell toed the official line by reassuring Gardiner that 'the king is merry and in perfect health'.[36] The fact that the king was up and about almost immediately suggests that he sustained no serious injury, at least none that was immediately apparent. What is clear from all the accounts is that the king fell from his horse and the horse tumbled on top of him. While there may not have been any immediate visible physical injuries, many modern commentators have attributed an acute change in Henry's personality to the head trauma he sustained in this fall.[37] It's also likely that the trauma to his legs caused an old leg ulcer to burst, an affliction that would plague him for the rest of his life.[38] Many historians have addressed Henry's deteriorating health, and there have been countless lively discussions and debates about the change in the king's personality, so these will not be examined here in detail.

What fewer historians have noted, though, is that the accident was a huge blow to Henry's honour as it effectively ended his jousting career. As Professor Suzannah Lipscomb points out, 'men at this time were intoxicated with honour, and with maintaining their reputations and good names... male honour was bound up with masculinity, upholding patriarchy, controlling women and defending one's good name'.[39] Henry, like all kings, was interminably preoccupied with his honour, and he told Francis I as much in 1544: 'thus touching our honour, which, as you know, we have hitherto guarded and will not have stained in our old age'.[40]

One way in which Henry could display his vigour and prove his masculinity in a public arena was in the tiltyard. Jousting was one of the king's great loves, and during his reign he participated in many tournaments and undertook countless hours of vigorous training. To try to understand just how injurious the accident was to Henry's honour and 'manhood', it's important to begin by noting that there is no record of a tournament having taken place at Greenwich in January 1536, which strongly implies that Henry's accident took place during a training exercise.[41] This suggestion is further supported by the fact that the queen was not present at the time, which she most certainly would have been had the king been competing in a tournament. Emma Levitt has suggested that Henry was training for the upcoming May Day jousts when he fell.[42] Wriothesley, in fact, specifies that the king was running at the ring at the time of the accident, an activity he had done countless times before. This exercise in developing accuracy involved a rider galloping full speed along the tiltyard barrier towards a post with a ring attached to it. The aim of the game was to spear the ring with one's lance. This is almost certainly what Henry was attempting to do when he plummeted from his horse, in front of his jousting companions and household servants. Why is this such a crucial detail? Simply because the accident was not an honourable defeat at the hands of a skilled opponent, it was an embarrassing fall which struck a shattering blow to Henry's ego and had disastrous long-term effects on the king and those around him. It was also another stark reminder of his mortality. The fact that he wasn't competing, though, probably saved his life, as it's unlikely that the horse would have been armoured.

It must be stressed that this event marked the end of Henry's jousting days. This was a difficult cross to bear as jousting was 'at the very heart of his identity as a king and as a man'.[43] Perhaps unsurprisingly, afterwards, he became increasingly jealous and wary of anyone who could still compete. Men like George Boleyn, Henry Norris, William Brereton and Francis Weston, all accomplished jousters, now posed a significant threat to Henry's honour and kingship. The king's 'jousting jealousy' proved instrumental to their downfall.[44]

Still reeling from the king's fall, Anne suffered the devastating loss of her baby. The details appear in Chapuys' letter to Charles V, dated 10 February.[45] He informed the emperor that on 29 January, the day of Katherine of Aragon's funeral, Anne miscarried 'a male child' of about three and a half months old. Once again, Charles Wriothesley's account agrees with Chapuys', although he claims the miscarriage occurred on 30 January. He also provides us with an additional detail about the length of gestation: the queen, he reported, 'had reckoned herself at that time but fifteen weeks gone with child'.[46] The slight discrepancy in the dates may point to Anne having suffered a long miscarriage. It's likely that she began experiencing the heartbreaking symptoms of miscarriage not long after the king's fall. This is supported by the Imperial ambassador's despatch of 29 January in which he reports the following:

this very morning, someone coming from the lady mentioned in my letter of the 21st of November ultimo, [Gertrude Courtenay, Marchioness of Exeter] and also from her husband, has stated that both had heard from the lips of one of the principal courtiers that this King had said to one of them in great secrecy, and as if in confession, that he had been seduced and forced into this second marriage by means of sortileges and charms, and that, owing to that, he held it as null. God (he said) had well shown his displeasure at it by denying him male children. He, therefore, considered that he could take a third wife, which he said he wished much to do.[47]

Henry would not have complained about a lack of male heirs, or toyed with the idea of taking another wife, had Anne's pregnancy still been progressing well. While Chapuys was clearly unaware of what had triggered the king's tirade at the time of penning the above note, we can be fairly confident that it was Anne's miscarriage. For news of the king's grumbling to have reached Chapuys on the morning of 29 January, Henry must have had the conversation at the very least the night before, which implies that by 28 January, although it was not yet publicly known at court, he already knew that Anne had lost the baby or was in the process of miscarrying. This would then allow time for 'the principal courtier' to whom Henry had 'confessed' to mention it to the Exeters' contact, who then presumably passed on the information to the marchioness and her husband, who, in turn, despatched their messenger from Greenwich to London, to deliver the news to the ambassador by the morning of 29 January. It's convoluted, but it fits the evidence. Furthermore, according to Chapuys, Anne blamed the miscarriage on the fright she got at hearing of the king's fall, suggesting that the symptoms began not long after she had received the news.[48]

So why did Chapuys report that Anne had miscarried on the day of Katherine's funeral? Because this was almost certainly what he had been told. It's not at all surprising that Anne's enemies at court – the very same people whispering in Chapuys' ear – would take advantage of the queen's loss in such a way. For what better evidence can there be of Anne's supposed wickedness, than the loss of her son on the very day of the 'good queen's' funeral? A deeply religious people would surely interpret this as a punishment from God and a sign that He was on Katherine's side, which is why the queen's opponents circulated the story. Furthermore, it served as a patriarchal morality tale, pitting the righteous Katherine against the sinful Anne Boleyn.

During Anne's daughter's reign, one Nicholas Sander, a Catholic recusant who revelled in smearing Anne's name in order to blacken Elizabeth's, made a number of outrageous claims, including that Anne had miscarried of 'a shapeless mass of flesh', which has given rise to the deformed foetus story.[49] It cannot be sufficiently stressed that there is absolutely no contemporary evidence to support Sander's theory, and let's not forget that he was only around 6 years old at the time of Anne's miscarriage. Therefore, hardly a reliable witness. At no point during Anne or Henry's lifetime, or during the reigns of Edward VI or Mary I for that matter, did anyone comment or remark on the appearance of the baby, or claim that it was in any way unusual.

There is also a good deal of confusion around exactly what Henry meant by 'sortileges'. Was the king implying that his wife was a witch? If he was, it would appear to lend credence to the deformed foetus story, as birth defects were at the time associated with witchcraft and sorcery, as well as moral and theological sins.[50] However, we've already established that there is no evidence to support this theory. Furthermore, the fact that Anne was neither accused of witchcraft nor charged with any such crime speaks for itself. As Eric Ives reminds us, the primary English meaning of the word at the time was 'divination'.[51] So, if Henry did in fact use the term (remembering that the information was passed on by at least three different people before it even reached Chapuys), he was probably referring to the 'premarital predictions that union with Anne would produce sons'.[52] Perhaps he was even referring to Anne's own promise of sons for the royal nursery, which would explain why after her miscarriage, he felt the need to unburden himself to one of his courtiers.

The king was understandably distressed by the loss of his heir, but he showed very little sympathy for his wife's delicate state. Before departing Greenwich for Westminster and the opening of Parliament, Henry coldly told Anne that 'he saw clearly that God did not wish to give him male children' before storming out.[53] Emotionally and physically exhausted by her ordeal, this must have shattered her already aching heart. Nevertheless, she soon composed herself and setting her overwhelming grief aside, she turned her attention to consoling her distraught ladies-in-waiting.[54] She told them that what had happened was for the best and assured them that she would soon fall pregnant again with a son. The English historian J.E. Neale concluded that Anne 'had miscarried of her saviour' and it's difficult to argue with this point of view.[55] But all that Anne knew at this point in time was that the tide had begun to turn. She sensed a shift in her relationship with Henry and was eager to set things right. Never one to capitulate without a fight, she found the courage to confront Henry about a woman he had been paying special attention to at court, one of her own ladies-in-waiting. She attributed her miscarriage, not just to the shock at the king's fall, but to the anguish she felt when she saw 'that he loved others'.[56] The name of this woman was Jane Seymour.[57]

Chapter 16

Mistress Seymour

O utwardly, life continued on as normal. The manors of Haseley and Collyweston were settled on Anne by Act of Parliament and her influence appeared undiminished.[1] It was to the queen that Anne Skeffington turned following the death of her husband, Sir William Skeffington, the former Lord Deputy of Ireland, in December 1535. Lady Skeffington was eager to return home from Ireland and hoped that the king would finance the journey and permit her to keep the fees and stipends due to her husband. She asked Anne to favour her petition and move the king on her behalf, and to remind him of Sir William's 'faithful, true, and diligent heart and service'.[2] Lady Skeffington felt that without Anne's support, and Cromwell's to whom she also appealed, she and her children would be 'utterly undone'.[3] Despite their efforts, it would be months before Lady Skeffington was able to return home.[4]

Another Act of Parliament that received the royal assent was the 'exoneration of Oxford and Cambridge from First Fruits and Tenths'.[5] Anne undoubtedly had a hand in this decision, as evidenced by a surviving letter from Cambridge University. It's clear that as far as the university was concerned, Anne was still in a position to sway the king on important matters.[6] George Boleyn's position also appeared uncompromised. As Lord Delaware had been excused from attending Parliament, the king chose George to cast his proxy vote, as he had also done in 1532.[7] Furthermore, early the following month, Thomas Boleyn was granted an extension of his lease on the Crown honour of Rayleigh in Essex, as well as the lordships and manors of Eastwood and Thundersley, and land called 'Lovedown' in Hockley.[8] The new lease also included George Boleyn as joint tenant. To all appearances, the king's marriage was progressing well.

Nevertheless, Chapuys watched and waited to see if there was any truth to the rumour that Henry was in the market for a new wife. He admitted that although the information had come from a reliable source, he was having a hard time believing it.[9] However, this did not stop him from using it as leverage in his dealings with Lady Shelton. He made sure that news of Henry's so-called 'confession' reached Mary's governess, and instructed his 'intermediary' to treat Lady Shelton 'in the most friendly terms possible', to convince her that should Mary regain her former status, 'she will experience no displeasure at her hands, but, on the contrary, shall be favoured and rewarded'.[10]

The idea that Mary might be reinstated in the line of succession was no longer as improbable as it had once been. Katherine's death had opened up new possibilities. All Henry needed to do was accept that his eldest daughter had been born in *bona fide parentum*, and she would once again be legitimate in the eyes of the law. As the eldest child, she would also supplant Elizabeth as heir presumptive. For now, though, she remained just Lady Mary, but there were signs that her father was softening towards her. On 10 February, Chapuys informed Charles V that Mary had been moved to another house, and that on the journey she had been better accompanied and provided for than ever before.[11] Henry gave his daughter permission to distribute alms along the way and placed a large sum of money at her disposal. Chapuys hoped that the rumours of the king's intention to increase Mary's train and 'exalt her position' were true, but he feared that a 'scorpion lurks under the honey'.[12] Cromwell, though, assured Chapuys that there was no better time to remedy her affairs and promised to do all he could on her behalf.[13] He also stressed that Henry, and his Council for that matter, desired nothing more than the emperor's friendship, especially now that Katherine, 'the only hindrance to cordial amity', was dead. Men like Thomas Boleyn, he claimed, were tired of the 'incredible ingratitude and wickedness of the French' and were greatly moved by Charles V's 'innumerable virtues'.[14] To demonstrate his goodwill towards the emperor, Henry sent Mary a little cross, which her mother had left her.[15] Granted, it was of little monetary value, but the gesture boded well for Mary. The fact that there was no male heir on the immediate horizon also meant that the pressure on her to take the oath of succession eased somewhat. This must have been a welcome reprieve. Anne, however, probably viewed this turn of events with some apprehension, but there was another more pressing threat for the queen to contend with – the matter of the king's new dalliance.

The first we hear of Henry's interest in Jane Seymour is in Chapuys' despatch of 10 February, in which he refers to her as 'Mistress Semel', and reports that the king has lately given her many great gifts.[16] It's likely that Henry chose her as his courtly 'mistress', not long after Anne fell pregnant in late 1535. This was certainly not an uncommon occurrence at the time, and custom dictated that Anne should simply turn a blind eye to her husband's diversions, but, as we shall see, this is not something she was in a position to do. In his biography of Cardinal Wolsey, George Cavendish observed that 'wise men in those days judged that her [Anne's] virtues was [*sic*] here her default', and that had she 'as well as the other queen' tolerated Henry's wandering eye 'she might have fallen into less danger'.[17] Cavendish also commented on Anne's 'too much love' for the king, which prevented her from following the norm. According to Chapuys, following her miscarriage, a heartbroken Anne herself asserted 'that the love she bore him was far greater than that of the late Queen', which is why it broke her heart to see him with others.[18]

Unlike Katherine and Henry, who had married primarily for diplomatic and dynastic reasons, Anne and Henry had married for love. This was virtually unheard of. The only other English monarch who defied contemporary mores in such a way was Henry's maternal grandfather, Edward IV. While there's little doubt that love eventually blossomed between Henry and Katherine, it was not the basis of their relationship. Royal marriages were about duty and alliances, with romance reserved for one's mistresses, but 'in marrying for love, Henry, in effect, confused the role of the wife and the mistress, with the result that personal emotion was the basis of his relationship with Anne and hers with him'.[19] Therefore, Anne could not afford to turn the other cheek and ignore her husband's philandering. There were no great alliances tying Henry to her, there was no son for her to raise in triumph, and no great European power waiting to fight her corner and support her should Henry stray. On the contrary, Anne's position was constantly being challenged and undermined both at home and abroad. The queen relied heavily on Henry's love and favour, and thus was prepared to fight to keep it.

According to Henry Clifford, the author of *The Life of Jane Dormer*, physical altercations were not beneath Anne. He claimed that there 'was much scratching and bye blows between the queen and her maid'.[20] The latter being, of course, Jane Seymour. He went on to assert that Anne's miscarriage was a result of the queen's 'anger and disdain' at espying Jane perched on the king's knee.[21] Another seventeenth-century commentator tells a similarly dramatic tale, in which Anne demands that Jane show her a 'jewel pendant' that she has hanging from her neck. Jane refuses, so Anne unceremoniously rips the jewel from her, injuring her own hand in the process, and is utterly heartbroken to discover that the locket contains a portrait of the king.[22] While these tales provide enticing fodder for novelists and screenwriters, there is absolutely no contemporary evidence to support them. In fact, we know virtually nothing about Anne's relationship with Jane. Furthermore, it's highly unlikely that Anne, who well understood the precarity of her situation, would have so willingly invited criticism by behaving in such an unqueenly way. It's equally unlikely that Anne's enemies at court would have failed to report such damaging incidents. While resorting to violence was out of the question, Anne would need to respond to her rival's challenge. It was time to mobilise her supporters and take her fight to the pulpit.

Part V

Spring 1536

Chapter 17

Power Play

The queen and her ladies spent Shrovetide at Greenwich Palace. This was traditionally a time of fun, frivolity and feasting before the austerity of the Lenten season. Court entertainments were typically performed, including plays, dances and masques, and jousts featured regularly. Like on Shrove Tuesday in 1526, for example, when the king 'kept a solemn joust at his manor of Greenwich', and rode out resplendent in cloth of gold and silver, 'richly embroidered, with a man's heart in a press, with flames about it, and in letters were written…Declare I dare not'.[1] His choice of motto suggests that the king had been struck by the dart of love. On this occasion, his new amour was none other than Anne Boleyn.

As always, music also formed an integral part of the festivities. In 1541, the French ambassador, Charles de Marillac, noted that a bout of illness had prevented the king from taking part in the usual celebrations and marvelled that he spent the whole of Shrovetide, 'without recreation, even of music, in which he used to take as much pleasure as any prince in Christendom'.[2] Anne's love of music and musical prowess are also well documented.[3] One contemporary observer noted that she 'knew how to sing and how to dance well…[and] how to play the lute and other instruments'.[4] Even Nicholas Sander, the Elizabethan recusant exile, acknowledged that 'she was handsome to look at, with a pretty mouth, amusing in her ways, playing well on the lute, and was a good dancer'.[5] But in March 1536, there was little cause for celebration. In fact, it's probable that Henry and Anne spent Shrovetide apart.

Chapuys informed the emperor that Henry had left Anne behind at Greenwich while he went to London, presumably to Whitehall Palace, 'whereas in former times he could hardly be one hour without her'.[6] He added that 'some courtiers' had told him that the king had not spoken to Anne more than ten times in the last three months, which smacks of exaggeration. Chapuys' own shock and disbelief at the news that Henry might take another wife is testament to how close the king and Anne were up until this point. Nevertheless, the celebrations were muted and unlike a decade earlier, when a besotted Henry could hardly remove his gaze from Anne, the king now sought out another.[7]

To complicate matters for Anne, the Seymour family were beginning to reap the rewards. Chapuys reported that in early March, the king 'put into his chamber the young lady's brother', Edward Seymour. [8] Before long, he would be raised to the peerage and showered with other prestigious offices and generous grants of land. As Sir John Seymour's eldest surviving son, one expects a certain number of rewards and favours to have gone his way, but the absence of any benefits for Jane's father has generated many questions over the centuries. An inscription above Sir John's tomb and effigy in St Mary's Church, Great Bedwyn, records his date of death as 21 December 1536, so why then were all the honours heaped upon Edward? Graham Bathe and Ian Purvis have very convincingly argued that the reason Sir John Seymour did not receive any recognition following his daughter's marriage to the king is because he was already dead.[9] The authors conclude that he probably died on 21 December 1535, which explains why he is absent from the sources in 1536.

Edward Seymour was certainly not the only person angling for rewards. As news spread that all monasteries with an income of less than £200 would be dissolved and their property returned to the Crown, the vultures descended. Cromwell's in-tray overflowed with letters from eager courtiers hoping to benefit from the closures. Lord Lisle in Calais enquired about Beaulieu Abbey, only to be promptly told that there was little likelihood that it or any other 'of like lands' would be dissolved any time soon.[10] Within a fortnight, he had turned his attention to the wealthy Glastonbury Abbey and received much the same response.[11] Sir Anthony Hungerford petitioned Cromwell for a small priory in Wiltshire, which he hoped would provide one of his ten sons with 'some honest livings'.[12] The Duke of Norfolk, the Earls of Westmorland and Essex, as well as Sir John Neville and Lord Delaware also hoped for a share in the spoils.[13] Even Archbishop Cranmer sought one of the suppressed houses for his brother-in-law.[14] The Act for the Dissolution of the Lesser Monasteries also stipulated that Henry could exempt any house from dissolution, which triggered another tidal wave of petitions.[15] It's little wonder that Thomas Warley concluded that 'it is as evil a time for suitors as can be, by reason the King and his Council have so many matters in hand daily'.[16]

The queen, too, was called upon to intercede, especially once her opposition to total secularisation was known. What's crucial to note here is that Anne was not opposed to reform itself, but rather to using the confiscated wealth of the monasteries to fill the royal coffers. She agreed that reform of the monasteries was sorely needed, but hoped that the legislation would ultimately benefit the poor and educational institutions, and she had every reason to believe this. The official line coming out of Cromwell's office asserted that religious houses were being dissolved for the 'maintenance of certain notable persons in learning and good qualities about his Highness'.[17] The bill also specified that the possessions of the dissolved religious houses shall be 'for the honour of this his [Henry's] Realm... used and converted to better uses'.[18] It seems, however, that Anne's definition of 'better uses' was strikingly different to that of her husband and his principal secretary. It was rumoured that Cromwell's main goal was to make Henry 'the richest prince in Christendom', an objective that Henry wholeheartedly supported.[19] Furthermore, a fresh injection of funds would finance much-needed building projects, including new coastal defences, and cover the cost of war, should the need arise. It would also 'dramatically increase royal (and ministerial) influence by multiplying the fund of royal patronage'.[20] There's evidence to suggest that the king attended the Commons in person to ensure the success of the bill, which was highly unusual.[21] These differing opinions led to an irretrievable and soon-to-be very public breakdown in Anne and Cromwell's already shaky relationship.

Anne responded by ordering her chaplain, William Latymer, 'to take some occasion in his next sermon to be made before the king to dissuade the utter subversion of the said houses and to induce the king's grace to the mind to convert them to some better uses', namely 'to places of study and good letters and to the continual relief of the poor', reported Latymer.[22] He also recounts that when the heads of other religious houses heard of where Anne's sympathies lay, they immediately sent a delegation 'of the gravest and sagest of the fraternity' to deliver a 'humble supplication' to the queen. In typical Latymer style, their pleas were met with another lengthy and stern rebuke, in which Anne upbraided them for their lewdness and blind ignorance, for their loyalty to Rome, for keeping their 'gates closed from the preachers of God's word', and for not adequately supporting 'needy students in the universities'.[23] While the passage of time may have blurred Latymer's memory somewhat, the overall message rings true and is in keeping with other accounts of Anne's social, religious and political convictions. We know that Anne's protection was definitely sought by the convent of Nun Monkton, and it's also possible that she interceded on behalf of the convent of Catesby.[24]

Despite the huge workload, Cromwell remained in regular communication with Chapuys, to whom he confided that 'before three months there would be [the] most perfect friendship between your Majesty [Charles V] and the King his master'.[25] In the same breath, he spoke of obstacles, so what was he hinting at? Given the state of Anne's marriage and the growing hostilities between queen and minister, it's tempting to conjecture that the only obstacle to 'perfect friendship' now that Katherine was dead, was Anne, and that Cromwell was hinting at her imminent removal. Of course, Chapuys could not have guessed at what was to come. He was, however, contented with the news that during Cromwell's meeting with Katherine's former physician, Cromwell 'put his hand to his bonnet' when the Lady Mary was mentioned, 'which he did not often do'.[26]

While the tempest brewed at home, rumours began circulating abroad that Anne had never really been pregnant. The Bishop of Faenza reported from France that Anne had only 'pretended to have miscarried of a son…and to keep up the deceit, would allow no one to attend on her but her sister'.[27] It's possible then that Mary Boleyn had been permitted to return to court, however, no other sources mention her. Similarly, Dr Ortiz informed the Empress Isabella that 'La Ana feared that the king would leave her, and it was thought that the reason of her pretending the miscarriage of a son was that the King might not leave her, seeing that she conceived sons'.[28] Surely, Anne must have known that such a deception would only serve to anger the king, and if it was just a trick to convince Henry that she was able to bear sons, why would she have pretended to miscarry the baby so early in the pregnancy, especially when Jane Seymour was still firmly in the picture? Anne's pregnancy was undoubtedly genuine, but the rumours did contain a kernel of truth – Anne was desperately concerned about the state of her marriage. If Henry had coolly turned his back on Katherine after more than two decades together, what did the future have in store for her?

Chapter 18

About the Throne the Thunder Rolls

The arrival of spring had done little to improve the unseasonable weather or the tense atmosphere at court. By late March, Chapuys was openly dining at his home with Anne's enemies, who, unsurprisingly, were vocal supporters of the Jane Seymour match and of the Lady Mary.[1] Among them was Henry Pole, Lord Montagu, who was the son of Sir Richard Pole and his wife Margaret Plantagenet, godmother and former governess of the Lady Mary. Through his mother, he was a grandson of George Plantagenet, Duke of Clarence, the younger brother of Edward IV and older brother of Richard III. Also present was Henry Grey, Marquess of Dorset, who was married to the king's niece, Frances Brandon. The couple would soon welcome their first child, a daughter named Jane Grey, who would grow up to famously occupy the throne before Mary I. The marquess's aunt, Elizabeth Grey, the widowed Countess of Kildare, also nailed her colours to the mast, as did a number of other courtiers. The dinner conversation quickly turned to Anne and Cromwell, whom all present asserted were on bad terms, and to rumours that Henry was thinking about a new marriage. This information agreed with letters Chapuys had recently received from France, which suggested the king was contemplating marrying Francis I's daughter.

Given the serious implications of such a match for his master, Chapuys immediately requested a meeting with Cromwell, who allayed his fears and promised 'that should the King, my master, want another wife, it is certainly not among the French that he will look for one.'[2] With one rumour seemingly put to bed, Chapuys fished for information about the state of Cromwell and Anne's relationship. On this, the statesman confided that he had only ever promoted the king's marriage to Anne, and 'paved the way towards it' because the king was 'so much bent upon it'. Importantly, he went on to reveal, 'in such a cold indifferent manner', that 'although the King, his master, was still inclined to pay his court to ladies… it was generally believed that in [the] future he would lead a more moral life than hitherto – a chaste and marital one with his present Queen.'[3] Tellingly, however, as he said this he leaned against a window and 'put his hand to his mouth to prevent the smile on his lips, or to conceal it altogether'. The principal secretary's manner and actions sufficiently convinced Chapuys that despite what Cromwell professed about

Anne and Henry's marriage, 'he meant just the contrary'.[4] The following day, the whole court learned of the rift between queen and minister when Anne's almoner, John Skipp, preached a highly controversial Passion Sunday sermon in front of the king at Greenwich Palace.

The sermon was based on the text *Quis ex vobis arguet me de peccato?*, 'Can any of you prove me guilty of sin?' John, chapter 8, verse 46.[5] According to one report, among other things, Skipp defended the clergy 'from their defamers and from the immoderate zeal of men in holding up to public reprobation the faults of any single clergyman as if it were the fault of all'.[6] He also warned against altering established customs that the people were contented with and lamented the decay of the universities, emphasising 'the necessity of learning'. Early in the sermon, he also cited the example of Solomon 'to show that he lost his true nobility towards the end of his life, by taking new wives and concubines', an audacious criticism of the king's interest in Jane Seymour.[7] It is unfathomable to think that any preacher would have dared express these views in public without the queen's specific approval. It was a bold and courageous move on Anne's part and her way of calling Cromwell to account for the 'barrage of attacks on the Church hierarchy… and the current passage of legislation about the lesser monasteries'.[8] Anne believed that moderate reform was the way forward, but vehemently opposed the programme of suppression which would see her husband's coffers filled with the wealth of the dissolved monasteries. The queen was adamant that the funds should be put to better uses, including allocating endowments to educational or charitable institutions, and instructed her clerics to fervently preach this message.[9]

Through her chaplain, Anne was using her voice to very publicly challenge the traditional – and deeply patriarchal – narrative. At a time when women were expected to behave modestly, obediently and discreetly, she refused to be silenced and found ways to make her opinions known. To use a popular modern expression, she was speaking truth to power, a tremendously brave act, not to mention a dangerous one. When Jane Seymour later attempted to speak up in favour of the monasteries, Henry warned Jane that her predecessor had died for interfering too much in the affairs of state. Jane quickly capitulated. Anne, on the other hand, would not be deterred.

What she hoped to achieve was probably something akin to the reforms that Matthew Parker had introduced at the college of Stoke by Clare in Suffolk, to which the queen had appointed him dean in 1535. As John Strype recalled, during Parker's tenure, 'he laboured to reform the superstitions here used' by implementing a number of reforms:

He founded a grammar school for children, to be instructed in good learning, and in the principles of Christian religion; and constituted a yearly stipend for a schoolmaster. And here youth were taught not only grammar, but brought up in all other studies of humanity. Thither soon flocked in great plenty the children as well of gentlemen as other poor men: and those of the poorer sort had their schooling gratis. The scholars here were taught also to sing, and to play upon the organs, and other instrumental music, with other exercises, according to their ages and capacities: and there were sundry teachers attending accordingly.[10]

Other reforms included the appointment of a person 'learned and able to read a lecture of Scripture four days a week' in both English and Latin, the employment of other highly educated and well-paid staff, and regular preaching. The queen, who saw this as a model of education and reformation worthy of emulation, was designated its founder.

During his sermon, Skipp also enlisted the biblical example of King Ahasuerus, who was tricked by his chief minister, Haman, into ordering a decree to kill all his Jewish subjects. The Jews were saved, however, by the intervention of the king's wise wife, Esther, who 'was a good woman (which the gentle king Ahasuerus loved very well and put his trust in because he knew she was ever his friend) and she gave unto the king contrary counsel'.[11] The wicked minister was then executed on the king's orders.

The allusions were obvious to a Tudor congregation well versed in Scripture: the gentle king was Henry VIII, his wicked minister was Cromwell, and the Jewish people were the clergy. The massacre symbolised the monastic suppressions. The good and wise woman was, of course, the king's wife, Anne Boleyn. Interestingly, Skipp alters an aspect of the original story. Instead of Haman offering to pay the king a large sum of money to finance the killings, Skipp's version has Haman assuring the king that the money would be raised as a result of the massacre. Unsurprisingly, the almoner's scarcely veiled attack on the king's chief minister landed him in hot water. He was accused of 'preaching seditious doctrines' and of slandering 'the King's highness, his counsellors, his lords and nobles, and his whole Parliament'.[12] Perhaps surprisingly, it appears he escaped punishment.

While Anne battled to improve the lives of her subjects, Jane Seymour looked to better her own. At the end of March, the king sent a messenger to Greenwich with a letter and a purse full of sovereigns for Jane. 'The young damsel', wrote Chapuys, 'after respectfully kissing the letter, returned it to the messenger without opening it, and then falling on her knees, begged the royal messenger to entreat the King in her name to consider that she was a well-born damsel, the daughter of good and honourable parents without blame or reproach of any kind'. She stressed that there was nothing that she valued more than her honour and requested that if the king wanted to gift her money, he 'reserve it for such a time as God would be pleased to send her some advantageous marriage'.[13] Jane had drawn a line in the sand: she would not become Henry's mistress. If the king wanted to be with her, he would have to make her his wife.

This theatrical display of piety and virtue was perfectly timed. According to the Marchioness of Exeter, Jane's well-rehearsed response 'marvellously increased' the king's love for her and he promptly declared that 'in order to prove the sincerity of his love, and the honesty of his views towards her, he had resolved not to converse with her in future, except in the presence of one of her relatives'.[14] To this end, the king ordered Cromwell to leave his room at Greenwich, which was connected to the king's apartment by a private gallery, and installed Jane's brother Edward and his wife there instead. The king's principal secretary was well recompensed; he received a fully furnished 'fine house' for his troubles.[15]

As Chapuys observed, Jane had been 'well tutored', namely by her ambitious brother, who, as we have already noted, was now the head of the Seymour family, and, as such, stood to gain a great deal from his sister's rise. She was also encouraged by the conservatives at court and Anne's enemies, who advised her to remind the king at every opportunity of how much his subjects deplored his marriage to Anne. They also stressed that she was not to give in to him unless he made her his queen. On this final point, Jane was 'quite resolved'.[16] It should be emphasised that all the evidence points to Jane having been 'willing to be used to oust Anne'.[17] Of course, she could not have foreseen the queen's brutal end. Like everyone else, she probably believed that her mistress would simply be banished from court and forced into obscurity.

Now, more than ever, Anne needed her family's support. Elizabeth and Thomas Boleyn spent Easter with their daughter at Greenwich. Their son, George, was also at court and determined not to venture too far from his sister's side.[18] While there are no contemporary descriptions of the 1536 Royal Maundy observances, we know that they took place at Greenwich and that the queen did indeed participate.[19]

On Good Friday, Thomas Warley, who was at court, noted in his letter to Lady Lisle that the Countess of Wiltshire 'heartily thanks your ladyship for the hosen [stockings worn to the knee]; and said you could not have devised to send her a thing that might be to her a greater pleasure than they were, considering how she was then diseased'.[20] He goes on to clarify that Anne's mother was suffering from a persistent cough 'which grieves her sore'. This must have greatly troubled Anne, but no doubt she was glad to have her at court, where the royal physicians and apothecaries could attend her.

On the Tuesday after Easter, Chapuys arrived at Greenwich for a private meeting with the king.[21] On arrival, he was warmly welcomed by all of the lords of the Council, including George Boleyn, with whom he spent some time in conversation. Shortly after, a message arrived from the king, inviting Chapuys to visit Anne and kiss her hand. The ambassador politely declined the offer and begged Cromwell to convey to the king that he had his reasons, which he would reveal at another time. Henry apparently took it all in good part. A little while later, when the king passed by Chapuys, he greeted him graciously and assured the ambassador that they would have time to discuss all the important matters of the day after dinner – namely a possible alliance between England and the Empire.

George Boleyn accompanied Chapuys to Mass. Courtiers and visitors alike flocked to the chapel to see how Anne and the ambassador would behave towards one another. The royal couple walked from the royal pew down to the altar to make their offerings, passing Chapuys who was standing behind the door through which they entered. According to Chapuys: 'I must say that she [Anne] was affable and courteous enough on the occasion'.[22] Importantly, he informed the emperor that 'she turned round to return the reverence which I made her when she passed' and in a later missive again refers to the 'mutual reverences' done at the church.[23] Popular history would have us believe that Chapuys was somehow tricked into standing in Anne's path and that she deliberately stopped in front of him, forcing the ambassador to acknowledge her. This is contradicted by Chapuys' own account, in which he says that he was already bowing as Anne and Henry passed, and that it was Anne who then returned the reverence. This was the first and last time Chapuys and Anne would come face to face.

After Mass, the king and Anne dined in her apartments, accompanied by members of the court and select ambassadors. Chapuys was the one notable absence. When Anne questioned Henry as to why the Imperial ambassador had not visited her lodgings like all the other ambassadors, the king curtly responded that 'it was not without good reason'. Despite her disappointment, she did her best to show her support for an Imperial alliance, boldly announcing after dinner that 'it was a great shame in the king of France to treat his uncle, the duke of Savoy, as he did, and to make war against Milan so as to break the enterprise against the Turks'. She wondered whether Francis I, 'weary of his life on account of his illnesses, wished by war to put an end to his days'. The queen's anti-French remarks promptly made their way to Chapuys, who had retreated to the king's presence chamber to dine with Lord Rochford and all the principal men of the court. When the king returned from dinner, he took Chapuys warmly by the hand and led him into his privy chamber, accompanied only by Cromwell and Thomas Audley, who stood discreetly aside as the king and Chapuys conversed by a window embrasure. At first, Henry listened without interruption as Chapuys presented the main points of an Imperial proposal, which included reinstating Mary into the line of succession and military support for the emperor should a war with France occur over Milan. Chapuys had already discussed these points at length with Cromwell, who had always responded favourably. Nevertheless, ever aware of the king's capricious nature, Chapuys took great care to speak 'as gently as possible, that he might not find grounds of quarrel or irritation'.[24] Despite the ambassador's best efforts, it wasn't long before the king lost his temper. When Chapuys declared that his master had renounced his claim to Burgundy because he desired above all things, peace in Christendom, Henry retorted that 'Milan belonged to the king of France, and the duchy of Burgundy also'.[25] The king then demanded that Chapuys repeat all that he had said in the presence of Cromwell and Audley, which he did so 'succinctly', before withdrawing to converse with Edward Seymour who was lingering nearby. By this point, the tension in the room must have been unbearable. Although for months, Cromwell had given Chapuys reason to hope that Mary's reinstatement was a real possibility, it was evident that Henry would not countenance the idea. The ambassador watched as the king and Cromwell disputed angrily, before the latter excused himself to get a drink and retreated to a bench out of the king's sight. Soon afterwards, the king followed and told Chapuys that he wanted all the aforementioned proposals in writing. The ambassador's reluctance to comply provoked another passionate tirade, in which the king dragged up numerous grievances from the past, including the allegation that after Charles V was elected emperor in 1519, he had neglected Henry, broken promises and attempted to deprive him of his kingdom.[26] A riled Henry also complained 'that he was no longer a child to be whipped in the first instance, and then caressed and, [sic] petted, and urged to come back and called all manner of sweet names'.[27] He insisted that he did not need the emperor to intercede with the Pope on his behalf and warned that as Mary was his daughter, he would treat her as he saw fit. Furthermore, as Cromwell and Audley watched on in silent disbelief, he suggested that the emperor should write him a letter essentially apologising for any past 'ingratitude, or any failing towards him' – a request that Chapuys deemed completely unreasonable.[28] In the end, Henry would only agree to look over the current treaties between the two nations and nothing more.

After paying his respects to the Duke of Norfolk, and other members of the king's Council, an exhausted Chapuys left court and went to meet Cromwell, who was so mortified by the day's events, he could hardly speak. 'Never in his life', he confessed, 'had he been so much taken aback as on hearing the [king's] said answer'.[29] Even so, he told Chapuys 'that the game was not entirely lost, and that he had still hopes of success'. Why would Henry abruptly turn his back on the Imperial proposal Cromwell had been negotiating for months? One suggestion is that he was expecting 'unconditional recognition of his marriage' to Anne, as evidenced by his invitation for Chapuys to kiss her hand.[30] While outwardly, Henry appeared to accept Chapuys' refusal to visit the queen, in truth, he was deeply offended by the slight. It's tempting to interpret this as evidence of the king's continued love for his wife and of his intention to remain in the marriage. However, we cannot overlook Henry's enormous ego and the fact that he utterly detested any show of defiance. His will was God's will – the significance of this statement, of this belief, cannot be sufficiently stressed. It is, in fact, one of the keys to unlocking all that was about to unfold. Henry fervently believed that it was the God-given responsibility and duty of everyone around him to carry out his will. It didn't matter if you were the king's childhood friend, his wife, a humble servant or the wealthiest nobleman in the realm. There were absolutely no exceptions. Although royal protocol often led him to pretend otherwise, not even foreign potentates were excluded – such was the king's grossly inflated sense of self-importance. Crucially, what this also meant is that Henry was constitutionally incapable of admitting mistakes. Any error in judgement or wrongdoing was unquestionably someone else's fault and the blame often fell on those closest to the Crown.

On Thursday, 20 April, Chapuys learned from Cromwell that at a Council meeting the previous day, each and every councillor had dropped to their knees to beg the king to continue talks with the emperor.[31] Despite the support for an Imperial alliance, Cromwell found himself in a dangerously vulnerable position, as he was deeply invested in the negotiations and had spent a great deal of time with Chapuys behind closed doors. Should relations continue to sour, Cromwell's involvement might be seen as overstepping the mark, especially given that at the end of 1535, the king had warned Chapuys that Cromwell was exceeding his authority.[32] The king's chief minister was afforded considerable free rein, but the reality was that his power, like everyone else's at court, 'was entirely dependent on the king's willingness to allow its exercise'.[33]

Additionally, it should not be forgotten that in June 1535, Cromwell told Chapuys that if Anne knew how close they were, she would 'see his head cut off'.[34] Considering the role she had played in Wolsey's downfall, this was no empty threat. Back then, he had been unperturbed by the queen's remarks because he felt confident in the king's protection. Now, that confidence was in freefall: 'whoever trusts in the words of princes who one day say one thing and on the next retract it, relies on them, or expects the fulfilment of their promises, is not a wise man, as I myself experienced last Tuesday', noted a disillusioned Cromwell.[35] His late mentor, Cardinal Wolsey, had made the grave error of underestimating Anne's influence on the king. Cromwell would not make the same mistake. Even though the queen had openly criticised the French and purported to support an Imperial alliance, he may still have suspected that she had something to do with the king's sudden change of heart. If she still held sway over Henry, she could easily whisper tales of hidden disloyalty in her husband's ear. After all, John Skipp had made the queen's position perfectly clear in his Passion Sunday sermon, comparing the minister to the biblical Haman who was hung for his treachery.

There was no denying it; Anne now posed a serious if not mortal threat to Cromwell. The minister responded by upping the ante. According to Chapuys, Cromwell took to his bed 'from pure sorrow', but in reality, he had retreated from court for a much more sinister reason – to plan the details of Queen Anne Boleyn's downfall.[36] Although physically absent from court, Cromwell remained as well informed as ever. Damage control was also high on his list. He vowed that in the future, he would 'not treat with foreign ambassadors unless he had with him one of his colleagues' and swore to Chapuys that he had never said or done anything without his master's express command.[37] We need not question his sincerity, especially in regard to the final point. The king was indubitably in charge, as the events of 18 April clearly demonstrated.

Despite the undercurrent of intrigue and politicking, court life continued. By the middle of April, news reached Calais that the king intended on visiting Dover with Anne.[38] Lord Lisle excitedly promised to bring over a cask of his own wine, 'supposing there shall be none found there so good'.[39] He had been granted a license to travel to Dover to meet the royal party, and would be accompanied by his wife, whose presence had been requested by the queen.[40] Henry and Anne had not visited Dover since November 1532, when they had stopped there on their way back from Calais and their meeting with Francis I. Anne prepared by ordering embellishments for her riding accoutrements, including 'round buttons of silk and gold for the bridle', 'silver and gold fringe, black silk fringe, and gold and silver buttons for a saddle', and 'leading reins with great buttons and long tassels'.[41] Red fringe was also requested to mend the harness of the Queen's mules and Anne's ladies-in-waiting were also provided for. 'Venice gold fringe and silk and gold points' were ordered for a saddle for 'my lady Margaret', possibly Lady Margaret Lee, the daughter of Sir Henry Wyatt and sister of the poet Thomas Wyatt, who was greatly favoured by the queen.

George Boleyn also turned his attention to preparations. On 17 April, he penned a hurried letter to Lord Lisle requesting that his servant be given access 'to all such things as he shall need for my provision'. He signed off, 'yours assuredly to my power, George Rochford'.[42] This brief note is George Boleyn's last surviving letter.

Lord Rochford hoped that he would have some good news to share with Lord Lisle on their meeting in Dover. The death of Lord Abergavenny in 1535 created a vacancy within the Order of the Garter, which the queen hoped George would be selected to fill. On 23 April, St George's Day, the yearly chapter meeting was held at Greenwich. The king attended, as did the Dukes of Richmond and Norfolk, and the Earls of Northumberland, Westmoreland, Wiltshire, Sussex, Rutland and Oxford. Lord Sandys and Sir William Fitzwilliam were also present.[43] As in 1535, George Boleyn was one of a number of men nominated. He received votes from Sir William Fitzwilliam, the Earls of Oxford and Sussex, and the Dukes of Norfolk and Richmond. The following day, however, the king announced that Sir Nicholas Carew had been elected because he had received the largest number of votes, (ten compared to George's five), and he was deemed to be 'highly fitting'.[44] Understandably, Lord Rochford was disappointed at the outcome, but it's important to reiterate that this was not the first time he had been overlooked. Moreover, he would have been well aware that in early 1535, Henry VIII had promised the French king that on the first vacancy, he would keep Carew in mind.[45] Therefore, what the queen and her family made of Carew's appointment is difficult to assess. Chapuys, however, firmly believed it was a victory for Anne's enemies and gloated that she 'had not had sufficient influence to get it for her brother'.[46] What's certain is that Nicholas Carew was no friend of the Boleyns. Following his appointment, he sent a messenger to the Lady Mary to tell her to be of good cheer because Henry was 'sick and tired' of Anne. He then dedicated himself to mentoring Jane Seymour on how to win over the king.[47]

Presumably, the king was so discontented with his wife that the following day he approved the setting up of two separate commissions of oyer and terminer to investigate offences committed in the counties of Middlesex and Kent, including 'unspecified treasons'.[48] Anne's uncle, Thomas Howard, was assigned to both commissions, whereas the queen's father, Thomas Boleyn, was only appointed to Middlesex. The commissions do not specifically mention Anne or any of her alleged 'lovers' and they are not signed by the king, although they are written in his voice.[49] While it seems highly unlikely that they could have been set up without Henry's knowledge or, as is often mooted, to deal with crimes unrelated to Anne, Eric Ives absolves Henry of responsibility and lays the blame solely with Thomas Cromwell.[50] He bases his argument on the fact that formal legal moves were usually only begun after the accused had been arrested and interrogated, and notes that the Crown did not need a special commission to authorise investigations or arrests. While this may be the case, the events of April and May 1536 were anything but *usual*. They were extraordinary in every way and thus required an innovative response.

If this was Henry's first formal move against his wife, exactly when, and why, did the game turn deadly? That Henry was looking for a way out of his marriage to Anne is undeniable. He had been toying with this idea since late January and had obviously expressed this desire to Cromwell, who was considering ways in which to make it happen. But what had suddenly prompted this decisive move on the king's part? The truth is as layered and complex as the people involved, and it is no coincidence that the impetus came just days after Cromwell's realisation that he was in fact dispensable and that he could not rely on Henry to side with him against the queen. Anne had made a very serious threat against Cromwell and now he would deliver a pre-emptive strike in return. While it does not appear that he had any substantial evidence against her at this point, it's possible that rumours about the queen's honour were circulating.[51] Whether or not Henry actually believed the rumours is a question we will explore in due course. But for now, a seed of doubt was all that was required because Henry was 'tremulously sensitive to the lightest breath of hidden disloyalty'.[52] By showing the king this new way out of his marital woes, Cromwell had inadvertently also reminded the king of the full breadth of his power – something that in 1532, Thomas More had portentously warned Cromwell against: 'ever tell him what he ought to do, but never what he is able to do. For if the lion knew his own strength, hard were it for any man to rule him'.[53]

Assuming that the commissions did relate to Anne, how then should we interpret the letter the king penned to his ambassador in Rome, Richard Pate, on Tuesday, 25 April, in which he expressed hope that 'God will send unto us heirs male to succeed us' and refers to Anne as 'our most dear and entirely beloved wife'?[54] Quite simply, such niceties were part and parcel of Tudor letter etiquette and should not be seen as incontrovertible proof of the king's intention to remain in the marriage. It was important for the king to maintain a facade of normality while Cromwell investigated any rumours and built a case against the queen.

An atmosphere of suspicion enveloped the court. Chapuys observed that the Council was spending entire days locked away behind closed doors and also noted that Richard Sampson, Dean of the Chapel Royal, had been closeted away with Cromwell 'for the last four days continually'.[55] It was rumoured that he was to be sent as an ambassador to the emperor, but Chapuys was far from convinced. The queen, too, had her doubts.

Anne was sufficiently unnerved and fearful to turn to her chaplain, Matthew Parker, for support. On Wednesday, 26 April, the pair met and although the exact details of their conversation are unknown, Parker later recalled that the queen had spoken to him about her daughter.[56] It's highly likely that Anne asked him to watch over Elizabeth, should anything happen to her. This is a conversation that Parker would never forget. He kept his promise to Anne and went on to serve Elizabeth as Archbishop of Canterbury from 1559 until his death in 1575. In 1572, he confessed to Lord Burghley that 'if I had not been so much bound to the mother, I would not so soon have granted to serve the daughter'.[57] Interestingly, he also referred to himself as Anne's 'countryman', meaning that they were both born in the same county or district.[58] Given that Matthew Parker was from Norfolk, this strongly suggests that Anne was born at her family's home in Blickling, not, as is so often assumed, at Hever Castle in Kent.

The following day, Parliament was suddenly summoned.[59] This was an ominous sign indeed considering that the Reformation Parliament had been dissolved only a fortnight earlier, and was clearly an 'emergency measure' put in place to deal with legal matters that Henry and Cromwell anticipated would arise following Anne's removal.[60] Among others, Anne's friend and ally, Thomas Cranmer, the Archbishop of Canterbury, was ordered to attend 'the first newly elected Parliament for seven years', which was to meet at Westminster on 8 June.[61] Unlike the commissions of oyer and terminer, there can be no doubt the king sanctioned this order. The very same day, the Bishop of London, John Stokesley, was consulted to see if Henry could 'abandon' Anne, which, if this line of questioning was instigated by the king, suggests that no substantial evidence had yet been uncovered to categorically prove any wrongdoing on Anne's part.[62] Diarmaid MacCulloch interprets these events as 'the stages of Anne's doom', and it's difficult to disagree.[63]

As the net closed around the queen, her characteristically sharp mind became jittery and clouded by fear. Her frayed nerves caused her to talk unguardedly and lash out in anger at those around her. On Saturday, 29 April, she found the court musician Mark Smeaton in her presence chamber looking despondent. When Anne asked him why he looked so sad, Smeaton responded that 'it was no matter'. The queen, in no mood for games, said reprovingly, 'you may not look to have me speak to you as I should do to a noble man, because ye be an inferior person'. To this Smeaton answered 'a look sufficeth me; and thus fare you well'.[64] Greg Walker suggests that this incident demonstrates that Smeaton 'harboured amorous feelings for the queen', and that he may have even seen himself as one of her courtly 'suitors'.[65] This would explain why the queen made a point of putting him in his place.

Anne's continental education ensured she was well versed in the rhetoric and conventions of courtly love. As queen, Anne was required to demonstrate the ideals of womanly behaviour, such as submissiveness and chastity, while simultaneously playing a central role in the culture of courtly love, which involved much flirtatious repartee. Anne struggled with treading the tightrope of these contradictory gender roles, which proved instrumental in her downfall. While it was commonplace for the high-ranking men who surrounded the queen to shower her with compliments and praise her beauty and virtues in sonnets and ballads, she needed to remain distant and appear at all times unattainable. But even someone of Anne's calibre could make mistakes while navigating this precarious balancing act.

Later the same day, or early Sunday morning, Anne accused Sir Henry Norris, a Boleyn supporter and her husband's Groom of the Stool, of delaying his marriage to her cousin and lady-in-waiting, Madge Shelton, because he wanted to marry her instead. 'You look for dead men's shoes', spat the queen recklessly, 'for if aught came to the King but good, you would look to have me'.[66] A dismayed Norris vowed that 'if he should have any such thought, he would his head were off'.[67] His response only further incensed the queen, who warned Norris that 'she could undo him' if she wanted to. No sooner had the words escaped her mouth than sanity returned. Aware that she had crossed a dangerous line, Anne later ordered Norris to go to her almoner and swear that 'she was a good woman', but in a court where ears pricked at the slightest impropriety, the damage was instantaneous and irreparable.[68] For according to the 1534 Treason Act, simply imagining the king's death was high treason. Hence, the queen had unwittingly handed her enemies the means with which to destroy her.

Courtiers carried whispers of Anne and Norris's falling out down the palace's privy gallery. It wasn't long before these words found the king's suspicious ear. This almost certainly explains what happened next. According to the Scottish theologian Alexander Ales, who had been at court on Sunday, 30 April, he witnessed a heated confrontation between Anne and Henry. In a letter sent to Elizabeth in September 1559, he recounted what he had seen.[69]

Never shall I forget the sorrow which I felt when I saw the most serene Queen, your most religious mother, carrying you, still a little baby, in her arms and entreating the most serene King, your father, in Greenwich

Palace, from the open window of which he was looking into the courtyard, when she brought you to him. I did not perfectly understand what had been going on, but the faces and gestures of the speakers plainly showed that the King was angry, although he could conceal his anger wonderfully well. Yet from the protracted conference of the Council, (for whom the crowd was waiting until it was quite dark, expecting that they would return to London,) it was most obvious to everyone that some deep and difficult question was being discussed.

The king's anger and Anne's desperation were almost certainly sparked by the earlier incident with Henry Norris. The situation was sufficiently serious to warrant the postponement of the royal couple's upcoming trip. Henry announced that he would be travelling to Dover the following week instead. As the new instructions contain no mention of Anne, one presumes that he intended on travelling alone. The decision, according to Thomas Warley, was made at 11 o'clock at night on Sunday, 30 April.[70] Whether or not Anne was immediately informed is uncertain. It's also unclear as to whether the queen noticed that Mark Smeaton was missing from court.

At some point following his encounter with the queen, the young musician was seized, presumably on Henry's orders, and taken to a house in Stepney for questioning.[71] He must have shuddered when he realised that it was the home of Thomas Cromwell and that the great man would be personally handling the interrogation. Imagine the broad smile that must have worked its way across the minister's face as he heard about the exchange between Anne and the musician. Unlike Sir Henry Norris, who was well-born and a seasoned courtier in his early fifties, Smeaton was probably only in his mid-twenties and a commoner at that. This made him wretchedly vulnerable and particularly susceptible to intimidation. If convicted of high treason, he would be hung, drawn and quartered, unless the king commuted the sentence to beheading. It's hardly surprising, then, that within hours of being detained, Smeaton had confessed to having committed adultery with the queen.[72]

Chapter 19

In Hope of Life

On May Day morning, England's queen carefully prepared for the
day's festivities in her apartments at Greenwich Palace, which
overlooked the glorious privy gardens and orchard beyond. A long
day of merriment and revelry stretched out before her and, like all public
appearances, delivered an opportunity to dazzle her subjects with a show of
wealth and magnificence. While there is no record of what the queen chose
to wear that day, it's possible that she dressed in one of the new gowns she
had recently purchased from the London mercer William Lok, who was often
in the queen's employ. Among a long list of items recorded on his bill for
January to April 1536 is a gown of tawny velvet lined with black sarsenet and
edged in black lambs' fur, a gown of tawny damask lined with tawny sarsenet,
one of tawny satin bordered with lizards, another of russet caffa (a rich silk
cloth) lined with russet sarsenet, and a gown of black velvet lined with satin.[1]
Perhaps the queen selected the gown of purple cloth of gold lined with silver
or the gown of tissue with sleeves of carnation satin from Bruges. Lok also
supplied Anne with embroidered nightgowns, cloaks, kirtles, stomachers,
partlets and detachable sleeves, in a variety of colours and fabrics, including
orange and black taffeta, crimson and black velvet, and white and russet satin.
Arnold the shoemaker was given plenty of black velvet for shoes and slippers.
Lok also provided Margaret Douglas, the king's niece and Anne's lady-in-
waiting, with black velvet for the edging of a kirtle of black damask, and the
queen's fool received a new gown and cap. Anne also spent a significant sum
of money on her daughter, who would go on to inherit her mother's exquisite
sartorial taste, as well as her penchant for colour.[2] Among the items made
for the 2-year-old Princess Elizabeth was a gown of orange velvet, purple
embroidered satin sleeves, partlets of black velvet and black satin, and kirtles
made of russet velvet, of yellow satin and of white damask.

Despite the unnerving events of the last 48 hours, Anne must have hoped
that the celebratory atmosphere of the day, and her and Henry's shared love
of theatre, would inspire a reconciliation between them. Their relationship
had always been tempestuous and emotionally charged, but past quarrels had
usually blown over quickly: 'storm followed sunshine and sunshine followed
storm'.[3] No doubt she yearned to feel the warmth of her husband's favour once

again, as she well understood that her security – and her family's – depended on it.

The day was traditionally celebrated at court with jousts and tournaments, music, dancing, plays and pageants – entertainments both she and Henry adored. The king was a perennial performer and had always loved to dress up. Throughout his reign, he financed and took part in countless elaborate disguises. In 1510, for example, he and a group of his favoured courtiers, Thomas Boleyn among them, burst into the queen's apartments one morning, dressed as Robin Hood and his men.[4] They danced and made merry with Katherine and her ladies, before departing as abruptly as they had arrived. The heroic outlaw was also a popular feature of the May Day festivities. Edward Hall recalled that on May Day 1515, Henry and Katherine, accompanied by many lords and ladies, had paused to 'take the air' on Shooter's Hill, when they came across a company of 200 men all dressed in green and brandishing bows and arrows.[5] Robin Hood himself then stepped forward and invited the royal couple to watch his men shoot, which they gladly did. The archers were, of course, yeomen of the king's guard, dressed up for the occasion. Following the display, which sounded both 'strange and great' on account of the whistling arrows used, they all retreated to a magnificent arbour in the woods to see how the outlaws lived. It was made of boughs and covered with flowers and sweet herbs, and contained a hall, a great chamber and an inner chamber 'which the king much praised'. Robin Hood and his merry men then served the royal couple an outlaw's breakfast of venison and wine, before escorting them back to the palace.

While there's no account of such elaborate entertainments taking place in 1536, there was high drama aplenty. The king may have cancelled the trip to Dover, but the May Day jousts were permitted to proceed. Anne and Henry watched from the stands, as according to Charles Wriothesley, Lord Rochford led the team of challengers and Sir Henry Norris, the defenders.[6] Lancelot de Carles, secretary to the French ambassador, who wrote a narrative poem about Anne's downfall, recorded that Francis Weston and William Brereton also participated.[7] Sources differ over exactly what happened at the conclusion of the joust. Edward Hall has Henry 'suddenly' departing and taking only six people with him. 'Of this sudden departing many men mused, but most chiefly the queen', observed the chronicler with hindsight.[8] John Stow echoes Hall's words: 'From these jousts King Henry suddenly departed to Westminster, having only with him six persons, of which sudden departure men marvelled.'[9] George Constantine recalled that after the joust, 'the king rode suddenly to Westminster', interrogating Norris along the way.[10] He promised Norris a pardon if he would speak the truth. But regardless of what the king said or did, 'Mr Norris would confess no thing to the king, whereupon he was committed to the Tower in the morning.'[11]

The May Day joust raises an important question. Why did the king allow the event to go ahead if he already knew about Mark Smeaton's confession and the incident with Sir Henry Norris? Similarly, it's also possible that the king knew of George Boleyn's alleged involvement, as Smeaton may have been pressured to implicate him. Certainly, even before the joust commenced, the young musician had been confined to the Tower, so why persist with the facade?[12] Once again, Henry's penchant for theatrics cannot be underestimated nor overlooked, neither can his inherently jealous and vindictive nature. As Emma Levitt has pointed out, 'the king now unable to actively participate in tournaments must have resented this display of continued vigour from his former jousting companions.'[13] In fact, she argues that it was Henry's 'jousting jealousy' that led to their downfalls, and not their relationship with the queen. In view of this, the most plausible explanation is that the king intentionally chose the May Day joust as the stage from which to make his carefully choreographed exit, in order to send a strong message to his subjects, reminding them that although he was no longer able to demonstrate his masculinity in the tiltyard, he was still very much in control. It also smacks of pure, unadulterated cruelty. The king put the men on a pedestal one final time, only to violently topple them. He was the ultimate puppeteer, and the fates of all his subjects rested, as they always had, firmly in his hands.

It's clear that the king believed his former jousting companions posed a threat to his masculinity and his kingship, but what about Anne? Did Henry believe Mark Smeaton's confession? Did he genuinely think that the queen's conversation with Norris was evidence of her murderous intentions and adulteries? The king's behaviour and actions throughout May suggest that he did not. This is not to say, however, that he did not think Anne was guilty of other grave offences. The riding accident had left Henry feeling especially insecure and vulnerable, which only exacerbated his jealousy over his wife's interactions with the virile men who surrounded her, including her own charismatic brother. Given Anne's allure and how adept she was at the art of coquetry, not to mention her infamously sharp tongue, it wasn't long before a wounded Henry began to wonder whether his wife was harbouring hidden desires for other men and laughing at him behind his back. It was this insidious and almost certainly fallacious thought that called Anne's loyalty into question, which contributed to the king's decision to close his heart to his wife. But in Henry's mind, this was not Anne's only betrayal.

Like everyone else at court, it was Anne's God-given duty to carry out the king's will and to help bring to life the fantasy in his head. Henry desperately wanted a son and heir, but she had failed in this regard, and, importantly, broken a promise she had made him years earlier. At some point during their courtship, Anne and Henry had penned notes to each other in a prayer book. Beneath the image of a wounded Christ, a besotted Henry wrote in French, 'If you remember my love in your prayers as strongly as I adore you, I shall hardly be forgotten, for I am yours. Henry R forever'. Anne responded with the following dutiful lines: 'By daily proof you shall me find To be to you both loving and kind'. She chose to write her couplet beneath an illustration of the Annunciation, when the Angel Gabriel announced to Mary that she would give birth to a son, thereby implicitly promising the king a son and heir. On the promise of boys and dynastic security, the king had risked his kingdom in order to marry her, but all she had brought him were troubles and another daughter. As Henry's mistress, Anne had ticked all of Henry's boxes, but as queen she had failed to live up to the king's impossible expectations. The interminable opposition to their marriage and immense stress of the previous twelve months, coupled with the king's intense disappointment at the lack of a male heir, eroded the great love he had once felt for Anne. Traits that he had once found irresistible, such as Anne's outspokenness, wit and vivacity, now grated on him. All that remained was raw anger and a deep sense of resentment at what he considered a devastating betrayal worthy of the harshest punishment. Where once he would have done anything to have her by his side, the king now urgently desired to be rid of her and to start afresh. He pursued this goal with the same vigour as he had once devoted to securing his marriage to Anne.

If Henry did not actually believe that Anne was guilty of the charges of adultery, there is one more important question to consider: why would someone so preoccupied with his honour and reputation willingly play the part of a cuckold? Quite simply because Henry preferred this over being wrong. If he found some grounds on which to annul his marriage to Anne, it would imply that he had made a mistake in marrying her and that his former wife, his daughter Mary, Charles V, the Pope and everyone else who had opposed their marriage had known better after all. The king also greatly feared that it would be seen as a validation of his first marriage and of the Pope's authority.[14] This was completely unacceptable, impossible, in fact, for a man unable to admit mistakes, which is why the king did not move against Anne until Cromwell presented him with an alternative way out.

Following the May Day joust, the king left Greenwich and made his way to Westminster with a small retinue. One can't help but wonder whether he hesitated as he walked away from Anne that day, knowing full well that the following day, she would be arrested and that he would never lay eyes on her again. It's unlikely, given Henry's knack for compartmentalising his life and moving on. What Anne thought of his departure is unknown. Similarly, there are no records detailing how Anne spent her last night of freedom, but considering that Elizabeth had been at court the previous day, it's possible that she enjoyed some time with her daughter before retiring to her apartments.

The following morning, Sir Henry Norris was imprisoned in the Tower. It was rumoured that he had concealed knowledge of Smeaton's alleged affair with the queen.[15] A few hours later, George Boleyn was apprehended at Whitehall Palace and transferred to the Tower.[16] The fact that George was at Whitehall and not at Greenwich when he was detained suggests that he may have been trying to reach the king to intervene on his sister's behalf.[17] Access to the king, however, was being strictly guarded and no doubt Cromwell ensured that the queen's most vehement supporters were quickly turned away.

All Lord Rochford's efforts were in vain because, late in the afternoon of 2 May, the queen herself was conducted in broad daylight to the Tower.[18] She was accompanied by members of the king's Privy Council, whom, according to Charles Wriothesley, included Thomas Audley, the Lord Chancellor; the queen's uncle, the Duke of Norfolk; William Kingston, the Constable of the Tower; and Thomas Cromwell.[19] Also present were the lord treasurer and the comptroller of the household, Sir William Fitzwilliam and Sir William Paulet respectively.[20] Chapuys gleefully reported that Anne was only permitted four ladies to wait on her and informed the emperor that she had been detained on charges of adultery with 'a spinet of her chamber'.[21] 'Even if the said crime of adultery had not been discovered', continued Chapuys, 'this king, as I have been for some days informed by good authority, had determined to abandon her', on the grounds that an alleged pre-contract existed between Anne and Henry Percy, the Earl of Northumberland.[22] This suggestion, the earl would later vehemently deny.[23]

The sombre delegation arrived at the Tower at around 5 o'clock and disembarked the barge at 'court gate', one of three riverside entrances.[24] Anne stepped off the boat and climbed a set of stairs, which led onto the wharf, before falling to her knees and protesting her innocence in front of the stony-faced lords. At this stage, all the queen knew was that she was being accused of having committed adultery with three men: Mark Smeaton, Sir Henry Norris and a third unnamed man. She implored Henry's councillors to 'beseech the king's grace to be good unto her', before being escorted across the drawbridge, through the Byward postern gate and into the outer ward of the Tower.[25] Anne feared that she would be lodged in a dungeon, so when Kingston informed her that she would, in fact, be housed in the royal apartments where she had stayed in such splendour prior to her coronation, Anne responded that it was too good for her. She then fell to her knees and wept, exclaiming 'Jesus, have mercy on me', before breaking out in uncontrollable laughter.[26] This, according to a baffled Sir William Kingston, 'she hath done so many times since'. Anne was clearly suffering from a form of emotional shock, as a result of not only her sudden incarceration, but also the months of stress, trauma and uncertainty she had endured.

Kingston, who was not without some sympathy for Anne, was under strict instructions to report all that the queen said and did during her imprisonment to Thomas Cromwell. His missives, albeit incomplete, are our best source of information regarding Anne's behaviour during this time.[27] Kingston was aided by the four main women chosen by the king to attend the queen or, more accurately, to spy on her. They were Mary Scrope, the wife of William Kingston; Margaret Dymoke, who was married to Sir William Coffin, Anne's master of the horse; Elizabeth Boleyn, who was the wife of Sir James Boleyn, Anne's paternal uncle; and a Mistress Stonor, possibly the wife of Sir Walter Stoner.[28] Kingston also recorded the presence of 'two other gentlewomen', whose identities remain unknown. Cromwell ordered Kingston to instruct Anne's attendants to have no communication with the queen unless Lady Kingston was present, however, as Kingston himself explained to Cromwell, this was impossible because 'my lady Boleyn and Mistress Coffin lie on the queen's pallet, and I and my wife at the door without'. He acknowledged that some conversation would obviously have to take place while Lady Kingston was out of the room, however, he assured Cromwell that Mistress Coffin would tell him everything 'that she thinks meet for me to know'.[29]

Once Anne recovered from the initial shock, she asked Kingston to 'move the king's highness that she might have the sacrament in the closet by her chamber that she might pray for mercy, for I am as clear from the company of man, as for [sic] sin'. This is clear evidence of Anne's opposition to radical Sacramentarian beliefs. She then declared before all those present that she was the king's true wedded wife. Kingston reported that a nervous Anne then peppered him with questions:

> Master Kingston, do you know wherefore I am here, and I said nay, and then she said when saw you the king? And I said, I saw him not since I saw him in the tiltyard, and then Master Kingston I pray you tell me where my Lord, my father is? And I told her I saw him afore dinner in the court. Oh, where is my sweet brother? I said I left him at York Place, and so I did.[30]

Anne was being intentionally kept in the dark and this only served to increase her anxiety. Her mind flitted from one thought to another, as she desperately tried to make sense of the situation. 'I hear say,' said she, 'that I should be accused with three men; and I can say no more but nay... O Norris, hast thou accused me, thou are in the Tower with me, and thou and I shall die together; and Mark, thou art here to.'[31] Her attention then turned to her mother, whom she feared would 'die of sorrow', and to her lady-in-waiting, the Countess of Worcester, whom Anne 'much lamented...for by cause that her child did not stir in her body'. Lady Kingston pressed her for more information, enquiring 'what should be the cause?' And [Anne] said, 'for the sorrow she took for me.'[32] Exactly what Anne was referring to is unclear. However, Lady Worcester was pregnant at the time, so perhaps Anne knew of some difficulties with the countess's pregnancy. It's possible that Anne and Lady Worcester were both pregnant in late January when Anne suffered the miscarriage, and that this tragedy had greatly grieved her lady-in-waiting. As Anne had attributed her miscarriage to the shock she suffered when Henry fell from his horse, perhaps she feared that the latest blow of her sudden imprisonment would cause Lady Worcester further grief – enough to cause her to lose her baby. The queen's remarks do appear to indicate a close bond between the two women. This is further evidenced by the fact that Anne made a secret loan of £100 to the countess.[33] Suddenly, Anne stopped fretting about others and turned to Kingston and asked, 'shall I die without justice?', to which Kingston responded, 'the poorest subject the king hath, hath justice'. The queen erupted in laughter.

Kingston left Anne with Mistress Coffin and Lady Boleyn, and retired for the evening. The queen continued to talk unguardedly, incessantly recounting the events of the previous weekend. She spoke of the incident with Henry Norris, but also admitted to being concerned about what Francis Weston would say. Her attendants encouraged her babbling and the following morning reported all to William Kingston. He, in turn, penned a letter to Cromwell to which he added a postscript:

> Sir since the making of this letter the Queen spoke of Weston, saying that she had spoken to him because he did love her kinswoman Mrs Skelton [Madge Shelton], and said he loved not his wife, and he made answer to her again that he loved one in her house better than them both. And the queen said, who is that? It is yourself. And then she defied him, as she said to me.[34]

Cromwell promptly ordered Weston's arrest, along with that of Sir William Brereton, another member of the king's privy chamber, Thomas Wyatt and Richard Page. Exactly who implicated the latter three is unknown, as Anne does not appear to have mentioned them in her recollections.

As news of the arrests spread throughout the city and abroad, the diplomatic rumour mill went into overdrive. The Bishop of Faenza reported that Anne's 'father, mother, brother, and an organist with whom she had been too intimate', had all been detained.[35] Similarly, on the day of the queen's arrest, Roland Bulkeley had penned a letter to his brother in North Wales, in which he erroneously stated that the queen was in the Tower with, among others, 'the earl of Wiltshire' and 'sundry ladies'.[36] Understandably, Bulkeley had assumed that if the queen was guilty of adultery, then her ladies must have been complicit and presumably facilitated the meetings. How else would the queen have managed to keep up the deceit for so long? Tellingly, however, there would be no arrests made among the queen's ladies, and many of them would go on to serve Anne's successor. Put simply, they suffered no disfavour because, like their mistress, they had committed no crime.

Anne's vice-chancellor, Sir Edward Baynton, also tried to make sense of the whole affair. He marvelled that 'no man will confess anything against her [Anne], but only Mark of any actual thing', and was concerned that this would 'much touch the king's honour'.[37] He also told William Fitzwilliam that Lady Margaret Lee, one of the queen's ladies 'hath used herself strangely toward me of late, being her friend as I have been', and noted the 'great friendship of late' between Margaret and Anne.

The bombshell of the queen's arrest must have left her friends, family and supporters utterly dumbfounded, not to mention infuriated at the injustice of it all. There was, of course, little they could do to help Anne, or any of the men for that matter, but this did not stop some brave individuals from trying. On 3 May, a shell-shocked Thomas Cranmer penned a careful letter to the king in which he expressed his sorrow over the allegations:

> I am in such a perplexity, that my mind is clean amazed; for I never had better opinion in woman, than I had in her; which maketh me to think, that she should not be culpable...Now I think that your grace best knoweth, that next unto your grace I was most bound unto her of all creatures living. Wherefore I most humbly beseech your grace to suffer me in that, which both God's law, nature, and also her kindness, bindeth me unto; that is, that I may with your grace's favour wish and pray for her, that she may declare herself inculpable and innocent.[38]

He was wise enough, though, to temper his words. After writing his letter, he was ordered to attend the Star Chamber, where he was informed of certain things which the king wanted him to know. Cranmer then dutifully added a postscript to his original letter, in which he lamented that 'such faults can be proved by the Queen'. He must have realised that the king was determined to be rid of Anne at all costs, and that there was little he could do but toe the line.

Lady Rochford, George Boleyn's wife, also intended on petitioning the king. She wrote a message to her husband in which she assured him that she would 'humbly [make] suit unto the king's highness'.[39] While the letter itself does not survive, Kingston mentions it in one of his despatches to Cromwell and notes that Lord Rochford gave thanks to his wife for her comforting words. Whether or not Lady Rochford kept her promise to George is uncertain.

According to Lancelot de Carles, Francis Weston's mother, 'weighed down by her great grief', also petitioned the king, as did Weston's wife, whom he claimed 'offered her entire wealth and income for his freedom'.[40] However, as Professor JoAnn DellaNeva has pointed out, 'Carle is the only source for this information concerning Weston's mother and wife'.[41] What is certain, however, is that some individuals did try to intervene on his behalf. On 13 May, John Husee informed Lord Lisle that if any shall escape execution, it will be Francis Weston 'for whose life there is importunate suit made'.[42] Unfortunately, he does not identify the petitioners. While it's possible that he was referring to Weston's family, he may also have been speaking about the French ambassadors Castelnau and Dinteville, whom we know tried to intervene on Weston's behalf.[43] In light of this, DellaNeva has proposed that de Carles may have altered the facts 'for the sake of adding melodrama to his tale, turning a political plea into a very personal one.[44] While we have no record of Brereton's family making such an impassioned plea for his life, we know that his wife believed in his innocence. One of the last gifts she had received from her husband was a bracelet, which she treasured until her own death in 1545. In her will she bequeathed to her son 'one bracelet of gold, the which was the last token his father sent me'.[45]

Back in the Tower, all eyes were on the queen. Just a day or two after her arrest, she learned that her brother was also in the Tower, along with Francis Weston and William Brereton. Kingston reported that upon receiving the news, Anne 'made very good countenance'.[46] By her own words, she was very glad to be so close to George, even in such dire circumstances, which again shines a light on the bond they shared. Kingston also informed the queen that Sir Richard Page and Sir Thomas Wyatt had also been detained. Unfortunately, at this point, Kingston's letter becomes illegible and so Anne's remarks have been lost. What we do know is that she requested to write a letter to Master Secretary, which Kingston offered to take down for her, and marvelled much that the king's Council had not come to see her. George, too, wondered when he would be called before the Council, and feared that it would not be until his trial. No doubt Anne had many matters which she wanted to address, including how she had been, in her own words, 'cruelly handled as was never seen' during the initial interrogations at Greenwich.[47] She told Kingston that the Duke of Norfolk had said to her condescendingly 'tut, tut, tut' and had shaken his head three or four times, but that 'Master Controller', Sir William Paulet, had behaved like a gentleman. At this point, she still believed that her incarceration was some sort of test and that the king did it to prove her innocence. 'I shall have justice,' asserted the queen, because 'if any man accuse me I can say but nay, and they can bring no witness'.

The queen fervently maintained her innocence throughout her incarceration, but her behaviour remained erratic. 'One hour she is determined to die,' wrote a perplexed Kingston, 'and the next hour much contrary to that'.[48] She also prophesised that there would be no rain until she was delivered from the Tower and foretold that her death would bring with it, 'the greatest punishment... that ever came to England'.[49] Then, in the same breath, she said, 'I shall be in heaven, for I have done many good deeds in my days'. If taken literally, this appears to indicate that Anne did not believe in justification by faith alone. However, Ives offers an alternative explanation in which he suggests that Anne's remark in fact adheres to the 'more moderate approaches to justification by faith alone', which 'saw faith as necessarily expressing itself in good works'.[50]

Anne also voiced her displeasure about the women whom the king had chosen to serve her. She thought it very unkind of the king to put 'such about me as I never loved', instead of women from her own privy chamber, which she favoured the most.

There's no doubt that the queen would have relished the opportunity to speak with her husband and plead her innocence in person. The powers that be, however, would never permit this, so the only other option left to Anne would have been to reach out to the king in a letter. It's true that Kingston makes no mention of one, but it's worth noting that the British Library is home to an intriguing missive, allegedly composed by Anne to Henry on 6 May 1536 [See Appendix 2]. Its authenticity has been hotly debated for centuries, with many historians concluding that it is an Elizabethan forgery. Others, however, fervently believe that Anne is the author. For example, Jasper Ridley asserted that the letter 'bears all the marks of Anne's character, of her spirit, her impudence and her recklessness'.[51] If these are Anne's words, then she believed the king's interest in Jane Seymour was the root of her troubles. We pick up the letter when Anne is pleading for a fair and open trial:

So that whatsoever God or you may determine of me, your grace may be freed from an open censure; and mine offence being so lawfully proved, your grace is at liberty, both before God and man, not only to execute worthy punishment on me as an unlawful wife, but to follow your affection already settled on that party, for whose sake I am now as I am, whose name I could some good while since have pointed unto: Your grace being not ignorant of my suspicion therein.

More recently, Sandra Vasoli convincingly argues in her book, *Anne Boleyn's Letter from the Tower*, that 'these are the final words from Anne Boleyn to Henry VIII'.[52] What is certain is that the letter is not written in Anne's own hand. Therefore, if she did indeed compose it, a scribe was used to record her poignant and courageous words. The closing paragraph is certainly in keeping with what we know of Anne's character and convictions. Furthermore, her deep concern for the men accused alongside her is corroborated by Kingston's letters and Chapuys' report of Anne's trial.

My last and only request shall be, that myself may only bear the burden of your grace's displeasure, and that it may not touch the innocent souls of those poor gentlemen, whom (as I understand) are likewise in strait imprisonment for my sake. If ever I have found favour in your sight; if ever the name of Anne Boleyn hath been pleasing in your ears, let me obtain this request; and so I will leave to trouble your grace any further, with mine earnest prayer to the Trinity to have your grace in his good keeping, and to direct you in all your actions. From my doleful prison the Tower, this 6th of May.
Your most loyal and ever faithful wife,
Anne Boleyn

The following day, Sunday, 7 May, the queen's chaplain, William Latymer, arrived at Sandwich where he was informed of Anne's arrest and imprisonment.[53] As he had been in Flanders on the queen's business, he was promptly searched by the authorities, who drew up a list of the books he was carrying and of those he had ordered on his trip. One Thomas Boys (or Boyce) then escorted Latymer to London. The Mayor of Sandwich's account specifies that Latymer was taken directly 'to the king', which points to Henry taking charge of the case against his wife. He was not simply leaving it all in Cromwell's hands, but rather personally overseeing and carefully managing every single detail. The fact that we hear nothing more of this suggests that Henry's men found no incriminating material amongst Latymer's belongings.

Like a predator on the scent of its prey, Henry was so consumed with securing his wife's conviction that little other business was transacted. On 8 May, Lord Lisle wrote to Cromwell in the hope of pocketing a share of the spoils that would result from the fall of Rochford and the other men, but John Husee advised his master that this 'is no time to make hot suit till time the matters which are now in hand be overblown'.[54] Lisle, however, was not the only courtier clamouring for rewards. Just hours after the first arrests, Richard Staverton wrote to Cromwell and blithely requested some of Norris's lands and perks.[55] The Duke of Richmond, on the other hand, coveted Norris's stewardship of Banbury for one of his servants, however, unbeknownst to the young duke, the office had already been offered to Thomas Cromwell.[56] It's quite chilling that the vultures descended even before Norris had been condemned, but as Richmond pointed out in a letter to the Bishop of Lincoln, 'it is presupposed with many men that there is no way but one with him [Norris]'.[57] The duke's assumption is understandable given that very few people were acquitted of high treason during his father's reign. As it transpired, Lord Lisle and the other eager suitors did not have long to wait for a formal conviction.

On 9 May, the sheriffs of London were commanded to assemble a grand jury at Westminster the following day, to examine the alleged offences committed by the accused parties in Middlesex and decide if there was sufficient evidence to proceed to trial.[58] Unsurprisingly, given the serious nature of the allegations, the queen, her brother, Norris, Weston, Brereton and Smeaton were all indicted. On 10 May, Sir John Dudley reported the news to Lady Lisle and informed her that in two days they would all be arraigned at Westminster, with the exception of the queen, whom he noted would be 'condemned by Parliament'.[59] Dudley, like everyone else at court, understood that the result of the trial was a foregone conclusion. He was, though, evidently unaware that like his sister, Lord Rochford would also be tried by a jury of his peers.

The same day, William Kingston was commanded to 'bring up the bodies' of Weston, Norris, Brereton and Smeaton on Friday, 12 May, to stand trial at Westminster Hall. As Earl Marshall and High Steward of England, Thomas Howard was ordered to make preparations for the trial of his niece and nephew, which would take place on Monday, 15 May, at the Tower of London. Things were now moving rapidly.

On Thursday, 11 May, a Kent grand jury met to examine the alleged crimes committed in the county, namely at Greenwich Palace. Predictably, they too ruled that the accused parties should proceed to trial.[60]

The following day, Sir William Kingston escorted the four men by barge to Westminster, where they were arraigned for high treason. As soon as Norris and the others caught sight of the jury, they knew they were dead men walking.[61] Among those selected to sit in judgement of the case were the likes of Walter Hungerford and Richard Tempest, who were utterly beholden to Cromwell. Others, like William Askew, were religious conservatives and supporters of the Lady Mary. Then there were men such as William Sidney, who were openly hostile to the Boleyns. This pliable panel was hand-picked by the king and Cromwell to deliver the desired verdict, and they did not disappoint. Despite the fact that only Smeaton pleaded guilty to adultery with the queen – and all pleaded not guilty to conspiring the king's death – all four men were found guilty of high treason and sentenced to be executed at Tyburn.[62] As they left the court, the ceremonial axe was turned towards them to let the public know that they had been condemned to death. Kingston returned his prisoners to the Tower to prepare their souls for the end. Almost immediately, people began to murmur about the integrity of the proceedings, with Chapuys concluding that apart from Smeaton, the men 'were condemned upon presumption and certain indications, without valid proof or confession'.[63]

At the conclusion of the trial, John Husee wrote to Lord Lisle that 'Mr Page and Mr Wyatt are in the Tower, but as it is said, without danger of death: but Mr Page is banished [from] the King's presence and Court for ever'.[64] However, the following day, he acknowledged that the court was a hotbed of rumour and suspicion, and that little was known for certain. 'Here are so many tales I cannot tell which to write,' began Husee.[65] 'Some saith young Weston shall escape; and some saith that none shall die but the Queen and her brother; and some other say that Wyatt and Mr Page are as like to suffer as the others'. Husee also noted that it was rumoured that one Harry Webbe would shortly be taken into custody. Husee told Lady Lisle that everything which had ever been 'penned, contrived, and written' against women since Adam and Eve, is 'nothing in comparison of that which hath been done and committed by Anne the Queen'. He did, however, confess that he did not believe everything that was being rumoured about her, only that 'which hath been by her confessed, and others, offenders with her'. Acts so 'abominable and detestable' that he thought they were not fit for the ear of 'any good woman'.[66] In reality, Anne had not confessed to any crime and neither had any of the men, with the exception of Smeaton. The queen and Lord Rochford had not even been tried yet. Nevertheless, the official line spun by the king and Cromwell was that they had already admitted their guilt. If further evidence was needed of the fact that Anne's guilt, and therefore George's too, was a foregone conclusion, on Saturday, 13 May, the queen's household was broken up and her servants were discharged of their offices.[67] Furthermore, on Sunday, 14 May, the king ordered Sir Nicholas Carew to move Jane Seymour to a house 'within a mile of his [the king's] lodging', where, according to Chapuys, a 'richly dressed' Jane was 'splendidly served by the King's cook and others'.[68] There can be little doubt that Mistress Seymour was being groomed to become Anne's successor.

The same day, Cromwell wrote to Stephen Gardiner and John Wallop, the king's ambassadors in France, to inform them of recent events involving the queen. What follows is the official government line.

> The Queen's incontinent living was so rank and common that ladies of her privy chamber could not conceal it. It came to the ears of some of the Council, who told his Majesty, although with great fear, as the case enforced. Certain persons of the privy chamber and others of her side were examined, and the matter appeared so evident that, besides that crime, 'there brake out a certain conspiracy of the King's death, which extended so far that all we that had the examination of it quaked at the danger his Grace was in, and on our knees gave him [God?] laud and praise that he had preserved him so long from it.' Certain men were committed to the Tower, including Marks [Mark Smeaton] and Norris, and the Queen's brother; then she herself was apprehended and committed to the same place; after her Sir Francis Weston and William Brereton. Norris, Weston, Brereton and Marks are already condemned to death, having been arraigned at Westminster on Friday last. The Queen and her brother are to be arraigned tomorrow, and will undoubtedly go the same way. I write no particularities; the things be so abominable that I think the like was never heard.[69]

There are, however, issues with the official story. Firstly, there are no records of any interrogations of Anne's ladies or other members of her household. Moreover, as we shall shortly see, most of the offences recorded on the indictment can be easily disproved. Finally, Henry's behaviour following Anne's arrest calls into question not only this version of events, but the credibility of the Crown's entire case against the queen and her alleged lovers. Chapuys told Charles V that since Anne's incarceration, the king 'had shown extravagant joy' and could be frequently found banqueting and partying late into the night accompanied by women and musicians.[70] 'It sounds ill in the ears of the people,' wrote Chapuys with characteristic insight. John Husee corroborated the ambassador's account and noted that 'it may become no man to prevent him'. This certainly does not sound like the behaviour of a grieving husband who has only just discovered that his wife has committed multiple acts of adultery and conspired to kill him and even to poison his children.[71] The king even openly alleged that his wife had slept with 'upwards of 100 gentlemen'.[72] This outrageous remark was part of a concerted effort to manipulate public opinion about the case and convince the people that

Anne's depravity and sexual voraciousness knew no bounds. The fact that the queen often flouted convention made her vulnerable to the charges. But the suggestion that she had committed adultery with hundreds of men was so farcical that it served the opposite purpose in the end. 'You never saw prince nor man who made greater show of his horns or bore them more pleasantly,' mused Chapuys.[73] 'I leave you to imagine the cause'. What the ambassador was hinting at was a growing general impression that the king had 'invented this device to get rid of her' and marry Jane Seymour.[74] The evidence for this is overwhelming.

On the day of Anne's show trial, the king sent a messenger to Jane to inform her that at three in the afternoon she would receive news of Anne's condemnation.[75] While Jane remained closeted away with her family, the queen and her brother prepared for one of the most important public performances of their lives. Inside the King's Hall at the Tower of London, an estimated 2,000 people were accommodated in special stands erected especially for the occasion.[76] Windsor Herald Charles Wriothesley described the scene as follows:

> There were made benches and seats for the lords, my Lord of Norfolk sitting under the cloth of estate, representing there the King's person as High Steward of England and uncle to the Queen, he holding a long white staff in his hand, and the Earle of Surrey, his son and heir, sitting at his feet before him holding the golden staff for the Earle Marshall of England, which said office the said duke had in his hands; the Lord Audley, Chancellor of England, sitting on his right hand, and the Duke of Suffolk on his left hand, with other marquesses, earls, and lords, every one after their degrees.[77]

This is the solemn sight that greeted Anne as she was brought into the hall by the constable and lieutenant of the Tower, Sir William Kingston and Sir Edmund Walsingham respectively. Of the queen's four attendants, only Lady Kingston and Lady Boleyn were present. Anne sat in the chair provided for her and calmly listened as her indictment was read out, before pleading 'not guilty' to all charges.[78] She was accused of 'despising her marriage, and entertaining malice against the King'. It was claimed that she followed daily 'her frail and carnal lust, [and] did falsely and traitorously procure by base conversations and kisses, touchings, gifts and other infamous incitations, divers of the King's daily and familiar servants to be her adulterers and concubines, so that several of the King's servants yielded to her vile provocations.' She was accused of having had intercourse on multiple occasions with Henry Norris, William Brereton, Francis Weston and Mark Smeaton, as well as committing incest with her brother, George Boleyn, and 'alluring him with her tongue in the said George's mouth, and the said George's tongue in hers'.

The alleged offences [see Appendix 3] are said to have occurred over a 27-month period beginning in October 1533, and to have taken place at Westminster, Greenwich, Hampton Court and Eltham Palace. But on close inspection, most of the allegations can be disproved because Anne Boleyn was elsewhere at the time, pregnant or recovering from childbirth.[79] Aware that their case was seriously flawed, the Crown inserted after each charge a catch-all phrase like, 'and divers days before and after'.[80] This made it very difficult for anyone to challenge the specific dates.

Apart from committing adultery, it was alleged that Anne had encouraged the men with gifts. This was said to have occurred on two occasions, one of which was laughably New Year's Eve in 1535, when the queen was, of course, required to give presents. It's also stated that she had plotted with them 'the death and destruction of the king', affirmed that she had never truly loved the king in her heart, and promised to marry one of them once Henry was dead. It was said that when the king became aware 'of the said abominable crimes and treasons against himself [he] took such inward displeasures and heaviness, especially from his said Queen's malice and adultery, that certain harms and perils have befallen his royal body'. In other words, Anne was being accused of physically harming the king. According to Chapuys, both Anne and George were also charged with having laughed at the king's dress and at 'certain ballads that the king had composed'.[81] He also stated that Anne was accused of poisoning Katherine of Aragon and of planning to poison the Lady Mary, however, these charges do not feature on the indictment.[82]

The accusations and lurid details of Anne's alleged crimes were intended to shock and annihilate Anne's reputation. A lesser person would have been completely crushed by the charges, but not Anne. According to the chronicler Charles Wriothesley, after her indictment was read, 'she made so wise and discreet answers to all things laid against her, excusing herself with her words so clearly, as though she had never been faulty to the same'.[83] The queen adamantly denied all the charges, but did admit to having given money to Francis Weston, as she had given to other men at court. But despite her eloquent defence, the twenty-six jurors reached a unanimous verdict – guilty. The Duke of Norfolk then gave the sentence:

> Because thou hast offended our sovereign the King's grace, in committing treason against his person, and here attainted of the same, the law of the realm is this, that thou hast deserved death, and thy judgment is this: That thou shalt be burned here within the Tower of London, on the

Greene, else to have thy head smitten of as the King's pleasure shall be further known of the same.[84]

According to Lancelot de Carles, Anne remained completely composed and once again, articulately addressed the court.

> I do not say that I have been such as I should have been, nor that I bore towards him the humility that I owed him, given his kindness and the great tenderness with which he treated me, and the great honour that he always bestowed on me, and that I didn't often harbour some notion of jealousy towards him. In this I know that I failed in virtue...But as for the rest, may God be my witness that I have done no more wrong against him.[85]

While it's highly likely that de Carles embellished parts of the speech to add to its emotional appeal, certain elements of what he wrote do agree with Chapuys' report of Anne's trial, namely that after hearing the sentence, Anne said 'that she was prepared to die, but was extremely sorry to hear that others, who were innocent and the king's loyal subjects, should share her fate and die through her.'[86] She then requested some time to prepare her soul for death and was escorted back to her apartments. The king, meanwhile, sent Sir Francis Bryan 'in all haste' to Jane Seymour, to inform her of the outcome.[87] It was now George Boleyn's turn.

He, like his sister, pleaded not guilty to all charges and put up a convincing and spirited fight. According to Charles Wriothesley, 'he made answer so prudently and wisely to all articles laid against him, that marvel it was to hear, and never would confess anything, but made himself as clear as though he had never offended.'[88] Chapuys added that all those present 'wagered 10 to 1 that he would be acquitted', especially as no witnesses had been produced at either trial.[89] Ludicrously, the fact that George had once spent a long time with his sister was the Crown's only evidence of incest between them. When he was handed a note regarding the king's sexual performance and warned not to read it aloud, George showed his mettle.

Aware that his days were numbered, Lord Rochford defied the court and did precisely what he was ordered not to. The queen, it was said, had told George's wife, Lady Rochford, that the king 'was not skilful in copulating with a woman, and he had neither virtue nor potency'.[90] All 2,000 onlookers were now privy to this sensitive and undoubtedly embarrassing information. Furthermore, it was claimed that George had 'spread reports' which questioned whether his niece, the Princess Elizabeth, was in fact Henry's daughter, 'to which he made no reply'.[91]

The glaring lack of substantive evidence made no difference to the outcome. The same twenty-six peers who had condemned the queen, now deliberated over George's fate. All with the exception of Henry Percy, Earl of Northumberland, who had 'suddenly taken ill' after Anne's conviction and was unable to continue in his duties. The verdict was once again unanimous: guilty. Norfolk then pronounced the grisly sentence:

> That he should go again to prison in the Tower from whence he came, and to be drawn from the said Tower of London through the City of London to the place of execution called Tyburn, and there to be hanged, being alive cut down, and then his members cut off and his bowel taken out of his body and burnt before him, and then his head cut off and his body to be divided in 4 pieces, and his head and body to be set at such places as the King should assign.[92]

George's thoughts immediately turned to his debts, which he asked the court to settle on his behalf, before being escorted back to his cell. In the face of such injustice and brutality, the fact that both Anne and George maintained their composure and wit throughout the proceedings, and defended themselves so ably, speaks volumes of their characters. They were formidable opponents. Their performance at their trials is a 'clear indication of their calibre and why they had to die'.[93] The trial records were immediately delivered to the Duke of Norfolk for safekeeping. No doubt the king was eager to lock away any evidence of royal impotence.

A note on the jurors; despite popular belief, Thomas Boleyn was not on the jury which condemned Anne and George, and was almost certainly not present at their trials.[94] It's likely that given the futility of the situation and his wife's illness, he had retreated to the family's home at Hever to grieve his children in private. There is also absolutely no contemporary evidence to suggest that Anne's sister-in-law, Jane Boleyn, had played any role in her husband's downfall, let alone that she had been his principal accuser.

On Tuesday, 16 May, Sir William Kingston informed the men that they would be executed the following day. His letter to Cromwell on that day betrays his nervousness and eagerness to do things by the book: 'I shall desire you further to know the king's pleasure touching the queen, as well for her comfort as for the preparation of scaffolds and other necessaries…the time is short'.[95] Kingston also reported that Archbishop Thomas Cranmer had been with the queen that day. It's been suggested that he visited to try to convince her to 'confess to an impediment to her marriage'.[96] This seems very probable given that that day at dinner, Anne told Kingston that she would go to a nunnery and that she was 'in hope of life'.[97] Perhaps Cranmer offered

Anne a deal: agree to an annulment and your life will be spared. If this is the promise that he made, was Cranmer aware of the king's duplicitous intentions? What is certain is that the day after Cranmer's visit, 'in a solemn court kept at Lambeth', he declared the marriage between Henry VIII and Anne Boleyn to be null and void, 'in consequence of certain just and lawful impediments'.[98] According to Wriothesley, Anne had confessed to having been pre-contracted to Henry Percy, Earl of Northumberland, a claim that the earl himself had vehemently denied just days earlier.[99] Chapuys, on the other hand, reported that the marriage had been annulled on account of the fact that the king had 'had connection with her [Anne's] sister'.[100] Either way, Henry was now a free man.

The king's preoccupation with overseeing every aspect of the executions, including the preparations for the scaffolds, bordered on obsessive. One Master Eretage was ordered to organise carpenters to build a scaffold on Tower Hill 'of such a height that all present may see it'.[101] Henry had decided to commute the men's sentences to beheading. The stage was now set for one of the bloodiest spectacles of Henry VIII's reign.

Chapter 20

Bloody Days

On the morning of Wednesday, 17 May 1536, Sir William Kingston delivered five of his prisoners into the custody of the sheriffs of London for execution.[1] George Boleyn, Henry Norris, Francis Weston, William Brereton and Mark Smeaton were led out of the Tower under close guard, to the scaffold on Tower Hill. Among the large crowd that had gathered were many familiar faces, some probably still reeling at the unprecedented turn of events. The onlookers watched as the men mounted the scaffold stairs. As the highest ranking of the group, the queen's brother was the first to be executed. Before placing his chin on the block, George delivered a lengthy speech, of which several versions survive, but which Wriothesley recorded commenced:

> Masters all, I am come hither not to preach and make a sermon, but to die, as the law hath found me, and to the law I submit me, desiring you all, and especially you my masters of the Court, that you will trust on God specially, and not on the vanities of the world, for if I had so done, I think I had been alive as you be now.[2]

Tudor scaffold etiquette dictated that the condemned should acknowledge their faults, confess their sins and the justness of their punishments, and request forgiveness and prayers, which is exactly what Lord Rochford did. He veered from convention, though, by omitting 'to say that he deserved death for the crimes alleged against him'.[3] George's speech had a great impact on those who heard it. Four months after his death, John Husee remembered how Lord Rochford had 'advised every man to beware of the flattering of the Court'.[4] Farewell speech done, Anne's beloved brother then laid his head on the block and was beheaded. One account states that it took the headsman three swings of the axe to sever George's head from his body.[5]

One by one, the other men followed – Norris, then Weston and Brereton. Each spoke a few words before submitting to the axe. Mark Smeaton was the last to die. The bloody scene that spilled out before those gathered would have resembled a slaughterhouse. It must have seemed incomprehensible that the butchered corpses and heads now unceremoniously piled onto a cart had once been robust, powerful and favoured men. As the crowds dispersed, the Tower officials then transported the remains to their final resting places: the Chapel Royal of St Peter Ad Vincula for Lord Rochford and the adjacent churchyard for the others.[6]

Chapuys reported that 'to aggravate her grief', Anne was made to watch the executions.[7] However, the ambassador is the only source for this claim. She certainly would not have been able to see the scaffold from her apartments in the south-east corner of the Tower, and while it's possible that she was moved to another building within the Tower complex, there's no record of it.

Another person who may have witnessed the executions from his cell in the Bell Tower is Thomas Wyatt. In his poem, *Innocentia Veritas Viat Fides Circumdederunt me*, he reflects on the reversal of fortune that so often afflicts those who draw too close to the throne. The third and fourth stanzas speak for themselves:

> These bloody days have broken my heart.
> My lust, my youth did them depart,
> And blind desire of estate.
> Who hastes to climb seeks to revert.
> Of truth, circa Regna tonat. [it thunders around the throne]
>
> The bell tower showed me such a sight
> That in my head sticks day and night.
> There did I learn out of a grate,
> For all favour, glory, or might,
> That yet, circa Regna tonat.[8]

With her brother now in his grave and her heart in pieces, Anne prepared for her own end, which she assumed would take place the following day. Unsurprisingly, sleep evaded her and she spent most of the night in prayer with her almoner. In the early hours of 18 May, Anne requested that Kingston hear Mass with her. He watched as she took the Sacrament and swore that she had never been unfaithful to the king. The constable promptly reported all to Cromwell: 'This morning she sent for me that I might be with her at such time as she received the good lord to the intent I should hear her speak as touching her innocence always to be clear.'[9] It wasn't long before Chapuys heard the news from one of the queen's own attendants, who was evidently spying for him. He wrote to the emperor that 'the lady in whose keeping she has been sends me word, in great secrecy, that before and after her receiving the Holy Sacrament, she affirmed, on peril of her soul's damnation, that she had not misconducted herself so far as her husband the King was concerned'.[10] For a deeply religious people, Anne's oath was almost irrefutable proof of her innocence.

On the same day, the king issued a writ from Westminster relating to how and where the queen would be dispatched.[11]

> The king to his trusty and welbeloved William Kyngston, knight, constable of his Tower of London, greeting.
>
> Whereas Anne late queen of England, lately our wife, recently attainted and convicted of high treason towards us by her committed and done, and adjudged to death, that is to say by burning of fire according to the statute, law and custom of our realm of England, or decapitation, at our choice and will, remains in your custody within our Tower aforesaid. We moved by pity do not wish the same Anne to be committed to be burned by fire. We, however, command that immediately after receipt of these presents, upon the Green within our Tower of London aforesaid, the head of the same Anne shall be caused to be cut off. And herein omit nothing [etc]. Witness the king at Westminster xviij day of May in the twenty-eighth year of our reign.

There's a current of urgency in the king's instruction that her beheading take place 'immediately after receipt' of his letter. Kingston, though, had much to prepare. He had been ordered to clear the Tower of foreigners and was probably still waiting for the swordsman to arrive from Calais, as the king had decided that Anne would be beheaded with a sword instead of an axe. Given the time it would have taken for a messenger to be sent to Calais and for the executioner to travel to London, it's possible, perhaps even likely, that he was ordered in advance of the queen's trial. When Kingston was told of the plan, he expressed his gladness, 'for he can handle that matter'.[12]

Was it genuine pity for Anne that moved the king to commute her sentence to the more merciful beheading or was he simply playing out a chivalric fantasy? Sarah Gristwood suggests that the choice might have had to do with the fact that 'the sword was the ultimate symbol of the chivalric code that had first bound, and then divided, them'.[13] There's no denying that Henry was a seasoned role player. During Anne and Henry's courtship, he had taken on the role of courtly suitor and now 'he'd morphed from Lancelot the wooer to Arthur the wounded'.[14] The king wanted to be seen in the best possible light, as a wronged yet merciful prince.

Later in the day, Anne sent for Kingston again. 'I hear say I shall not die afore noon, and I am very sorry therefore; for I thought to be dead and past my pain'.[15] The constable then assured Anne that there would be no pain, to which she responded: 'I heard say the executioner was very good, and I have a little neck'. She then put her hands around her throat and laughed heartily. A perplexed Kingston told Cromwell that in all the executions he has witnessed, he had never seen anyone take so much 'joy and pleasure in death'. This was not the only example of the queen's gallows humour. She reputedly jested with her ladies that the people will have no problem finding a nickname for her and would call her *la Royne Anne Sans Tete*, or Queen Anne Lackhead, and then burst out laughing.[16] This was clearly Anne's way of coping with the darkness that ensnared her. The endless hours of waiting and wondering, however, were about to come to an end.

The following morning, Kingston returned to the queen's apartments to inform her that her execution would take place imminently. After all she had endured and the hours she had spent on her knees in prayer, Anne was ready. As she made the short journey from her apartments to the scaffold that had been newly erected on the north side of the White Tower, she distributed the £20 in alms the king had sent her.[17] Gathered around the scaffold were around a thousand Englishmen and women, many of whom she knew well: Thomas Audley, the Lord Chancellor; Charles Brandon, Duke of Suffolk; Henry Fitzroy, the king's illegitimate son; the Mayor of London, with the aldermen and sheriffs; and most of the king's Council, including Thomas Cromwell.[18] Kingston escorted Anne up the scaffold steps and her four attendants followed discreetly behind. As always, she was impeccably dressed. Resplendent in an ermine mantle and an English gable hood, she ensured that she would go to her death every inch the English queen. Anne made her way to the front of the scaffold and addressed the hushed crowd 'with a goodly smiling countenance'.[19]

Good Christian people, I am come hither to die, for according to the law and by the law I am judged to die, and therefore I will speak nothing against it. I am come hither to accuse no man, nor to speak anything of that whereof I am accused and condemned to die, but I pray God save the king and send him long to reign over you, for a gentler nor a more merciful prince was there never: and to me he was ever a good, a gentle, and sovereign lord. And if any person will meddle of my cause, I require them to judge the best. And thus I take my leave of the world and of you all, and I heartily desire you all to pray for me.[20]

Convention demanded such a submissive speech, but it was also in the best interests of the loved ones she was leaving behind, who were undoubtedly at the front of her mind. Those gathered, however, would not have failed to notice that Anne had made no public admission of sin, and that like her brother she had not admitted to deserving the punishment. These omissions would have spoken volumes. As custom dictated, Anne paid the executioner and offered him her forgiveness. With the formalities over, the ermine mantle was removed and Anne took off her headdress. One of her attendants then stepped forward and handed her a linen cap, into which she tucked her hair.[21] It's possible that she was also blindfolded. The queen then knelt down, as did many in the crowd, and repeated, 'To Christ I commend my soul, Jesu receive my soul'. Swiftly, it was done.

Anne's attendants, whom Lancelot de Carles described as 'bereft of their souls', quickly covered the head and body with a white sheet and carried her remains to the chapel of St Peter. There they carefully undressed their mistress one final time and buried her before the altar, not far from where her brother's remains had just recently been interred.[22] Their tears and reverence seem a world away from the first days of Anne's incarceration, when the queen had grumbled about the women. Perhaps, by the end, they had bonded, or at the very least, navigating together the harrowing experience of the last couple of weeks had softened their opinions of one another.

Sir William Kingston was paid £100 'for such jewels and apparel as the late Queen had in the Tower' and the executioner of Calais received £23 6s. 8d. for 'his reward and apparel'.[23] This was less than what Kingston had spent on feeding Anne during her imprisonment.

It's traditionally said that as no provision had been made for a coffin, the queen's remains were 'placed in an elm chest which had contained bow-staves for Ireland'.[24] The original source of this story is 'an old…diary or journal' of one Mr Anthony Anthony, surveyor of the ordnance at the Tower of London at the time of Anne's execution.[25] What modern historians rarely note is that the diary has been lost for centuries and is only known through marginal notes made by one Thomas Torneur in his seventeenth-century copy of *The Life and Reign of King Henry VIII* by Herbert of Cherbury. According to Torneur's annotations, as soon as Anne's head was 'smitten off', her remains were wrapped in a linen sheet and carried into the chapel within the Tower. After her clothing was removed, she was placed in a chest of elm wood, designed to transport bows into Ireland, and buried by the high altar at midday. Without the original diary, it's impossible to verify Torneur's recollections.

This story went on to be embellished and popularised in soldier-turned-historian G.J. Younghusband's book, *The Tower from Within*, published in 1918, in which he wrote that 'a kindly yeoman warder' upon seeing how distressed Anne's ladies were at the lack of a 'decent casket', fetched an old arrow chest from the nearby armoury.[26] Unfortunately, Younghusband does not list his sources.

A contemporary Italian account, possibly written by a Venetian diplomat, states that one of Anne's attendants covered her remains and placed them in a 'coffin' that was by the scaffold.[27] He makes no mention of an 'arrow chest', therefore it's possible that a simple coffin was provided by the Tower officials.

While the majority of the Tudor court turned their back on the events of May 1536, some brave souls chose to honour the dead. An elegy, frequently accredited to Thomas Wyatt, but which Nicola Shulman believes is almost certainly not his work, shows that they were remembered.[28] The author dedicates a stanza to each man. Of George Boleyn, he wrote,

> Rochford, haddest thou been not so proud,
> For thy great wit each man would thee bemoan,
> Since as it is so, many cry aloud
> It is a great loss that thou art dead and gone.

He concludes his poem by saying that he can hardly write as his paper is soaked with tears. Anne does not feature among the victims eulogised; perhaps it was too dangerous to name her or perhaps there were simply no words to describe the poet's immeasurable grief. Anne's death was a shattering and incomprehensible loss. Not just for Elizabeth, who would now be forced to navigate life at court without her mother, and for her family and friends who loved her dearly, but for the English people, whose lives she genuinely wanted to improve. Henry attempted to obliterate Anne's memory, but in the end he failed. Death would immortalise her.

Each year, on the anniversary of her execution, a basket of red roses is delivered anonymously to the chapel of St Peter at the Tower of London. The accompanying handwritten card simply reads, 'Queen Anne Boleyn, 19th of May 1536'. It's a poignant and powerful tribute to a remarkable woman whose extraordinary story has left an indelible mark on history and on the hearts of many.

Chapter 21

The Aftermath

Despite the king's attempts to control public opinion, news quickly spread that the queen had died 'boldly'.[1] Immediately following Anne's execution, the king boarded his barge and went to see Jane Seymour. The next day, the couple were formally betrothed. [2] Henry hoped to keep the news secret until Whitsunday, but Chapuys was already a step ahead. He wrote that 'everybody begins already to murmur by suspicion, and several affirm that long before the death of the other there was some arrangement which sounds ill in the ears of the people'.[3] John Husee had also heard some whispers. On 24 May, he told Lord Lisle that 'it is presumed that there shall be by Midsummer a new coronation'.[4] One disgruntled Londoner, presumably a Boleyn supporter, even wrote a derisive ballad about the king and Jane. Henry told Jane to pay no attention to it and warned that when the author was discovered, he would be severely punished.[5]

In the frenzy of correspondence that ensued, further details of the official version of events emerged. Husee wrote to Lady Lisle that 'the first accusers, [were] the Lady Worcester, and Nan Cobham, with one maid more. But the Lady Worcester was the first ground.'[6] The following day he repeated the information: 'Touching the Queen's accusers, my Lady Worcester beareth name to be the principal'.[7] Evidently he felt quite confident of the accuracy of the statement. Husee's letters are unique because they are the only contemporary documents which have survived that specifically name or mention any of the queen's accusers.

Lady Worcester was, of course, the woman that Anne showed such concern for during her imprisonment. Elizabeth was the wife of Henry Somerset, Earl of Worcester, and through her mother, was a half-sister of Sir William Fitzwilliam.[8] The identity of Nan Cobham is unknown. Muriel St. Clare Byrne asserted that Husee would not refer to Anne, the wife of George Brooke, Lord Cobham, in such a familiar way. Thus, it's likely that he was referring to a Mrs Cobham, who received a New Year's gift from the king in 1534.[9] The identity of the unnamed maid is another mystery. If these women were formally examined, the records do not survive, and thus we have no way of knowing whether they provided any evidence against the queen. Similarly, no documentation survives to shed light on why Lady Worcester might have turned on her mistress, especially given their close friendship.

This official version of events inspired several stanzas of Lancelot de Carles' narrative poem about the life and death of Anne Boleyn, in which a 'close advisor to the king' admonishes his sister for 'showing many signs of loving some men with an impure love'.[10] When he challenged her, she retorted that her sins were nothing compared to the queen's! She then advised him to see Mark Smeaton for the whole story and also implicated George Boleyn. Afraid of what would happen to him if he kept such scandalous information secret, the poem continues that the brother then confided in 'two of the most favoured friends of the king' and, in turn, all three men informed Henry.

Thanks to Husee's letters, we know that the sister referenced in the poem was the Countess of Worcester, whose brother was Anthony Browne, a gentlemen of the king's privy chamber. Regarding Lord Rochford's trial, de Carles has George say that he is judged 'on the word of one woman'.[11] This has long been thought to be a reference to his wife Jane Boleyn, but within the context of the poem, it must refer to Lady Worcester. It's worth reiterating that no contemporary evidence survives to suggest that Lady Rochford was in any way involved in the downfall of her husband and sister-in-law. In fact, their deaths left her in financial dire straits. It's time we put this pernicious myth to bed.

Importantly, as JoAnn DellaNeva reminds us in her groundbreaking book, *The Story of the Death of Anne Boleyn*, de Carles' letter is no ordinary diplomatic despatch, 'it is clearly intended to be a work of art, and, as such, it demands to be read for its aesthetic qualities.'[12] In regards to the exchange between brother and sister, she emphasises its 'highly theatrical quality' and cautions that it 'should not be read as if it were a transcript of actual utterances'.[13] When addressing the important question of what the poem tells us about Anne's guilt or innocence, DellaNeva explains that while Anne is initially portrayed as capable of having committed the alleged crimes, this view shifts dramatically in the second half of the poem, where she is portrayed much more sympathetically. Furthermore, DellaNeva's discovery of a number of previously unknown verses 'explicitly paint a picture of an innocent Anne', and of a repentant people who, in the end, came to realise that they had seriously misjudged their queen. This would explain why Henry became so enraged when he read the poem in June 1537 and why he insisted on its eradication.

When Chapuys met with Cromwell in early June 1536, the minister made the momentous confession that 'it was he who, in consequence of the disappointment and anger he had felt on hearing the King's answer to me on the third day of Easter [18 April], had planned and brought about the whole affair'.[14] Despite engineering the queen's downfall, he went on to extoll Anne and George's intelligence, spirit and courage. The dignity, strength and wit they had shown throughout their incarceration had evidently earned Cromwell's respect, perhaps even his admiration. Importantly, he also clarified Henry's role in the proceedings, admitting that he had 'been authorised and commissioned by the King to prosecute and bring to an end the mistress's trial'. Cromwell had done his duty by his king, and, like many others, was duly rewarded. In July 1536, he became Lord Privy Seal following Thomas Boleyn's resignation, and within days of his new appointment, he was raised to the peerage as Baron Cromwell of Wimbledon.

Thomas Wyatt and Richard Page were both eventually released from the Tower. Contrary to the reports that stated the latter would be forever banished from court, within months, he was welcomed back with open arms. Henry even later appointed him to several important positions within Prince Edward's household. It does appear that they were only ever detained to demonstrate the integrity of the Tudor judicial system: the 'guilty' are punished, but the 'innocent' are released.

As for the king's new love, on 30 May 1536, just eleven days after Anne's execution, Henry VIII married Jane Seymour in a private ceremony in the Queen's Closet at Whitehall Palace.[15] The following day, Jane presided over the court for the first time.[16] The Lady Mary sent her hearty congratulations to the couple and requested leave to wait upon the new queen.[17] With Anne gone, Mary mistakenly assumed that her situation would improve. Instead, the pressure to submit to her father's will only intensified.

Midsummer 1536 came and went with no sign of a coronation. At the end of October, during the popular uprising known as the Pilgrimage of Grace, it was reported that the new queen 'threw herself on her knees before the king and begged him to restore the abbeys'.[18] The king callously ordered her to get up and warned her not to interfere with state business. Henry instead suggested she 'attend to other things' and reminded her that Anne Boleyn had died in consequence of 'meddling too much with State affairs'.[19] Jane dutifully heeded her husband's warning.

Twelve months later, in October 1537, Queen Jane gave birth to a son at Hampton Court Palace, but died just twelve days later, probably from a post-partum infection. Henry's quest for a male heir had claimed yet another victim. History would show that the last Tudor queen consort to be crowned at Westminster Abbey was Anne Boleyn.

For two decades following her death, her name was only spoken in whispers. This all began to change on 15 January 1559 when Anne's daughter, Elizabeth, was crowned queen of England and Ireland.

Against all odds, a Boleyn woman was once again on the throne.

Epilogue

At around 2 o'clock in the afternoon, on Saturday, 14 January 1559, Elizabeth left the Tower of London and processed through the City towards Westminster, where she would be crowned the following day. The new queen was carried on a golden litter through the crowd-lined streets of London, which reverberated with the sound of cheers and unbridled joy. At Fenchurch Street, a child waited to officially welcome her on the city's behalf. Elizabeth asked the musicians to stop playing so she could hear the boy's speech. 'O peerless sovereign Queen, behold what this thy town hath thee presented with at thy first entrance here', he began. The subsequent two verses presented the queen with two gifts: 'blessing tongues, which many a welcome say which pray thou mayest do well, which praise thee to the sky', and 'true hearts, which love thee from their root whose suit is triumph now, and ruleth the game'.

After listening to the boy's moving oration, the royal procession made its way to Gracechurch Street, to the first of five pageants staged in the queen's honour. It was designed to show Elizabeth's descent from Henry VII and her namesake, Elizabeth of York, and emphasise her 'Englishness' in contrast to her predecessor's 'Spanishness'. At the end of the street, near the Spread Eagle Tavern, a great arch had been erected and a stage was made which extended from one side of the street to the other. The stage had three vaults and three entrances. Over the middle entrance rose a series of three stages or levels, described in some detail in a contemporary pamphlet:

> Upon the lowest stage was made one seat royal [a throne], wherein were placed two personages representing King Henry the seventh and Elizabeth his wife, daughter of the King Edward the fourth, either of these two princes sitting under one cloth of estate in their seats, not otherwise divided, but that the one of them which was King Henry the seventh, proceeding out of the house of Lancaster, was enclosed in a red rose, and the other which was Queen Elizabeth, being heir to the house of York, enclosed with a white rose, each of them royally crowned and decently apparelled as appertaineth to princes, with sceptres in their hands, and one vault surmounting their heads, wherein aptly were

placed two tables, each containing the title of those two princes. And these personages were so set that the one of them joined hands with the other, with the ring of matrimony perceived on the finger. Out of the which two roses sprang, two branches gathered into one, which were directed upward to the second stage or degree wherein was placed one representing the valiant and noble prince King Henry the eighth, which sprang out of the former stock, crowned with a crown imperial, and by him sat one representing the right worthy Lady Queen Anne, wife to the said King Henry the eighth and mother to our most sovereign Lady Queen Elizabeth that now is, both apparelled with sceptres and diadems and other furniture [equipment] due to the estate of a king and queen, and two tables surmounting their heads wherein were written their names and titles. From their seat also proceeded upwards one branch directed to the third and uppermost stage or degree, wherein likewise was planted a seat royal, in which was set one representing the Queen's most excellent Majesty Elizabeth now our most dread sovereign Lady, crowned and apparelled as the other princes were.

This was the first time that Anne Boleyn had been publicly honoured in almost 23 years. Resting on 'a little hill' near the late queen's image was her badge – a white falcon, with a crown on its head and sceptre in its talon, surrounded by branches with little roses in front. The royal regalia Henry VIII had unjustly stripped from Anne Boleyn was now hers once more.

Elizabeth would go on to reign for 45 years – a period traditionally viewed as a golden age in English history. Although Elizabeth did not often speak about her mother in public, she honoured her memory in other subtle, yet important ways. Apart from using Anne's falcon badge, she also adopted one of her mottoes and greatly favoured and promoted her Boleyn relatives at court. Perhaps most touchingly, tucked inside one of her bejewelled rings was a tiny portrait of a smiling woman, almost certainly Anne Boleyn. From her birth to her death, Elizabeth embraced and cherished her mother's memory, and carried within her heart a spark of her bold spirit, courage and vivacity.

Appendix I

The 1535 'giests'

[The King's g]estes the xx[vii. year of] his reign, from [Windsor to] Bristowe.
– Monday, 5 July, Windsor to Reading, and there Tuesday and Wednesday,
St. Thomas Day; three days, 12 miles. Thursday, 8 July, Reading to Ewelme,
and there Friday, 2 days, 10 m. (*In the margin*, [M]yssenden.) Saturday, 10th
July, to Abingdon, and there till Monday, 3 days, 8 m. (*In the margin*,...
arringden [p]ark, [W]odstock.) Tuesday, 13 July, to Langley, and there till
Friday, 12 m. (*In the margin*,.... wnell.) Saturday, 17 July, to Sydley, and there
till Thursday, 14 m. (*In the margin*,...... mbe.... aylles.) Friday, 23 July, Sedley
to Tewkesbury, and there till Monday, 7 m. (*In the margin*,...... gtor the.... ttes
place.) Tuesday, 27 July, Tewkesbury to Gloucester, and there till Sunday, 7
m. (*In the margin*,...... eyerd the.... ttes place.) Monday, 2 Aug., Gloucester
to Berkeley Heron, and there till Sunday, 15 m. (*In the margin*,...... Pointz.)
Monday, 9 Aug., Berkley Heron to Thornbury, and there till Monday, 5 m.
(*In the margin*, [Mr. W]alshes.) Tuesday, 17 Aug., Thornbury to Bristowe, and
there till Friday, 10 m. Saturday, 21 Aug., Bristowe to Acton, Mr. Poyntz's
place, and there Sunday, 7 m. Monday, 23 Aug., Acten to Mr. Walshe's,
where he dwelleth, and there till Wednesday, 6 m. Thursday, 26 Aug., from
Mr. Walshe's to Bromham, and there till Wednesday, 12 m. (*In the margin*,....
stock.) Thursday, 2 Sept., Bromham to Whofall, there till Monday... m.
Tuesday, 7 Sept., Whofall to Thrukstone, there till Thursday, 12 m. Friday,
10 Sept., Thruckeston to Pryor's Horsborne, and there a night, 8 m. Saturday,
11 Sept., Priors Horsborne to Winchester, and there till Wednesday, 10 m.
Thursday, 16 Sept., Winchester to Bishop's Waltham, and there till Tuesday,
7 m. Wednesday, 22 Sept., Waltham to Alsford, 7 m. Thursday, 23 Sept.,
Alsford to Alton, to dinner, that night to Farnham, and there till Sunday, 14
m. Monday, 27 Sept., Farnham to Esthamstede, and there till Thursday, 12
m. Friday, 1 Oct., from Esthamstede to Windsor, and there during the King's
pleasure, 6 m.

Source

L&P, vol. 8, no. 989

Appendix II

Anne Boleyn's Letter from the Tower

Sir, your grace's displeasure, and my imprisonment, are things so strange unto me, as what to write, or what to excuse, I am altogether ignorant. Whereas you send unto me (willing me to confess a truth, and to obtain your favour) by such an one whom you know to be my ancient professed enemy; I no sooner received this message by him, than I rightly conceived your meaning; and if, as you say, confessing a truth indeed may procure my safety, I shall with all willingness and duty perform your command.

But let not your Grace ever imagine that your poor wife will ever be brought to acknowledge a fault, where not so much as a thought thereof proceeded. And to speak a truth, never a prince had wife more loyal in all duty, and in all true affection, than you have ever found in Anne Boleyn, with which name and place I could willingly have contented myself, if God, and your grace's pleasure had been so pleased. Neither did I at any time so far forget myself in my exaltation, or received queenship, but that I always looked for such an alteration as now I find; for the ground of my preferment being on no surer foundation than your grace's fancy, the least alteration was fit and sufficient (I know) to draw that fancy to some other subject. You have chosen me, from a low estate, to be your queen and companion, far beyond my desert or desire. If then you found me worthy of such honour, good your grace let not any light fancy, or bad counsel of mine enemies, withdraw your princely favour from me; neither let that stain, that unworthy stain of a disloyal heart towards your good grace, ever cast so foul a blot on your most dutiful wife, and the infant princess your daughter: try me good king, but let me have a lawful trial, and let not my sworn enemies sit as my accusers and judges; yea, let me receive an open trial, for my truth shall fear no open shame; then shall you see, either mine innocency cleared, your suspicion and conscience satisfied, the ignominy and slander of the world stopped, or my guilt openly declared. So that whatsoever God or you may determine of me, your grace may be freed from an open censure; and mine offence being so lawfully proved, your grace is at liberty, both before God and man, not only to execute worthy punishment on me as an unlawful wife, but to follow your affection already settled on that party, for whose sake I am now as I am, whose name I could some good while since have pointed unto: Your grace being not ignorant of my suspicion therein.

But if you have already determined of me, and that not only my death, but an infamous slander must bring you the joying of your desired happiness; then I desire of God, that he will pardon your great sin herein, and likewise my enemies, the instruments thereof; and that he will not call you to a strait account for your unprincely and cruel usage of me, at his general judgment-seat, where both you and myself must shortly appear, and in whose judgment, I doubt not, (whatsoever the world may think of me) my innocency shall be openly known, and sufficiently cleared.

My last and only request shall be, that myself may only bear the burden of your grace's displeasure, and that it may not touch the innocent souls of those poor gentlemen, whom (as I understand) are likewise in strait imprisonment for my sake. If ever I have found favour in your sight; if ever the name of Anne Boleyn hath been pleasing in your ears, let me obtain this request; and so I will leave to trouble your grace any further, with mine earnest prayer to the Trinity to have your grace in his good keeping, and to direct you in all your actions. From my doleful prison the Tower, this 6th of May.

Your most loyal and ever faithful wife,

Anne Boleyn

[PostScript on reverse side of original letter in the same handwriting]

The King sending a message to Queen Anne, being prisoner in the Tower, willing her to confess the Truth, she said she could confess no more than she had already spoken. And she said she must conceal nothing from the King, to whom she did acknowledge herself so much bound for so many favours, for raising her first from a mean woman to be a Marquess, next to be his Queen, and now, seeing he could bestow no further honour upon her on earth, for purposing to make her, by martyrdom, a saint in heaven.

Sources

BL, Cotton Otho CX f232r-f232v
Burnet, G. *The History of the Reformation*, vol. iv, 291–292
Vasoli, S. *Anne Boleyn's Letter from the Tower*, 18–24

Appendix III

The Alleged Offences

Henry Norris – *6 and 12 October 1533 at Westminster
(At this time, the court was actually at Greenwich and the queen had only recently given birth to Princess Elizabeth)

Henry Norris – *12 and 19 November 1533 at Greenwich

William Brereton – *16 and 27 November 1533 at Greenwich

William Brereton – *3 and 8 December 1533 at Westminster and Hampton Court respectively
(On 8 December, the court was at Greenwich, not Hampton Court)

Francis Weston – *8 May and 20 May 1534 at Westminster
(On 20 May, Queen Anne Boleyn was at Richmond Palace, not Westminster. Furthermore, it's worth noting that as early as January 1534, the queen is reported as being pregnant. In late April, George Taylor writes that the queen has a 'goodly belly', and in late June, we hear that the couple are 'merry'. It's doubtful that a heavily pregnant Anne would have engaged in sexual liaisons with three different men at this time)

Mark Smeaton – *13 and 19 May 1534 at Greenwich
(On 17 or 18 May, the court departed Greenwich and travelled to Richmond, where they remained for Whitsuntide, which began on Sunday, 24 May)

Francis Weston – *6 and 20 June 1534 at Greenwich
(From 4–11 June, the court was at Hampton Court Palace and the queen was heavily pregnant)

Mark Smeaton – *12 and 26 April 1535 at Westminster
(On 26 April, the court was at Greenwich)

31 October 1535 at Westminster – The queen and her alleged lovers are said to have 'compassed and imagined the King's death'
(By 30 October, members of the court were at Windsor Castle)

George Boleyn – *2 and 5 November 1535 at Westminster
(By early November, the court was at Windsor Castle and the queen was in the early stages of pregnancy)

27 November 1535, 'and other days at Westminster' – Anne is alleged to have given all five men 'gifts and great rewards to inveigle them to her will' (The court remained at Windsor throughout November 1535)

George Boleyn – *22 and 29 December 1535 at Eltham Palace (The queen was pregnant and unlikely to have engaged in sexual intercourse)

31 December 1535 at Eltham – The queen is said to have given the men gifts (The queen always gave gifts at New Year!)

8 January 1536 – Anne is said to have conspired the king's death with her alleged lovers and promised to marry one of them (This was probably the day that Anne learned of Katherine of Aragon's death. Would she really have conspired to murder the king on this very day?)

* On these days the queen is said to have 'procured and incited' the men 'by sweet words, kisses, touches, and otherwise', with intercourse taking place on the date that follows.

Sources

L&P, vol. 6, no. 1221, 1227, 1231, 1252, 1293
ibid, no. 1500
L&P, vol. 7, nos. 556, 682, 693, 707, 775, 795, 820, 823, 824, 888
L&P, vol. 8. nos. 592, 594
L&P, vol. 9. nos. 710, 779, 817, 820, 823, 838, 850

Notes

Chapter 1

1. Morris, S., & Grueninger, N., *In the Footsteps of Anne Boleyn,* 167.
2. L&P, VIII, no. 514.
3. L&P, VII, nos. 362–363.
4. L&P, VIII, no. 514.
5. Mackay, L., *Inside the Tudor Court,* 25.
6. L&P, VIII, no. 189.
7. L&P, VIII, no. 429.
8. L&P, VIII, nos. 263 & 684.
9. For threats of excommunication, see L&P, V, no. 27 and L&P, IX, no. 207. For talk of the Bull of Deprivation, see L&P, IX, no. 249 and L&P, X, no. 82.
10. L&P, VIII, no. 901.
11. L&P, VIII, nos. 343 and 793.
12. Lennon, C., *Sixteenth Century Ireland,* 110 and Ellis, Steven G., *The Kildare Rebellion and the Early Henrician Reformation,* 810.
13. L&P, VIII, no. 189.
14. L&P, VIII, no. 263.
15. L&P, VIII, nos. 189 and 556.
16. L&P, VIII, no. 263.
17. L&P, VIII, no. 590.
18. *Documents Illustrative of the History of the English Church* (https://archive.org/stream/documentsillustrx00geeh#page/238/mode/2up). See also the proclamation issued on 30 March 1536, L&P, VII, no. 390.
19. ibid., 242.
20. ibid., 243.
21. Wriothesley, *A Chronicle During the Reign of the Tudors,* Vol. I, 29.
22. *Documents Illustrative of the History of the English Church,* 245–6.
23. Reynolds, E.E., *Margaret Roper,* 73.
24. *Documents Illustrative of the History of the English Church,* 243.
25. *Documents Illustrative of the History of the English Church,* 248.
26. Marshall, P. *Heretics and Believers: A History of the Reformation,* 214.
27. L&P, VIII, no. 856.
28. Craik, G., & MacFarlane, G. *The Pictorial History of England,* Vol. 2, 369. See also L&P, VIII, no. 254.
29. ibid., 369.
30. L&P, VIII, no. 196.
31. L&P, VIII, no. 278.
32. L&P, VIII, no. 737.
33. L&P, VII, no. 1609, which it appears should be dated June 1535. See also L&P, VIII, 844.

34. L&P, VIII, no. 844.
35. L&P, VIII, no. 324.
36. ibid.
37. L&P, VIII, no. 738.
38. L&P, VIII, no. 838.
39. L&P, VIII, no. 838. 'Pilling and polling' was a common expression that referred to financial extortion. It was similar in meaning to fleecing and plundering.
40. L&P, VIII, no. 565.
41. L&P, XII (2), no. 952.
42. Ives, E., *The Life and Death of Anne Boleyn*, 200.
43. L&P, VIII, no. 567.
44. For a summary of the evidence and discussion surrounding Henry Carey's paternity, see chapter 7 in *Mary Boleyn* by Josephine Wilkinson, chapter 5 in *Lady Katherine Knollys* by Sarah-Beth Watkins and chapter 8 in *Mary Boleyn* by Alison Weir.
45. L&P, VII, no. 1554.
46. Ives, E., *The Life and Death of Anne Boleyn*, 210.
47. Wood, M.A.E. (ed.), *Letters of royal and illustrious ladies of Great Britain, from the commencement of the twelfth century to the close of the reign of Queen Mary*, Vol. 2, 193–197.
48. L&P, VIII, no. 1.
49. L&P, VIII, no. 121.
50. L&P, VIII, no. 263.
51. L&P, VII, no. 464.
52. Duffy, E., *The Stripping of the Altars*, 381.
53. Burnet, G., *The History of the Reformation of the Church of England*, Vol. 4, 166.
54. ibid., 166. See also the Memorandum issued on 15 January 1535, L&P, VIII, no.52.
55. Burnet, G., *The History of the Reformation of the Church of England*, Vol. 4, 166–167.
56. Duffy, E., *The Stripping of the Altars*, 392.
57. Burnet, G., *The History of the Reformation of the Church of England*, Vol. 4, 171.
58. Marshall, P., *Heretics and Believers: A History of the Reformation*, 240.
59. Naphy, W., *The Protestant Revolution: From Martin Luther to Martin Luther King Jr.*, 96.
60. Lipscomb, S., *1536: The Year that Changed Henry VIII*, 107.

Chapter 2
1. Thurley, S., *Hampton Court: A Social and Architectural History*, 102.
2. ibid.
3. Thurley, S., 'Henry VIII and the Building of Hampton Court', 14.
4. Thurley, S., *Hampton Court: A Social and Architectural History*, 55.
5. Thurley, S., 'Henry VIII and the Building of Hampton Court', 14–16.
6. L&P, VIII, no. 327.
7. There is some confusion as to whether the Admiral of France proposed a marriage between Mary and the Dauphin or Mary and the Duke of Angoulême. In L&P, VII, nos. 1482 and 1507, Chapuys states that the match was between the former, however, a few weeks later he asserts that the admiral had in fact proposed a match between the latter, see L&P, VII, no. 1554. Entry no. 1369 mentions the Duke of Angoulême but no. 1483 states that the intended groom was, in fact, the Dauphin. The confusion appears to have arisen as a result of the secret nature of the negotiations.

8. L&P, VII, no. 1482.
9. L&P, VII, no. 1483.
10. L&P, VIII, no. 48.
11. ibid. no. 174.
12. Ives, Eric W., 'Anne Boleyn and the Entente Évangélique', 83–102.
13. L&P, VIII, nos. 309 and 327.
14. L&P, VIII, nos. 336, 338, 339, 340, 341.
15. L&P, VIII, no. 336.
16. L&P, VIII, no. 337.
17. ibid. no. 340 (2).
18. ibid. no. 341.
19. Lerer, S., *Courtly Letters in the Age of Henry VIII*, 87.
20. L&P, VIII, no. 330.
21. Beer, M., *Practices and Performances Of Queenship: Catherine Of Aragon and Margaret Tudor, 1503–1533*, 111.
22. ibid., 112.
23. Byrne, M. St. C. (ed.)., *The Lisle Letters*, Vol. 1, pg. 351.
24. Byrne, M. St. C. (ed.)., *The Lisle Letters*, Vol. 4, no. 830.
25. Mikhaila, N. and Malcolm-Davies, J., *The Tudor Tailor*, 36. See also Johnson, C., *The Queen's Servants: Gentlewomen's dress at the accession of Henry VIII*, 22.
26. Byrne, M. St. C. (ed.), *The Lisle Letters*, Vol. 1, no. 833.
27. Byrne, M. St. C. (ed.), *The Lisle Letters*, Vol. 3, no. 658.
28. CSP(Spain), IV, (1), no. 547; Ives. E., *The Life and Death of Anne Boleyn*, 141–143.
29. Huth, Henry., Ellis, Frederick Startridge & Hazlitt, William Carew, *The Huth library. A catalogue of the printed books, manuscripts, autograph letters, and engravings*, 1679.
30. L&P, X, no. 1009.
31. L&P, IV, no. 5366. See also *Lisle Letters*, Vol. 1, 333 & 518–519.
32. L&P, VIII, no. 632 (3).
33. *Statutes of the Realm*, Vol. 3, 441.
34. CSP (Venice), II, no. 887.
35. SP I/85 f. 135, L&P, VII, no. 1126.
36. MacCulloch, D., *Thomas Cromwell*, 27.
37. L&P, XIV (Part 1), no. 579.
38. L&P, VII, no. 1126.
39. MacCulloch, D., *Thomas Cromwell*, 587, BL MS Cotton Otho C/X. f. 176, L&P, VII, no. 1126(2).
40. SP I/85 f. 135; L&P, VII, no.1126.
41. L&P, VIII, no. 327.
42. L&P, VIII, no. 432.
43. ibid. no. 556.
44. CSP(Spain), IV, (2), nos. 1144, 1161, 1164.
45. Guy, J., *The Children of Henry VIII*, 82.
46. L&P, VIII, no. 263.
47. L&P, XI, no. 203.
48. Ives, E., *The Life and Death of Anne Boleyn*, 256.
49. L&P, VIII, no. 429.
50. L&P, VIII, no. 355.
51. L&P, VIII, no. 171.

52. ibid.
53. L&P, VII, no. 296.
54. ibid., no. 871.
55. L&P, VIII, no. 431.
56. L&P, X, no. 699.
57. L&P, VII, no. 296; CSP(Spain), V, (1), no. 22.
58. ibid.
59. Byrne, M. St. C. (ed.), *The Lisle Letters*, Vol. 2, 169.
60. L&P, VII, no. 556.
61. Clifford, H., Stevenson, J., Estcourt, E.E. (eds.), *The Life of Jane Dormer, Duchess of Feria*, 81–82.
62. CSP(Spain), V, (1), nos. 86.
63. CSP(Spain), V, (1), nos. 31, 32.
64. CSP(Spain), V, (1), nos. 86.
65. CSP(Spain), V, (1), nos. 32.
66. Ives, E., *The Life and Death of Anne Boleyn*, 198.
67. CSP(Spain), V, (2), no. 9.
68. CSP(Spain), V, (2), no. 13.
69. L&P, IX, no.873.
70. L&P, VIII, nos. 422, 438; Byrne, M. St. C. (ed.), *The Lisle Letters*, Vol. 2, 352.
71. Byrne, M. St. C. (ed.), *The Lisle Letters*, Vol. 2, 454.

Chapter 3
1. Colvin, H.M. (ed.), *The History of the King's Works: Volume IV 1485–1660*, Part II, 222.
2. Thurley, S., *The Royal Palaces of Tudor England*, 27.
3. ibid., 28.
4. Kipling, G., *The Receyt of the Ladie Kateryne*, 73. A contemporary description of Richmond Palace can be found in this book, edited by Gordon Kipling, see pages 70–76.
5. ibid.
6. Bernard, G.W., *The King's Reformation: Henry VIII and the Remaking of the English Church*, 151.
7. L&P, VIII, nos. 422, 438.
8. Hayward, M., *Dress at the Court of King Henry VIII*, 132.
9. Byrne, M. St. C. (ed.), *The Lisle Letters*, Vol. 2, 352.
10. Quoted in Robinson, B., *The Royal Maundy*, 23–24.
11. Levin, C., '"Would I Could Give You Help and Succour": Elizabeth I and the Politics of Touch', 194.
12. ibid.
13. ibid.
14. Hayward, M., *Dress at the Court of King Henry VIII*, 132–133.
15. Hayward, M., *Dress at the Court of King Henry VIII*, 133.
16. Beer, M., *Practices and Performances Of Queenship: Catherine Of Aragon and Margaret Tudor, 1503–1533*, 269.
17. L&P, X, no. 772.
18. Dowling, M. (ed.), *William Latymer's Chronickille of Anne Boleyn*, see introduction.
19. Ives, Eric W., 'Anne Boleyn and the Entente Évangélique', 83–102.
20. Dowling, M. (ed.), *William Latymer's Chronickille of Anne Boleyn*, 53.

21. L&P, X, no. 772 and Hayward, M., *Dress at the Court of King Henry VIII*, 133.
22. L&P, VIII, no. 428.
23. Beer, M., *Practices and Performances Of Queenship: Catherine Of Aragon and Margaret Tudor, 1503–1533*, 276.
24. L&P, VII, no. 469.
25. Beer, M., *Practices and Performances Of Queenship: Catherine Of Aragon and Margaret Tudor, 1503–1533*, 269.
26. L&P, VIII, no. 435.
27. Byrne, M. St. C. (ed.), *The Lisle Letters*, Vol. 5, 1415.
28. Kisby, F. "'When the King Goeth a Procession": Chapel Ceremonies and Services, the Ritual Year, and Religious Reforms at the Early Tudor Court, 1485–1547', 62–63.
29. Colvin, H.M. (ed.), *The History of the King's Works: Volume IV 1485–1660*, Part II, 227.
30. Kipling, G., *The Receyt of the Ladie Kateryne*, 73.
31. Thurley, S., *The Royal Palaces of Tudor England*, 199. Also, see figure 262.
32. ibid., 198–199. See also L&P, VIII, no. 189, where Chapuys mentions that Henry asked him for a copy of his letters to read while he was at mass.
33. L&P, VIII, no. 826. See also L&P, V, no. 564, where Chapuys describes arriving at court on a Sunday and being conducted to the great hall 'full of people waiting for the King to go to mass.'
34. L&P, VIII, no. 468 and L&P, IV, no. 6654 (20).
35. Wriothesley, C., *Chronicle*, Volume 1, 43.
36. L&P, VII, no. 9 (II).
37. L&P, VIII, no. 416.
38. CSP(Spain), V, no. 97. See also L&P, VII, no. 1257.
39. CSP(Spain), V, no. 118. See also L&P, VII, no. 1554.
40. CSP(Spain), V, no. 118. See also L&P, VII, no. 1554.
41. Ives, E., *The Life and Death of Anne Boleyn*, 195.
42. CSP(Spain), V, no. 118. See also L&P, VII, no. 1554.
43. ibid.
44. L&P, VIII, no. 263.
45. Ives, E., *The Life and Death of Anne Boleyn*, 195.
46. Grueninger, N., *Discovering Tudor London*, 109–110.

Chapter 4

1. L&P, VI, no. 890.
2. Colvin, H.M. (ed.), *The History of the King's Works: Volume IV 1485–1660*, Part II, 105.
3. Starkey, D., *Elizabeth: The Struggle for the Throne*, 2.
4. Licence, A., *In Bed with the Tudors*, 146.
5. Cressy, D., *Birth, Marriage & Death*, 54.
6. Colvin, H.M. (ed.), *The History of the King's Works: Volume IV 1485–1660*, Part II, 105.
7. *Privy Purse Expenses*, XXIV.
8. *Privy Purse Expenses*, XLII.
9. *Privy Purse Expenses*, see examples on pages 98, 131 and 216.
10. ibid., 216.
11. ibid., 113.
12. *Eltham Ordinances*, 233.

13. Quoted in *Lives of the Queens of England*, Volume 4, 129.
14. *Privy Purse Expenses*, 274.
15. ibid., 275–276.
16. Cavendish, G., *The Life of Cardinal Wolsey*, 428.
17. Colvin, H.M. (ed.), *The History of the King's Works: Volume IV 1485–1660*, Part II, 102.
18. Colvin, H.M. (ed.), *The History of the King's Works: Volume IV 1485–1660*, Part II, 105.
19. L&P, VIII, no. 554.
20. Byrne, M. St. C. (ed.), *The Lisle Letters*, Vol. 2, 373.
21. See previous entry for Cromwell's illness and L&P, VIII, no. 666.
22. L&P, VIII, no. 666.
23. L&P, VIII, no. 524.
24. L&P, VIII, no. 587.
25. *The Register of the Most Noble Order of the Garter*, 396–397.
26. L&P, VIII, no. 69.
27. *The Register of the Most Noble Order of the Garter*, 394.
28. *The Register of the Most Noble Order of the Garter*, 387 & 389.
29. Brears, P., *All the King's Cooks: The Tudor kitchens of King Henry VIII at Hampton Court Palace*, 9.
30. *Eltham Ordinances*, 137.
31. *Eltham Ordinances*, 160.
32. *Letters of the Kings of England*, Volume 1, 361–363 and L&P, VIII, no. 623.
33. L&P, VIII, no. 592.
34. L&P, VIII, no. 609.

Chapter 5
1. L&P, VIII, no. 661.
2. L&P, VIII, no. 666.
3. L&P, VIII, no. 726.
4. L&P, VIII, no. 661.
5. ibid.
6. L&P, VIII, no. 666 & CSP(Spain), V, Part 1, no. 156.
7. Wood, M., *Letters*, Volume 2, 191–192; L&P, VIII, no. 710.
8. Ives, E., *The Life and Death of Anne Boleyn*, 286.
9. Dowling, M. (ed.), *William Latymer's Chronickille of Anne Boleyn*, 56.
10. ibid.
11. *Privy Purse Expenses*, 23.
12. L&P, VII, no. 964.
13. Dowling, M. (ed.), *William Latymer's Chronickille of Anne Boleyn*, 57.
14. ibid.
15. L&P, X, no. 345.
16. *Statutes of the Realm*, Vol. 3, 599; *Annals of Cambridge*, Vol. 1, 379.
17. L&P, VIII, no. 722.
18. Wood, M., *Letters*, Volume 2, 189; L&P, VII, no. 693.
19. Dowling, M., *Fisher of Men: a Life of John Fisher, 1469–1535*, 112.
20. L&P, V, no. 148.
21. ibid.
22. Brodie, R.H., 'The Case of Dr. Crome', 299.

23. Ives, Eric W., 'Anne Boleyn and the Entente Évangélique', 83–102.
24. Dowling, M. (ed.), *William Latymer's Chronickille of Anne Boleyn*, 62.
25. ibid.
26. Dowling, M. (ed.), *William Latymer's Chronickille of Anne Boleyn*, 63.
27. Translation quoted in Ives, *The Life and Death of Anne Boleyn*, 269; Original in the BL, Royal MS 20. B XVII f. 1.
28. Ives, 269.
29. For an in-depth discussion of George Boleyn's religious beliefs, see Cherry, C. & Ridgway, C., *George Boleyn*, 55–66.
30. L&P, VIII, no. 826.
31. ibid.
32. L&P, VIII, no. 760.
33. ibid.
34. L&P, VIII, no. 826.
35. In 1585, government correspondence travelling from Dover to London could take 10 hours and, in 1605, a trip from North Yorkshire to London involved around fourteen changes of horses and took three days. This was around three times the distance from Dover to Greenwich. See *The Material Letter in Early Modern England*, pages 113 and 122.
36. Daybell, J., *The Material Letter in Early Modern England*, 113.
37. L&P, VIII, no. 763.
38. Berglar, P., *Thomas More: A Lonely Voice Against the Power of the State*, 195–196.
39. Byrne, M. St. C. (ed.), *The Lisle Letters*, Vol. 2, no. 396.
40. L&P, VIII, no. 846.
41. *Annales*, 963.
42. L&P, VIII, no. 826.
43. L&P, VIII, no. 793.
44. L&P, VIII, no. 826.

Chapter 6
1. L&P, VIII, no. 683.
2. Ives, E., *The Life and Death of Anne Boleyn*, 207–209.
3. MacCulloch, D., *Thomas Cromwell*, 114.
4. For examples, see L&P, VI, nos. 1370, 1371; L&P, VII, no. 1436 (2); L&P, VIII, no. 892.
5. CSP(Spain), V, (i), no. 170. L&P, VIII, no. 826.
6. L&P, IX, no. 478.
7. Ives, E., *The Life and Death of Anne Boleyn*, 175; L&P, V, nos. 1086, 1307, 1432, 1467, 1487, 1719, 1781.
8. L&P, IX, no. 358.
9. L&P, IX, no. 272.
10. L&P, VI, no. 562 & 563; de Worde, Wynkyn., *The Maner of the Tryumphe of Caleys and Bulleyn and The Noble Tryumphant Coronacyon of Quene Anne, Wyfe unto the Most Noble Kynge Henry VIII, 1532–33*, edited by Edmund Goldsmid, 20–25.
11. MacCulloch, D., *Thomas Cromwell*, 169.
12. L&P, VIII, no. 673.
13. CSP(Spain), V, (i), no. 102.
14. ibid.
15. L&P, VIII, no. 556.

16. CSP(Spain), V, (i), no. 174; L&P, VIII, no. 876.
17. ibid.
18. Livingstone, A., *Medieval Lives c. 1000–1292: The World of the Beaugency Family*.
19. CSP(Spain), IV, (ii), no. 1003. For information on Hanworth, see Morris, S., & Grueninger, N., *In the Footsteps of Anne Boleyn*, 111–113.
20. L&P, VII, no. 352.
21. L&P, V, no. 1207 (7); *Statutes of the Realm*, Vol. 3, 479–481; L&P, V, no. 1370 (3).
22. L&P, VII, no. 419 (25); *Statutes of the Realm*, Vol. 3, 479–481.
23. *Statutes of the Realm*, Vol. 3, 479–481; Beer, M., *Practices and Performances Of Queenship: Catherine Of Aragon and Margaret Tudor, 1503–1533*, 47; L&P, VII, no. 419 (26).
24. L&P, VII, nos. 352 & 543. (In no. 352, Thomas Combe is recorded as '*auditor of the ministers' accounts for divers lands, 61l. 3s. 4d*'.
25. L&P, VII, no. 352.
26. Dowling, M. (ed.), *William Latymer's Chronickille of Anne Boleyn*, 49.
27. L&P, XI, no. 117.
28. L&P, VII, no. 352.
29. L&P, IV, no. 2972; L&P, VI, no. 1541.
30. L&P, VIII, no. 1007.
31. Warnicke, R.M., *Elizabeth of York and Her Six Daughters-in-Law*, 65.
32. ibid., 63.
33. L&P, VII, no. 352.
34. L&P, III, no. 851; L&P, IV, no. 6121, f.51.
35. Warnicke, R.M., *Elizabeth of York and Her Six Daughters-in-Law*, 63.
36. Hamilton, D.L., 'The Learned councils of the Tudor queen consort' in *State, Sovereigns & Society*, 87–88.
37. L&P, VIII, no. 149 (30); Ives, E., *The Life and Death of Anne Boleyn*, 211 & Bindoff, S.T. (ed.), *House of Commons*, Vol. 1, 666; L&P, X, no.914.
38. L&P, IX, no. 477; RO: The National Archives, Kew: SC 6/HENVIII/6680.
39. Hamilton, D.L., 'The Learned councils of the Tudor queen consort' in *State, Sovereigns & Society*, 89.
40. L&P, II, no.1363; L&P, XV, no. 21 (2).
41. Hamilton, D.L., 'The Learned councils of the Tudor queen consort' in *State, Sovereigns & Society*, 89.
42. Ives, E., *The Life and Death of Anne Boleyn*, 215.
43. L&P, X, no. 914.
44. L&P, VIII, no. 937.
45. L&P, VIII, no. 800.
46. L&P, VIII, nos. 814, 815.
47. L&P, VIII, no. 815.
48. L&P, VIII, no. 886.
49. L&P, VIII, no. 837.
50. *Hall's Chronicle*, 817.
51. ibid. 817.
52. CSP(Spain), V, (i), no. 179.

Chapter 7
1. L&P, VIII, no. 909.
2. ibid.

3. L&P, VIII, no. 847.

4. L&P, VIII, no. 911. Court was at Windsor by 16 June, L&P, VIII, no. 882.

5. Thurley, S., *The Royal Palaces of Tudor England*, 34.

6. Robinson, James (ed.), *Readings in European History*, Vol II, 137.

7. L&P, III, no. 950.

8. CSP(Spain), IV, (ii), no. 765.

9. L&P, V, no. 1187.

10. L&P, IV, Appendix, no. 256.

11. *Privy Purse Expenses*, 47.

12. ibid., 50.

13. ibid., 74.

14. ibid., 245.

15. L&P, VIII, no. 957.

16. Roberts, J., *Royal Landscapes: The Gardens and Parks of Windsor*, 9–10.

17. Sim, Alison, *Food and Feast in Tudor England*, 118.

18. *Eltham Ordinances*, 175.

19. Thurley, S., *The Royal Palaces of Tudor England*, 68.

20. Samman, N., 'The Progresses of Henry VIII, 1509–1529' in *The Reign of Henry VIII: Politics, Policy and Piety*, 59.

21. L&P, IV, no. 4367; Thurley, S., *The Royal Palaces of Tudor England*, 67.

22. Thurley, S., *The Royal Palaces of Tudor England*, 67.

23. L&P, VIII, no. 954.

24. L&P, VIII, no. 989.

25. ibid.

26. Samman, N., 51–52; Brears, P., *All the King's Cooks: The Tudor kitchens of King Henry VIII at Hampton Court Palace*, 21.

27. Samman, N., 52.

28. L&P, III, no. 851.

29. Society of Antiquaries of London. (1790). *A collection of ordinances and regulations for the government of the royal household, made in divers reigns: From King Edward III to King William and Queen Mary. Also receipts in ancient cookery*, 53.

30. Cavendish, G., *The Life of Cardinal Wolsey*, (S.W. Singer edition), 193–194.

31. Samman, N., 51.

32. L&P, VIII, no. 988.

33. L&P, VIII, no. 996.

Chapter 8

1. Account Book of Sir William Paulet, Controller of the Household, TNA E101/422/1, ff. 001r-036v.

2. Samman, N., 73.

3. L&P, VIII, 1018.

4. L&P, VIII, 1020.

5. L&P, VIII, 921; Strype, J., *Ecclesiastical Memorials*, Vol. 1, 184–185.

6. L&P, VIII, 1020.

7. L&P, VIII, 1024.

8. L&P, VIII, 1025.

9. L&P, IX, 37.

10. *Hall's Chronicle*, 840.

11. Daybell, J., *The Material Letter in Early Modern England*, 27.

12. L&P, VIII, no. 1130.
13. *A History of the County of Oxford*, Volume 18, 192–234; L&P, IV, 1615.
14. L&P, VIII, no. 1101.
15. *Lisle Letters*, Vol. 4, no. 836.
16. L&P, VIII, no. 1034.
17. *Hall's Chronicle*, 592.
18. Creighton, C., *A History of Epidemics in Britain*, 241.
19. Dyer, A., 'The Influence of Bubonic Plague in England', 309.
20. Creighton, C., *A History of Epidemics in Britain*, 241.
21. For Henry VIII's love letter that he wrote to Anne upon discovering that she had fallen ill, see Stemmler, T.B., *Die Liebesbriefe Heinrichs VIII an Anna Boleyn*, 120–121; for George Boleyn, see Stemmler, 116–117; for Thomas Boleyn, see L&P, IV, no. 4409.
22. L&P, IV, no. 4408.
23. L&P, IV, nos. 4424 & 4438.
24. MacCulloch, D., *Thomas Cromwell*, 36 and 591. Caroline Angus suggests that Elizabeth Cromwell's death happened in late 1528. See Angus, C., *My Hearty Commendations*, 54.
25. MacCulloch, D., *Thomas Cromwell*, 540.
26. Paulet's accounts, TNA E101/422/1, ff. 001r-036v.
27. Cox, John, *The Royal Forests of England*, 1.
28. ibid, 2.
29. L&P, VIII, no. 1062.
30. Anne was referring to the monastery of Vale Royal in Cheshire. (See L&P, VII, nos. 868 & 1037, which probably belong to this period).
31. Add MS 19398 f. 48-48v, British Library; L&P, VIII, no. 1056. Also published in Wood, M.A.E. (ed.), *Letters of royal and illustrious ladies of Great Britain, from the commencement of the twelfth century to the close of the reign of Queen Mary*, Vol. 2, 190–191.
32. There is no evidence to suggest that the unnamed candidate put forward by the queen was the same man that Dr Adam Becansaw proposed. L&P, VII, no. 1094 (misdated in L&P); *The Ledger Book of Vale Royal Abbey*, 23.
33. L&P, IX, nos. 34(2) & 35.
34. L&P, V, nos. 479 & 496.
35. Thornton, T., *Cheshire and the Tudor State: 1480–1560*, 207.
36. Add MS 19398 f. 49r-50v, British Library; L&P, VIII, no. 1057.
37. Hurstfield, J., *The Revival of Feudalism in Early Tudor England*, 142; L&P, V, nos. 1327 & 1447.
38. For Thomas's elevation, see L&P, IV, nos. 6083 & 6085. For the wardship grant, see L&P, V, (Miscellaneous), no. 11.
39. *Lisle Letters*, Vol. 2, no. 421; L&P, VIII, no. 1084.
40. *Lisle Letters*, Vol. 2, no. 290a.
41. ibid.
42. Hayward, Maria, 'Gift Giving at the Court of Henry VIII: the 1539 New Year's Gift Roll in Context', 17.
43. In the collection of the Duke of Buccleuch and Queensberry KT.
44. Grosvenor, B., 'Happy Birthday Katherine of Aragon' in *Art History News*, 16 December 2011 (www.arthistorynews.com/articles/897).

45. Author unknown, 'Portrait of Queen Katherine of Aragon'. *Historical Portraits Image Library*, Philip Mould Ltd., no date. (www.historicalportraits.com/Gallery. asp?Page=Item&ItemID=32&Desc=Queen-Catherine-of-Aragon-%7C--English-School).

46. L&P, VIII, nos. 1078 & 1111.

47. Shaw, Anthony, N., *The Compendium Compertorum and the Making of the Suppression Act of 1536*, 2003, 22–23.

48. MacCulloch, D., *Thomas Cromwell: A Life*, 269.

49. For a full list, see Shaw, Anthony, N., *The Compendium Compertorum and the Making of the Suppression Act of 1536*, 2003, 33.

50. ibid., 36 & L&P, VIII, nos. 1059.

51. L&P, VIII, no. 1127. L&P dates this letter to 28 July, but the court did not arrive at Berkeley until Saturday, 7 August, so this letter must have been written at midnight on Wednesday, 11 August.

52. L&P, VIII, no. 76 (2) & (3).

53. Knowles, D., *The Religious Orders in England*, Volume 3, 274–277. This includes a list of the standard version used and reproduced by historians. However, Anthony Shaw identified two additional injunctions not included in the above list: Hospitality for the wayfarer and Master to teach the novices grammar. This version also concluded with a list of penalties for non-observance of the twenty-nine injunctions. See Shaw, A., 287–289.

54. *William Latymer's Chronickille of Anne Boleyn*, 61.

55. L&P, VI, no. 247.

56. ibid.

57. Vincent, N., *The Holy Blood: King Henry III and the Westminster Blood Relic*, 198.

58. *William Latymer's Chronickille of Anne Boleyn*, 61.

59. Latimer, *Sermons*, II, 407–408.

60. Wriothesley, *A Chronicle During the Reign of the Tudors*, Vol. I, 90.

61. L&P, VIII, no. 989. In the margin next to Sudeley, is written: '…aylles'. The margin contains the name of places the king intended on visiting en route to the main staging posts.

62. L&P, VIII, no. 1130.

63. For details please see, Morris, S., & Grueninger, N., *In the Footsteps of Anne Boleyn*, 193.

64. CSP(Spain), V, (i), no. 183.

65. ibid.

66. CSP(Spain), V, (i), no. 184.

67. Southworth, J., *Fools and Jesters at the English Court*, 90; Hayward, M., *Dress at the court of King Henry VIII*, 265–266.

68. Weir, A., *The Six Wives of Henry VIII*, 284–285.

69. *Archaeologia*, Volume 9, 249. Calendared in L&P, VIII, no. 937.

70. L&P, X, no. 181.

71. *Praise of Folly and Letter to Maarten van Dorp 1515*, 57.

Chapter 9

1. (I am indebted to Sarah Morris for bringing this under-used account to my attention.) Douglas, A. & Greenfield, P. (eds.), *Records of Early English Drama*, 293–296; Stevenson, W.H. (ed.), 'The Records of the Corporation of Gloucester' in *The 12th Report of the Manuscript Commission*, Appendix, Part 9, 443–445.

2. Douglas, A. & Greenfield, P. (eds.), *Records of Early English Drama*, 483.
3. Samman, 34.
4. L&P, IX, no. 53; *Lisle Letters*, Vol. 2, nos. 403 & 434.
5. Baggs, A.P., Jurica, A.R.J., and Sheils, W.J., 'Painswick: Manors and other estates' in *A History of the County of Gloucester: Volume 11*, 65–70.
6. *Lisle Letters*, Vol. 2, nos. 198, 246 & 434.
7. *Lisle Letters*, Vol. 2, no. 434.
8. Douglas, A. & Greenfield, P. (eds.), *Records of Early English Drama*, 483.
9. St Claire Baddeley, W., *A Cotteswold Manor being the History of Painswick*, (preface).
10. ibid., 145.
11. Morris, S. & Grueninger, N., *In the Footsteps of Anne Boleyn*, 197.
12. Douglas, A. & Greenfield, P. (eds.), *Records of Early English Drama*, 295.
13. Hayward, M., *Dress at the Court of King Henry VIII*, 168–169.
14. *Privy Purse Expenses of Elizabeth of York*, 68–69.
15. 'A slit up from the hem on coats and shirts', Hayward, 435.
16. Hayward, M., *Dress at the Court of King Henry VIII*, 169.
17. Douglas, A. & Greenfield, P. (eds.), *Records of Early English Drama*, 295.
18. *A History of the County of Gloucester*, Volume 11, pp. 49–52; L&P, VII, no. 352.
19. L&P, XX1, part II, no. 60.
20. *Leland's Itinerary*, Part V, p. 57.
21. L&P, IX, no. 52.
22. L&P, IX, no. 52 (2).
23. 'Houses of Benedictine monks: Priory of St Mary, Worcester' in *A History of the County of Worcester: Volume 2*, 94–112.
24. *The Compendium Compertorum and the Making of the Suppression Act of 1536*, 74.
25. L&P, IX, no. 51.
26. L&P, IX, no. 5.
27. L&P, IX, no. 497.
28. L&P, IX, no. 52.
29. ibid.
30. L&P, X, no. 216; Thornton, D., 'The Last Monks of Worcester Cathedral Priory' in *Midland History*, Vol, 43, no. 1, 9–10.
31. Thornton, D., 'The Last Monks of Worcester Cathedral Priory' in *Midland History*, Vol, 43, no. 1, 10.
32. *Records of Early English Drama*, 485.
33. *Records of Early English Drama*, 295; Account Book of Sir William Paulet, TNA E101/422/1.
34. L&P, IX, nos. 66 & 118.
35. L&P, VIII, no. 633 (i).
36. L&P, VIII, no. 1127. (Misdated in L&P. 'This Wednesday at midnight', must refer to Wednesday, 11 August, when the court was at Berkeley).
37. L&P, VIII, no. 1127; Shaw, A., *The Compendium Compertorum*, 37–38.
38. L&P, VIII, no. 1127; Shaw, A., *The Compendium Compertorum*, 38. Diarmaid MacCulloch notes that 'buried quick' meant buried alive.
39. CSP, Spain, V, part 1, no. 193.
40. L&P, IX, no. 48.
41. ibid.
42. L&P, IX, no. 71.
43. L&P, IX, no. 175.

44. L&P, IX, no. 178.
45. ibid. & no. 107.
46. L&P, IX, no. 41.
47. L&P, IX, no. 119.
48. L&P, IX, no. 47.
49. L&P, IX, no. 209.
50. Account Book of Sir William Paulet, Controller of the Household, TNA E101/422/1.

Chapter 10
1. Britton, J., *The Architectural Antiquities of Great Britain*, Vol. 4, 156–158; L&P, III, no. 1286 & Hawkyard, A.D.K., 'Thornbury Castle' in *Transactions of the Bristol and Gloucestershire Archaeological Society*, Vol. 95, 51–58.
2. Hawkyard, A.D.K., 'Thornbury Castle' in *Transactions of the Bristol and Gloucestershire Archaeological Society*, Vol. 95, 52.
3. *Leland's Itinerary*, Parts VII & VIII, 106.
4. Lipscomb, S., *A Visitor's Companion to Tudor England*, 154.
5. L&P, III, no. 1286.
6. Hawkyard, A.D.K., 'Thornbury Castle' in *Transactions of the Bristol and Gloucestershire Archaeological Society*, Vol. 95, 52.
7. L&P, III, no. 1286.
8. Britton, J., *The Architectural Antiquities of Great Britain*, Vol. 4, 157.
9. Phillpotts, C., *Park Farm, Thornbury, South Gloucestershire Documentary Research Report*, p. 15.
10. L&P, III, no. 1286.
11. Phillpotts, C., *Park Farm, Thornbury, South Gloucestershire Documentary Research Report*, pp.16 & 24.
12. L&P, IX, no. 163; *Ricart's Calendar*, 53–54.
13. *Ricart's Calendar*, 53–54.
14. ibid; *Aurum Reginae*, pp. 2, 122–126.
15. Warnicke, R.M., *Elizabeth of York and Her Six Daughters-In-Law*, 81.
16. L&P, IX, no. 163.
17. Seyer, S. (ed.), *Memoirs historical and topographical of Bristol and its neighbourhood; from the earliest period down to the present time*, Vol. 2, p. 214.
18. L&P, IX, no. 169; Document Ref.: SP 1/95 f.156.
19. *Leland's Itinerary*, Vol. 5, pp. 100–101, 159.
20. Burton, J., *A history of Bewdley; with concise accounts of some neighbouring parishes*, 11.
21. ibid.
22. Cunningham, S., *Prince Arthur*, 165 and 189; *Rymer's Foedera*, Vol. 12, 756–762.
23. L&P, IX, no. 186.
24. L&P, VIII, no. 989.
25. L&P, IX, no. 157.
26. Morris, S. & Grueninger, N., *In the Footsteps of Anne Boleyn*, 233–236.
27. Hawkyard, Alasdair, 'Poyntz, Sir Robert (b. late 1440s, d. 1520), courtier and landowner' in *Oxford Dictionary of National Biography*. 23 September 2004; Accessed 7 September 2020. (https://www.oxforddnb.com/view/10.1093/ref:odnb/9780198614128.001.0001/odnb-9780198614128-e-70796).
28. L&P, I, no. 82; Beer, M., *A Queenly Affinity? Catherine of Aragon's Estates and Henry VIII's Great Matter*, 13.

29. L&P, VII, no.1167.
30. L&P, VIII, no. 149 (37) & L&P, IX, no. 914 (22).
31. Faulkner, Neil. "'A goodly howse": the rebuilding of Acton Court' in *Current Archaeology*, Issue 218, 16.
32. ibid., 20.
33. Bell, R., 'The Royal Visit to Acton Court in 1535' in Starkey, D. (ed.), *Henry VIII: A European Court in England*, 123.
34. ibid., 123.
35. L&P, IX, no. 178.
36. L&P, IX, nos. 218 & 219.
37. Norris, H., *Tudor Costume and Fashion*, 131.
38. Bolland, C., *Italian Material Culture at the Tudor Court*, 192.
39. *Statutes of the Realm*, Vol. 3, 430.
40. L&P, IX, nos. 165, 184 & 217.
41. *State Papers*, Volume 5, King Henry VIII, Part IV, 39–41.
42. L&P, IX, no. 182.
43. Daniell, D., 'Tyndale, William (c. 1494–1536), translator of the Bible and religious reformer' in *Oxford Dictionary of National Biography*. 19 May 2011. Retrieved 18 September 2020. (https://www.oxforddnb.com/view/10.1093/ref:odnb/9780198614128.001.0001/odnb-9780198614128-e-27947).
44. ibid.
45. *Narratives of the Reformation*, 52–57; Extracts from the life of Anne Boleyn by George Wyatt in Singer (ed.), *Wolsey*, 438–441.
46. Extracts from the life of Anne Boleyn by George Wyatt in Singer (ed.), *Wolsey*, 440.
47. *Narratives of the Reformation*, 56.
48. ibid.
49. *The Works of the English Reformers: William Tyndale and John Frith*, Vol. 1, ed. Russell, 212–213.
50. ibid.
51. *Narratives of the Reformation*, 56.
52. L&P, V, nos. 65, 246 & 248.
53. L&P, V, no. 248.
54. ibid.
55. L&P, V, no. 533.
56. L&P, V, no. 574.
57. L&P, IX, no. 275 & 498.
58. *Foxe's Book of Martyrs*, 488.
59. L&P, IX, no. 498.
60. *The New Testament* (Antwerp 1534), BL, Shelfmark: C.23 a.8.
61. Ives, E., *The Life and Death of Anne Boleyn*, 269.
62. *William Latymer's Chronickille of Anne Boleyn*, 55.
63. *William Latymer's Chronickille of Anne Boleyn*, 55–56, note 16.
64. Elton, G. R., *An Early Tudor Poor Law*, 66; Ives, E., *The Life and Death of Anne Boleyn*, 284–285.
65. Elton, G. R., *An Early Tudor Poor Law*, 66.

Chapter 11
1. Bathe, G. and Holley, R., *A Re-appraisal of the Architectural and Historic Significance of Wolfhall, Wiltshire*, 1.

2. ibid.
3. L&P, VII, no. 9 (ii).
4. L&P, IX, nos. 620, 639.
5. L&P, IX, no. 729 (6, 7, 8).
6. *Lisle Letters*, Vol. 2, no. 451.
7. L&P, IX, nos. 203, 252, 272–273, 342.
8. CSP, Spain, V, Part 1, no. 201. See also L&P, IX, no. 243.
9. L&P, IX, no. 274.
10. L&P, IX, no 358.
11. L&P, VIII, no. 658; L&P, IX, nos. 383, 384.
12. L&P, IX, no. 310.
13. Paulet's accounts: arrived 9 September and departed 11 September.
14. L&P, IX, no. 326.
15. L&P, VIII, no. 989.
16. Malory, T. and Pollard, A. W. (ed.), *Le Morte d'Arthur: Sir Thomas Malory's Book of King Arthur and of his Noble Knights of the Round Table*, p. xi.
17. *Lisle Letters*, Vol. 2, no. 451. Husee's testimony is contradicted by Cranmer's certificates of consecration, which suggest that Latimer and Hilsey were consecrated together on 23 September and Edward Fox on 20 September. See L&P, IX, no. 729 (6, 7 & 8).
18. Starkey, D., *Six Wives*, 539.
19. L&P, IX, nos. 203, 252, 272; L&P, X, no. 1257 (ix); L&P, XI, no. 117 (7).
20. L&P, IX, no. 203 & 272.
21. L&P, VII, no. 589 (viii); L&P, XI, no. 117 (7).
22. L&P, IX, no. 378.
23. L&P, VII, no. 958.
24. Ives, E., *The Life and Death of Anne Boleyn*, 32–33; L&P, VI, no. 692.
25. L&P, IX, no. 434.
26. L&P, IX, no. 420.
27. L&P, VIII, no. 1117.
28. L&P, IX, no. 434.
29. L&P, IX, nos. 442, 741.
30. L&P, IX, no. 398.
31. L&P, IX, no. 437.
32. L&P, IX, no. 386.
33. L&P, IX, no. 217. (Misdated in L&P, as Henry Brandon was not born until 18 September).
34. *Lisle Letters*, Vol. 2, no. 446.
35. *State Papers*, II, 273–275.
36. L&P, IX, no, 434.
37. *Lisle Letters*, Vol. 2, no. 446.
38. L&P, IX, no. 873.
39. *Lisle Letters*, Vol. 2, no. 451. (See also notes on pp. 589–590)
40. *Lisle Letters*, Vol. 2, nos. 455, 468.
41. L&P, IX, nos. 460, 467.

Chapter 12
1. L&P, IX, nos. 460, 525, 527, 532, 535.
2. *Eltham Ordinances*, 160.

3. Stevens, J. E., *Music and Poetry in the Early Tudor Court*, 297.
4. *Eltham Ordinances*, 160–161.
5. *Privy Purse Expenses* (see index for full list). For example, 11, 18, 53, 75.
6. ibid., 173.
7. ibid., 14, 121, 262.
8. Cavendish, G., *The Life of Cardinal Wolsey and Metrical Visions*, 36–38.
9. Ives, E., *The Life and Death of Anne Boleyn*, 325.
10. Collins, B.M., *The Royal Progress and Anne Boleyn's Visit to Winchester in 1535*, 6.
11. Kings MS 9, f. 231v and f. 66r.
12. L&P, IX, no. 729 (2).
13. Hurren, E.T., *King Henry VIII's Medical World*, 2.
14. L&P, VI, no. 562 (2).
15. Sloane MS 1047.
16. CSP, Spain, V, part 1, no. 205. L&P, IX, no. 436.
17. *Lisle Letters*, Vol. 2, no. 399.
18. L&P, IX, nos. 527, 528.
19. L&P, IX, no. 609.
20. L&P, IX, no. 168.
21. ibid.
22. Cressy, D., *Birth, Marriage & Death*, 22.
23. ibid, no. 458.
24. ibid, no. 460.
25. L&P, VIII, no. 989.
26. L&P, IX, nos. 525, 555, 571, 639.
27. *Lisle Letters*, Vol. 2, no. 455.
28. L&P, IX, no. 555.
29. *Lisle Letters*, Vol. 2, no. 459.
30. L&P, IX, no. 639.
31. L&P, IX, nos. 467, 525, 594, 642. *Lisle Letters*, Vol. 2, no. 455, 463.
32. L&P, IX, nos. 467, 568.
33. Morris, S. & Grueninger, N., *In the Footsteps of Anne Boleyn*, 255; Benson, R. and Hatcher, H., *Old and New Sarum, or Salisbury*, 236–237, quoting from the City muniments Ledger B, fol. 280.
34. L&P, IX, no. 579.
35. L&P, IX, no. 568.
36. ibid.
37. L&P, IX, no. 577; *Letters of Royal and Illustrious Ladies*, Vol. 2, 121.
38. L&P, X, no, 416.
39. CSP, (Spain) Vol. 5, part 1, no. 213.
40. L&P, IX, nos. 587, 588.
41. L&P, IX, no. 594.
42. CSP, (Spain) Vol. 5, part 1, no. 213.
43. The National Library of France, MSS Dupuis, Volume 547, folio 200.
44. Froude, J., *The Pilgrim*, 100–103.
45. L&P, IX, no. 566; Camusat, N., *Meslanges Historiques*, [Lettres de Roy Francois Premier...pour le dit Roy d'Angleterre] 21–23.
46. L&P, IX, no. 729 (1).
47. *The Pilgrim*, 102.
48. MSS Dupuis, Volume 547, folio 200.

49. Ives, E., *The Life and Death of Anne Boleyn*, 293; Fox, J., *Jane Boleyn*, 172; Friedmann, P., *Anne Boleyn*, 184.
50. Fox, J., *Jane Boleyn*, 349–350.
51. The printed version by Camusat reads: 'au desceu de leurs maris'. 'Desceu' means despair. Friedmann writes 'in spite of their husbands'. L&P, 'unknown to their husbands'.
52. The original MS almost certainly says, 'au desir de leurs maris', which loosely translates to 'at their husband's desire' or 'at their husband's wish'. I'm grateful to Dr Sean Cunningham for taking the time to look over this passage.
53. L&P, VIII, no. 948; CSP, Spain Vol. 5, part 1, no. 178.
54. L&P, IX, no. 663.
55. Morris, S. & Grueninger, N., *In the Footsteps of Anne Boleyn*, 261.
56. Howard, M. & Wilson, E., *The Vyne: A Tudor House Revealed*, 145.
57. ibid., 145–146.
58. L&P, IX, nos. 619, 620, 639, 650.
59. ibid, no. 639.
60. Cope, W., *Bramshill: Its history and architecture*, 9–10.
61. L&P, IX, no. 576.
62. *Latymer's Chronickille of Anne Boleyn*, 54.
63. L&P, IX, nos. 619, 639, 650, 682.
64. L&P, IX, nos. 619, 620.
65. *Annals of Cambridge*, Vol. 1, 376.
66. ibid., nos. 650, 783, 823.

Chapter 13

1. L&P, IX, no. 819.
2. L&P, IX, no. 779.
3. L&P, X, no. 243 (13 & 24).
4. *Lisle Letters*, Vol. 2, no. 477; CSP, Spain, Vol. 5, part 1, no. 229.
5. CSP, Spain, Vol. 5, part 1, no. 229.
6. ibid.
7. The National Library of France, MSS Dupuis, Volume 547, folio 200.
8. L&P, IX, nos. 841, 949.
9. L&P, IX, no. 786.
10. ibid, no. 791.
11. L&P, IX, no. 846.
12. CSP, Spain, Vol. 5, part 1, no. 213.
13. CSP, Spain, Vol. 5, part 1, no. 222.
14. CSP, Spain, Vol. 5, part 1, no. 213.
15. CSP, Spain, Vol. 5, part 1, no. 222; L&P, IX, no. 733; MSS Dupuis, Volume 547, folio 200.
16. CSP, Spain, Vol. 5, part 1, no. 219.
17. Ives, E., *The Life and Death of Anne Boleyn*, 105 & 185.
18. L&P, IX, no. 776.
19. L&P, IX, no. 861.
20. L&P, IX, no. 776.
21. L&P, IX, nos. 777, 861.
22. Friedmann, P., *Anne Boleyn*, 187–188.
23. L&P, IX, no. 594.

24. L&P, IX. no. 754.
25. L&P, IX. no. 1036.

Chapter 14
1. L&P, IX, nos. 897, 935, 976.
2. Jones, E.A., *England's Last Medieval Monastery*, 20.
3. Jones, E.A., *England's Last Medieval Monastery*, 4 & 25–26.
4. ibid., 25–26.
5. Norton, E., *The Lives of Tudor Women*, 171.
6. Dowling, M. (ed.), *William Latymer's Chronickille of Anne Boleyn*, 61.
7. L&P, IX, nos. 954, 986; Shaw, Anthony, N., *The Compendium Compertorum and the Making of the Suppression Act of 1536*, 65.
8. L&P, IX, no. 986.
9. ibid, no. 954.
10. ibid, no. 986.
11. Ives, E., *The Life and Death of Anne Boleyn*, 266.
12. Jones, E.A., *England's Last Medieval Monastery*, 50.
13. L&P, IX, nos. 897, 1038.
14. Stowe, J., *A Survey of London*, 37.
15. Streitberger, W.R., 'Devising the Revels' in *Early Theatre*, Vol. 1, 1998, 55–74. *JSTOR*. Accessed 24 November 2020. (www.jstor.org/stable/43499080).
16. Feuillerat, A. (ed.), *Documents Relating to the Revels at Court in the Time of King Edward VI and Queen Mary*, 89–90.
17. L&P, VI, no. 1508; Colvin, H.M. (ed.), *The History of the King's Works: Volume IV 1485–1660*, Part II, 102.
18. Hayward, M., *Dress at the Court of King Henry VIII*, 131.
19. L&P, IX, no. 870.
20. L&P, IX, no. 991; *Lisle Letters*, Vol. 2, no. 331. (This letter is attributed to 1535 in L&P and 18 December 1534 in the *Lisle Letters*).
21. L&P, IX, no. 964.
22. ibid, nos. 964, 966, 967.
23. ibid, no. 970.
24. L&P, IX, nos. 1037, 1050.
25. L&P, IX, no. 1036.
26. CSP, Spain, Vol. 5, part 1, no. 246.

Chapter 15
1. Society of Antiquaries of London. (1790). *A collection of ordinances*, 120.
2. *The Inventory of King Henry VIII*, no. 1046.
3. L&P, XIV, part 1, no. 330b; L&P, XVI, no. 580(53).
4. *The Inventory of King Henry VIII*, no. 1046.
5. L&P, VII, no, 1668.
6. See the following examples from August 1537: L&P, XI, nos. 203–204, 207, 211, 213–214.
7. L&P, V, no. 686; L&P, VII, no, 9.
8. CSP, Spain, Vol. 4, part 2, no. 880; Ives, E., *The Life and Death of Anne Boleyn*, 10.
9. L&P, V, no. 686.
10. ibid.
11. L&P, VII, no, 9.

12. L&P, V, no. 696.
13. L&P, X, nos. 28, 59.
14. L&P, X, no. 28; Strype's *Memorial*, Vol. 1, 241.
15. L&P, X, no. 28.
16. L&P, X, no. 37.
17. Tremlett, G., *Catherine of Aragon*, 424.
18. L&P, X, nos. 141, 208.
19. ibid., no. 59.
20. CSP, Spain, Vol. 5, part II, no. 9.
21. ibid.
22. *Hall's Chronicle*, 818.
23. CSP, Spain, Vol. 5, part II, no. 13.
24. ibid., nos. 38–39, 41, 65, 75, 76; L&P, X, no. 128. Katherine's goods were inventoried and valued at 5,000 marks.
25. L&P, X, no. 141.
26. ibid., no. 65.
27. CSP, Spain, Vol. 5, part II, no. 9.
28. ibid., nos. 9, 13.
29. L&P, X, no. 307.
30. ibid.
31. CSP, Spain, Vol. 5, part II, no. 9.
32. ibid, no. 13.
33. L&P, X, no. 200.
34. L&P, X, no. 427.
35. Wriothesley, *A Chronicle During the Reign of the Tudors*, Vol. I, 33
36. L&P, X, no. 255.
37. For a summary of arguments, see Lipscomb, S., *1536: The Year that Changed Henry VIII*, 23–26.
38. Lipscomb, S., *1536: The Year that Changed Henry VIII*, 58–59; Chalmers, C.R. & Chaloner, E.J., '500 years later: Henry VIII, leg ulcers and the course of history', 514–517.
39. Lipscomb, S., *1536: The Year that Changed Henry VIII*, 55.
40. L&P, XIX, part II, no. 19.
41. Young, A., *Tudor and Jacobean Tournaments*, 200.
42. Levitt, E., 'Did Jousting Jealousy Bring Down a Queen?' On the Tudor Trail, 30 May, 2019. (onthetudortrail.com/Blog/2019/05/30/did-jousting-jealousy-bring-down-a-queen)
43. ibid.
44. ibid.
45. L&P, X, no. 282. Dated 17 February in CSP, Spain, Vol. 5, part II, no. 21.
46. Wriothesley, *A Chronicle During the Reign of the Tudors*, Vol. I, 33
47. CSP, Spain, Vol. 5, part II, no. 13.
48. L&P, X, no. 199.
49. Ives, E., *The Life and Death of Anne Boleyn*, 296–297. See chapter 8 in Warnicke, R.M., *The Rise and Fall of Anne Boleyn*.
50. Walters, L., *Monstrous Births and Imaginations*, pp.122/134.
51. Ives, E., *The Life and Death of Anne Boleyn*, 298.
52. ibid.
53. L&P, X, no. 351.

54. L&P, X, no. 352.
55. Neale, J.E., *Queen Elizabeth I*, 5.
56. L&P, X, no. 351.
57. L&P, X, no, 282.

Chapter 16
1. L&P, X, no. 243 (13 & 24).
2. *State Papers*, Volume 2, King Henry VIII, Part III, pp. 302–303; L&P, X, no. 26.
3. L&P, X, no. 27.
4. L&P, XI, no. 1150.
5. L&P, X, no. 243 (14).
6. L&P, X, no. 345.
7. Lehmberg, S.E., *The Reformation Parliament*, 57.
8. L&P, X, no. 597 (3 & 4); Loades, D., *The Boleyns*, 110.
9. L&P, X, no. 199.
10. CSP, Spain, Vol. 5, part II, no. 13.
11. L&P, X, no. 282.
12. L&P, X, no. 282.
13. L&P, X, no. 351.
14. ibid.
15. L&P, X, no. 351.
16. L&P, X, no. 282.
17. Cavendish, G., *The Life of Cardinal Wolsey*, 444.
18. L&P, X, no. 351.
19. Ives, E., *The Life and Death of Anne Boleyn*, 303.
20. Clifford, H., Stevenson, J., Estcourt, E.E. (eds.), *The Life of Jane Dormer, Duchess of Feria*, 41.
21. ibid., 79.
22. Fuller, T., *History of the Worthies of England*, Vol. 3, 320.

Chapter 17
1. Hall, Edward, *Chronicle*, 707–708.
2. L&P, XVI, no. 589.
3. Urkevich, L.A., *Anne Boleyn, A Music Book, and the Northern Renaissance Courts*, 98–101.
4. ibid., 100; DellaNeva, J., *The Story of the Death of Anne Boleyn: A Poem by Lancelot de Carle*, 157.
5. Sander, N., *Schism*, 25.
6. CSP, Spain, Vol. 5, part II, no. 29.
7. L&P, X, no. 495.
8. ibid.
9. Bathe, G. & Purvis, I., 'A Revised date for the death of Sir John Seymour of Wolfhall', 285–288.
10. L&P, X, no. 339.
11. *Lisle Letters*, Vol. 3, no. 650.
12. L&P, X, no. 382.
13. L&P, X, nos. 381, 531, 633, 552, 599.
14. L&P, X, no. 547.
15. *Statutes of the Realm*, Vol. 3, 577. For an example of a petition see L&P, X, no. 384.

16. *Lisle Letters*, Vol. 3, no. 668.

17. *Lisle Letters*, Vol. 3, no. 650.

18. *Statutes of the Realm*, Vol. 3, 576.

19. MacCulloch, D. (ed.), *The Reign of Henry VIII*, 41–42.

20. Ives, E., *The Life and Death of Anne Boleyn*, 309.

21. Lehmberg, S., *The Reformation Parliament*, 227.

22. Dowling, M. (ed.), *William Latymer's Chronickille of Anne Boleyn*, 57.

23. ibid., 57–59.

24 L&P, XII, (i), no. 786, (15); L&P, X, no. 383 – as this letter is undated, 'the Queen' may in fact be Jane Seymour. See also ibid, X, no. 858.

25. L&P, X, no. 429.

26. ibid.

27. L&P, X, no. 450.

28. L&P, X, no. 528.

Chapter 18

1. CSP, Spain, Vol. 5, part II, no. 43.

2. ibid.

3. ibid.

4. ibid.

5. L&P, X, no. 615.

6. ibid.

7. L&P, X, no. 615 (4).

8. MacCulloch, D., *Thomas Cromwell: A Life*, 331.

9. Dowling, M. (ed.), *William Latymer's Chronickille of Anne Boleyn*, 57.

10. Strype, J., *The Life and Acts of Matthew Parker*, Vol 1, 16–17.

11. Ives. E., *The Life and Death of Anne Boleyn*, 308.

12. L&P, X, no. 615 (5).

13. CSP, Spain, Vol. 5, part II, no. 43.

14. ibid.

15. L&P, X, no. 699.

16. CSP, Spain, Vol. 5, part II, no. 43.

17. Ives, E., *The Life and Death of Anne Boleyn*, 305.

18. *Lisle Letters*, Vol. 3, no. 673; L&P, X, no. 675.

19. L&P, X, no. 772.

20. *Lisle Letters*, Vol. 3, no. 673.

21. CSP, Spain, Vol. 5, part II, no. 43a; L&P, X, no. 699.

22. CSP, Spain, Vol. 5, part II, no. 43a.

23. L&P, VIII, no. 720.

24. L&P, X, no. 699.

25. ibid.

26. L&P, X, no. 699.

27. CSP, Spain, Vol. 5, part II, no. 43a.

28. ibid.

29. CSP, Spain, Vol. 5, part II, no. 43a.

30. Ives, E., *The Life and Death of Anne Boleyn*, 313.

31. CSP, Spain, Vol. 5, part II, no. 43a; L&P, X, no. 699.

32. Ives, E., *The Life and Death of Anne Boleyn*, 315.

33. Head, D.M., '"If a Lion Knew His Own Strength": The Image of Henry VIII and His Historians', 105.
34. L&P, VIII, no. 826.
35. CSP, Spain, Vol. 5, part II, no. 43a & 61.
36. L&P, X, no. 700; CSP, Spain, Vol. 5, part II, no. 61.
37. CSP, Spain, Vol. 5, part II, no. 43a.
38. L&P, X, nos. L&P, X, nos. 673, 675, 738, 742, 747, 748, 751.
39. *Lisle Letters*, Vol. 3, no. 676.
40. *Lisle Letters*, Vol. 3, no. 687.
41. L&P, X, no. 913.
42. *Lisle Letters*, Vol. 3, no. 677.
43. *The Register of the Most Noble Order of the Garter*, 398; L&P, X, no. 715.
44. *The Register of the Most Noble Order of the Garter*, 399–401.
45. L&P, VIII, no.174. Francis I had first favoured Carew's appointment in 1533: L&P, VI, no. 555.
46. L&P, X, no. 752.
47. ibid.
48. Palgrave. F., et al. *The 1st Annual Report of the Deputy Keeper of the Public Records*, 242–245; Mackay, L., *Among the Wolves of Court*, 210.
49. I'm indebted to Dr Daniel Gosling of The National Archives in London for clarifying these matters and taking the time to discuss them with me.
50. Walker, G., 'Rethinking the Fall of Anne Boleyn', 3; Ives, E., *The Life and Death of Anne Boleyn*, 322.
51. DellaNeva, J., *The Story of the Death of Anne Boleyn – A Poem by Lancelot de Carle*, 190–191.
52. John Richard Greene quoted in Head, D.M., '"If a Lion Knew His Own Strength": The Image of Henry VIII and His Historians', 100.
53. Roper, W., 'The Life of Sir Thomas More' in *Two Early Tudor Lives*, 228.
54. L&P, X, nos. 725, 726; State Papers, Volume 7, King Henry VIII, Part V, 683–688.
55. L&P, X, no. 752–753. 'The last four days' equates to around 25–29 April.
56. *Correspondence of Matthew Parker, D. D., Archbishop of Canterbury*, 59 & 400.
57. ibid., 391.
58. ibid., 400.
59. L&P, X, no. 736.
60. Ives. E., *The Life and Death of Anne Boleyn*, 320.
61. MacCulloch, D., *Thomas Cranmer: A Life*, 156.
62. L&P, X, no. 752.
63. MacCulloch, D., *Thomas Cranmer: A Life*, 156.
64. L&P, X, no. 793.
65. Walker, G., 'Rethinking the Fall of Anne Boleyn', 18.
66. L&P, X, no. 793; Cavendish, G., *The Life of Cardinal Wolsey*, 450–461.
67. ibid.
68. ibid.
69. *Calendar of State Papers Foreign, Elizabeth*, Vol. 1, no. 1303.
70. L&P, X, no. 789.
71. Constantine, G., *Archaeologia, or, Miscellaneous Tracts Relating to Antiquity*, Vol 23, p.64.
72. ibid.

Chapter 19

1. Loke, W. 'Account of materials furnished for the use of Anne Boleyn and Princess Elizabeth, 1535–1536', in *Miscellanea of the Philobiblon Society*, (1862).
2. ibid. For Elizabeth I's love of colours, see 'Rainbow for a Reign: The Colours of a Queen's Wardrobe' in *Costume*, Vol. 41.
3. Ives, E. *The Life and Death of Anne Boleyn*, p.196.
4. *Hall's Chronicle*, p. 513.
5. ibid, p. 582.
6. *Wriothesley's Chronicle*, p. 35.
7. DellaNeva, J. *The Story of the Death of Anne Boleyn – A Poem by Lancelot de Carle*, 207.
8. *Hall's Chronicle*, p. 819.
9. Stowe, J. *Annales*, p. 572.
10. Constantine, G. *Archaeologia, or, Miscellaneous Tracts Relating to Antiquity*, Vol 23, p.64.
11. ibid.
12. ibid.
13. Levitt, E., 'Did Jousting Jealousy Bring Down a Queen?' On the Tudor Trail, 30 May, 2019. (onthetudortrail.com/Blog/2019/05/30/did-jousting-jealousy-bring-down-a-queen).
14. L&P, X, no. 782.
15. L&P, X, no. 782.
16. Singer (ed.), *Wolsey*, 451.
17. Ives, E., *The Life and Death of Anne Boleyn*, 328. The other possibility, as noted by Ives, is that George was unaware of the other arrests and simply moved to join the king and court.
18. *Wriothesley's Chronicle*, 36; L&P, X, no. 782.
19. *Wriothesley's Chronicle*, 36
20. Singer (ed.), *Wolsey*, 456.
21. L&P, X. no. 782.
22. ibid.
23. L&P, X. 864.
24. *Wriothesley's Chronicle*, 36. Stow refers to the same entrance as 'Towergate', p. 572. This entrance was located near the Byward Tower, confirming that Anne did not enter the Tower via the 'Traitor's Gate', as is so often assumed.
25. *Wriothesley's Chronicle*, 36.
26. Singer (ed.), *Wolsey*, 451.
27. The manuscript was damaged in the infamous Cotton Library fire of October 1731. However, the historian John Strype saw the letters before they were burned in the fire and Singer uses his work to fill in the gaps.
28. Cavendish, G., *The Life of Cardinal Wolsey*, 452–453, 454.
29. ibid., 453.
30. ibid., 451; L&P, X, no. 793.
31. ibid., 451–452.
32. Singer (ed.), *Wolsey*, 452; L&P, X, no. 793.
33. L&P, XIII, (i), 450.
34. Singer (ed.), *Wolsey*, 453; L&P, X, no. 793.
35. L&P, X, no. 838.
36. ibid, no. 785.
37. L&P, X, no. 799.

38. ibid, no. 792; Cranmer, T., *Miscellaneous Writings and Letters*, 323–324.
39. Singer (ed.), *Wolsey*, 454; L&P, X, no. 798.
40. DellaNeva, J., *The Story of the Death of Anne Boleyn – A Poem by Lancelot de Carle*, 241.
41. ibid.
42. *Lisle Letters*, Vol. 3, no. 695.
43. L&P, X, 908.
44. DellaNeva, J., *The Story of the Death of Anne Boleyn – A Poem by Lancelot de Carle*, 241 (note 810).
45. Ives, E., *The Life and Death of Anne Boleyn*, 342.
46. Singer (ed.), *Wolsey*, 454; L&P, X, no. 798.
47. Singer (ed.), *Wolsey*, 456–457; L&P, X, no. 797.
48. Singer (ed.), *Wolsey*, 456; L&P, X, no. 797.
49. Singer (ed.), *Wolsey*, 457; L&P, X, no. 797.
50. Ives, Eric W., 'Anne Boleyn and the Entente Évangélique', 83–102.
51. Ridgway, C., *The Fall of Anne Boleyn*, 134.
52. Vasoli, S., *Anne Boleyn's Letter from the Tower*, 43. This is the most in-depth study of the letter to date and an invaluable resource for those wanting to explore the question of its authenticity further.
53. L&P, X, 827.
54. *Lisle Letters*, Vol. 3, nos. 691a & 694.
55. L&P, X, 791.
56. ibid, no. 891.
57. Murphy, B., *Bastard Prince: Henry VIII's Lost Son*, 175; L&P, X, no. 891(2).
58. Hardy, W. Duffers, et al., *The 1st Annual Report of the Deputy Keeper of the Public Records*, 242.
59. *Lisle Letters*, Vol. 3, no. 692.
60. Hardy, W. Duffers, et al., *The 1st Annual Report of the Deputy Keeper of the Public Records*, 242.
61. For a list of jurors, see the appendix to Vol. 1 of *Wriothesley's Chronicle*.
62. L&P, X, no. 848; *The 1st Annual Report of the Deputy Keeper of the Public Records*, 242–243.
63. L&P, X, no. 908.
64. *Lisle Letters*, Vol. 3, no. 694.
65. *Lisle Letters*, Vol. 3, no. 695.
66. *Lisle Letters*, Vol. 4, no. 845a.
67. *Wriothesley's Chronicle*, 37.
68. L&P, X, no. 908.
69. L&P, X, no. 873.
70. L&P, X, no. 908.
71. For the claim that Anne tried to poison the Lady Mary and Henry Fitzroy, see L&P, X, no. 908.
72. CSP, Spain, Vol. 5 (ii), no. 54.
73. L&P, X, no. 909.
74. ibid, no. 965.
75. L&P, X, no. 908; CSP, Spain, Vol. 5 (ii), no. 55.
76. *Wriothesley's Chronicle*, 37; L&P, X, no. 908.
77. *Wriothesley's Chronicle*, 37.
78. L&P, X, no. 876.

79. See appendix 3.

80. L&P, X, no. 873.

81. L&P, X, no. 908.

82. CSP, Spain, Vol. 5 (ii), no. 55; Ives, E., *The Life and Death of Anne Boleyn*, 345.

83. *Wriothesley's Chronicle*, 37–38.

84. *Wriothesley's Chronicle*, 38.

85. DellaNeva, J., *The Story of the Death of Anne Boleyn – A Poem by Lancelot de Carle*, 263/265.

86. CSP, Spain, Vol. 5 (ii), no. 55.

87. L&P, X, no. 908.

88. *Wriothesley's Chronicle*, 39.

89. L&P, X, no. 908.

90. Quoted in L&P, X, no. 908: 'nestoit habile en cas de soy copuler avec femme, et quil navoit ne vertu ne puissance'. The English translation is quoted in Lipscomb, S., *1536: The Year that Changed Henry VIII*, 83.

91. L&P, X, no. 908.

92. *Wriothesley's Chronicle*, 39.

93. Ives, E., *The Life and Death of Anne Boleyn*, 341.

94. For a list of the peers, see L&P, X, no. 876.

95. Singer (ed.), *Wolsey*, 459–460; L&P, X, no. 890.

96. Ridgway, C., *The Fall of Anne Boleyn: A Countdown*, 193.

97. L&P, X, no. 890.

98. *Wriothesley's Chronicle*, 40–41; L&P, X. no. 896.

99. L&P, X, no. 864.

100. ibid., no. 909.

101. ibid., no. 902.

Chapter 20

1. Cunningham, S., 'How to kill a queen? Preparing for the execution of Anne Boleyn in May 1536', The National Archives blog, 25 November 2020 (https://blog.nationalarchives.gov.uk/how-to-kill-a-queen-preparing-for-the-execution-of-anne-boleyn-in-may-1536/)

2. *Wriothesley's Chronicle*, 39–40.

3. Ives, E., *The Life and Death of Anne Boleyn*, 343.

4. L&P, XI, no. 467.

5. *The Spanish Chronicle*, 67.

6. *Wriothesley's Chronicle*, 40.

7. L&P, X, no. 908.

8. Shulman, N., *Graven with Diamonds*, 197.

9. Singer (ed.), *Wolsey*, 461.

10. CSP, Spain, Vol. 5 (ii), no. 55.

11. TNA: C 193/3, fol. 80; TNA blog (see note 1 above). I'm indebted to Dr Sean Cunningham for providing me with a translation and transcription of the writ.

12. L&P, X. no. 902.

13. Gristwood, S., *The Tudors in Love*, 188.

14. ibid., p. 186.

15. Singer (ed.), *Wolsey*, 461.

16. L&P, X, no. 1070.

17. L&P, XI, no. 381 (a).

18. *Lisle Letters*, Vol. 3, no. 697; *Wriothesley's Chronicle*, 41.
19. *Wriothesley's Chronicle*, 42.
20. *Hall's Chronicle*, 819.
21. *The Pilgrim*, 116.
22. *Wriothesley's Chronicle*, 42; L&P, X, no. 911; *The Pilgrim*, 117.
23. L&P, XI, no. 381 (a).
24. Ives, E., *The Life and Death of Anne Boleyn*, 359. He lists three sources, two of which make no mention of the 'arrow chest', see note 10 on page 423 of his book. The third source is the lost journal of Anthony Anthony, a Surveyor of the Ordnance of the Tower and a groom of the chamber, known only through the notes made by one Thomas Tourneur in his copy of *Henry VIII* by Herbert of Cherbury, published in the late seventeenth century.
25. Bodleian Library, Fol. Delta 624, 384–385.
26. Younghusband, G. J., *The Tower from Within*, 135–136.
27. Hamy, A., *Entrevue*, p. CCCCXXXVI.
28. Shulman, N., *Graven with Diamonds*, 204–206.

Chapter 21
1. *Lisle Letters*, Vol. 3, no. 698.
2. L&P, X, no. 926.
3. L&P, X, no. 926.
4. *Lisle Letters*, Vol. 3, no. 703.
5. *Letters of the Kings of England*, 353.
6. *Lisle Letters*, Vol. 3, no. 703a.
7. *Lisle Letters*, Vol. 4, no. 848.
8. *Lisle Letters*, Vol. 3, p.379.
9. ibid., 381; L&P, VII, no.9 (ii).
10. DellaNeva, J., *The Story of the Death of Anne Boleyn*, 187.
11. ibid., 247.
12. ibid., 305.
13. ibid., 335.
14. CSP, Spain, Vol. 5, part II, no. 61.
15. L&P, X, nos. 993/1000.
16. L&P, X, no. 1047.
17. L&P, X, no. 1022.
18. L&P, XI, no. 860.
19. ibid., no. 1250.

Epilogue
Warkentin, G. (ed.), *The Queen's Majesty's Passage & Related Documents*, 78–79.

Bibliography

Archival Sources
The National Archives, Kew
SP I/85 f. 135
SC 6/HENVIII/6680
SP 1/95 f.156
SP 1/103 SP1/103 ff. 322–7
Account Book of Sir William Paulet, Controller of the Household: E 101/422/1, ff. 001r–036v.
The British Library
Add MS 19398 f. 48-48v, 49r-50v
Kings MS 9, f. 231v and f.66r.
Sloane MS 1047
Bodleian Library
Fol. Delta 624, pp. 384–385
The National Library of France
MSS Dupuis, Volume 547, folio 200

Printed Primary Sources
Ashmole, E. (ed.), *The Register of the Most Noble Order of the Garter*, Volume 1 (1724)
Brewer, J.S. (ed.), *Letters and Papers, Foreign and Domestic, Henry VIII*, Volume 1 (1920)
Brewer, J.S. (ed.), *Letters and Papers, Foreign and Domestic, Henry VIII*, Volume 2 (1864)
Brewer, J.S. (ed.), *Letters and Papers, Foreign and Domestic, Henry VIII*, Volume 3 (1867)
Brewer, J.S. (ed.), *Letters and Papers, Foreign and Domestic, Henry VIII*, Volume 4 (1875)
Brown, R. (ed.), *Calendar of State Papers Relating to English Affairs in the Archives of Venice*, Volume 2 (1867)
Bruce, J. & Perowne, T. (eds.), *Correspondence of Matthew Parker, D.D. Archbishop of Canterbury: comprising letters written by and to him, from A.D. 1535, to his death, A.D. 1575*, (Cambridge University Press, 1853)
Burnet, G. (ed.), *The History of the Reformation of the Church of England*, Volume 4 (1865)
Byrne, M. St. C. (ed.), *The Lisle Letters*, 6 Volumes (The University of Chicago Press, Chicago and London, 1981)
Camusat, N., *Meslanges Historiques*, [Lettres de Roy Francois Premier…pour le dit Roy d' Angleterre], 1619
Cox, J.E. (ed.), *Miscellaneous Writings and Letters of Thomas Cranmer*, (Cambridge University Press, 1844–1846)
De Gayangos, P. (ed.), *Calendar of State Papers, Spain*, Volume 4 Part 1 (1879)
De Gayangos, P. (ed.), *Calendar of State Papers, Spain*, Volume 4 Part 2 (1882)
De Gayangos, P. (ed.), *Calendar of State Papers, Spain*, Volume 5 Part 1 (1886)
De Gayangos, P. (ed.), *Calendar of State Papers, Spain*, Volume 5 Part 2 (1888)
Dowling, M. (ed.), *William Latymer's Chronickille of Anne Boleyn*, (Camden Society, London, 1990)

Froude, J.A. (ed.), *The pilgrim: a dialogue on the life and actions of King Henry the Eighth by William Thomas*, (London, 1861)

Gairdner, J. (ed.), *Letters and Papers, Foreign and Domestic, Henry VIII*, Volume 5 (1880)

Gairdner, J. (ed.), *Letters and Papers, Foreign and Domestic, Henry VIII*, Volume 6 (1882)

Gairdner, J. (ed.), *Letters and Papers, Foreign and Domestic, Henry VIII*, Volume 7 (1883)

Gairdner, J. (ed.), *Letters and Papers, Foreign and Domestic, Henry VIII*, Volume 8 (1885)

Gairdner, J. (ed.), *Letters and Papers, Foreign and Domestic, Henry VIII*, Volume 9 (1886)

Gairdner, J. (ed.), *Letters and Papers, Foreign and Domestic, Henry VIII*, Volume 10 (1887)

Gairdner, J. (ed.), *Letters and Papers, Foreign and Domestic, Henry VIII*, Volume 11 (1888)

Gairdner, J. (ed.), *Letters and Papers, Foreign and Domestic, Henry VIII*, Volume 12, Part 2 (1891)

Gairdner, J. (ed.), *Letters and Papers, Foreign and Domestic, Henry VIII*, Volume 14, Part 1 (1894)

Gairdner, J. (ed.), *Letters and Papers, Foreign and Domestic, Henry VIII*, Volume 15 (1896)

Gairdner, J. & Brodie, R. (eds.), *Letters and Papers, Foreign and Domestic, Henry VIII*, Volume 16 (1898)

Gairdner, J. (ed.), *Letters and Papers, Foreign and Domestic, Henry VIII*, Volume 21, Part 2 (1910)

Gee, H. & Hardy, W.J. (ed.), *Documents Illustrative of the History of the English Church*, (Macmillan and Co., London, 1914)

Great Britain Record Commission, *State papers, published under the authority of His Majesty's Commission. King Henry the Eighth*, Volume 2 (London, 1830)

Great Britain Record Commission, *State papers, published under the authority of His Majesty's Commission. King Henry the Eighth*, Volume 7, Part V (London, 1849)

Hall, E, *Hall's Chronicle*, (London, 1809)

Halliwell-Phillipps, J.O. (ed.), *Letters of the Kings of England, Volume 1*, (London, 1848)

Hamilton, W.D. (ed.), *A Chronicle of England During the Reigns of the Tudors by Charles Wriothesley, C. Windsor Herald*, Volume 1, (London, 1838–1901)

Hamy, A., *Entrevue de François Ier avec Henry VIII à Boulogne-sur-Mer, en 1532*, (1899).

Hume, M. (ed.), *Chronicle of King Henry VIII. of England: Being a Contemporary Record of Some of the Principal Events of the Reigns of Henry VIII and Edward VI* [known as the Spanish Chronicle], (London, 1889)

Kipling, G. (ed.), *The Receyt of the Ladie Kateryne*, (Oxford University Press, 1990)

Luders, A. (ed.), *The Statutes of the Realm: Printed by Command of His Majesty King George the Third, In Pursuance of an Address of the House of Commons of Great Britain. From Original Records And Authentic Manuscripts.* (London: Dawsons of Pall Mall, 1810–1828)

Milner, J. (ed.), *Foxe's book of martyrs: a complete and authentic account of the lives, sufferings, and triumphant deaths of the primitive and Protestant martyrs in all parts of the world, with notes, comments and illustrations*, (London, 1856)

Nichols, J.G. (ed.), *Narratives of the days of the reformation: chiefly from the manuscripts of John Foxe the martyrologist; with two contemporary biographies of Archbishop Cranmer*, (The Camden Society, 1859)

Nicolas, N.H. (ed.), *The Privy Purse Expenses of Elizabeth of York*, (London, 1830)

Nicolas, N.H, (ed.), *The Privy Purse Expenses of King Henry the Eighth, from November 1529 to December 1532, with introductory remarks and illustrative notes*, (London, 1827)

Palgrave, F., Lyte, H. C. Maxwell., Hardy, W., Hardy, W. Duffers, *The 1st Annual Report of the Deputy Keeper of the Public Records*, (London: H.M. Stationery Office. 1840)

Philobiblon Society (Great Britain), *An account of materials furnished for the use of queen Anne Boleyn, and the princess Elizabeth: by William Loke, 'the king's mercer'*, (London, 1862–1863)

Radice, B. (translator) & Levi, A.H.T. (ed.), *Praise of Folly and Letter to Maarten van Dorp 1515 by Erasmus Desiderius*, (Penguin Books, 1993)

Russell, T. (ed), *The Works of the English Reformers: William Tyndale and John Frith Volume I*, (London, 1831)

Rymer, T. (ed.), *Rymer's Foedera*, Volume 12, (London, 1739–1745)

Singer, S. (ed.), *The Life of Cardinal Wolsey by George Cavendish*, (London, 1827)

Singer, S. (ed.), *The Life of Cardinal Wolsey by George Cavendish and Metrical Visions from the original autograph manuscript*, Volume 2, (Chiswick, 1825)

Smith, L.T. (ed.), *The Itinerary of John Leland in or about the Years 1535–1543*, (London: G. Bell, 1907)

Smith, L.T. (ed.), *The Maire of Bristowe is Kalendar* [Ricart's Calendar], (Camden Society, 1872)

Society of Antiquaries of London, *A collection of ordinances and regulations for the government of the royal household, made in divers reigns: from King Edward III to King William and Queen Mary, also receipts in ancient cookery*. (London, 1790)

Society of Antiquaries of London, *Archaeologia, or, Miscellaneous tracts relating to antiquity*. Volume 9, (London, 1789)

Society of Antiquaries of London. *Archaeologia, or, Miscellaneous tracts relating to antiquity*, Volume 23, (London, 1831)

Starkey, D. (ed.), *The Inventory of King Henry VIII*, (London, 1998)

Stemmler, T. (ed.), *Die Liebesbriefe Heinrichs VIII an Anna Boleyn*, (Zurich, 1998)

Stevenson, J. (ed.), *Calendar of State Papers Foreign: Elizabeth*, Volume 1, (1863)

Stowe, J, *Annales, or, a general chronicle of England*, (London, 1631)

Strype, J, *Ecclesiastical Memorials*, Volume 1, (London, 1721)

Strype, J. (ed.), *The Life and Acts of Matthew Parker*, Volume 1, (Oxford, 1821)

Sylvester, R.S. & Harding, D.P. (eds.), *Two Early Tudor Lives*, (New Haven and London: Yale University Press, 1967)

Thoms, W.J. (ed.), *A Survey Of London By John Stowe 1598*, (London, 1842)

Warkentin, G. (ed.), *The Queen's Majesty's Passage & Related Documents,* (Centre for Reformation and Renaissance Studies, 2004)

Wood, M.A.E. (ed.), *Letters of royal and illustrious ladies of Great Britain, from the commencement of the twelfth century to the close of the reign of Queen Mary*, Vol. 1 & 2, (Henry Colburn, London, 1846)

Secondary Sources

Baggs, A.P., Jurica, A.R.J., and Sheils, W.J., 'Painswick: Manors and other estates', in *A History of the County of Gloucester: Volume 11*, pp. 65–70

Bathe, G. & Holley, R., *A Re-appraisal of the Architectural and Historic Significance of Wolfhall, Wiltshire* (May 2017)

Bathe, G., & Purvis, I., 'A Revised date for the death of Sir John Seymour of Wolfhall' in *The Wiltshire Archaeological and Natural History Magazine*, 2019

Beer, M., 'A Queenly Affinity? Catherine of Aragon's Estates and Henry VIII's Great Matter' in *Historical Research*, Volume 91, Issue 253, August 2018

Beer, M., *Practices and Performances Of Queenship: Catherine Of Aragon and Margaret Tudor, 1503–1533,* (Ph.D. dissertation, University of Illinois at Urbana-Champaign, 2014)

Bell, R., 'The Royal Visit to Acton Court in 1535' in Starkey, D. (ed.), *Henry VIII: A European Court in England*, (Cross River Press, New York, 1991)

Berglar, P., *Thomas More: A Lonely Voice Against the Power of the State*, (Cologne, 1999)

Bernard, G.W., *The King's Reformation: Henry VIII and the Remaking of the English Church*, (Yale University Press, London, 2007)

Bindoff, S.T., *The House of Commons, 1509–1558*, Volume 1 (London, 1982)

Bolland, C., *Italian Material Culture at the Tudor Court*, (Ph.D. thesis, Queen Mary University of London, 2011)

Brears, P., *All the King's Cooks: The Tudor kitchens of King Henry VIII at Hampton Court Palace*, (Souvenir Press, London, 1999)

Britton, J., *The Architectural Antiquities of Great Britain*, Vol. 4, (London: Printed for Longman, Hurst, Rees, and Orme, 1807–1826)

Brodie, R.H., 'The Case of Dr. Crome' in *Transactions of the Royal Historical Society*, Vol. 19, 1905, pp. 295–304. *JSTOR*.

Brownbill, J. (ed.), *The Ledger Book of Vale Royal Abbey*, (Manchester, 1914)

Burton, J., *A history of Bewdley with concise accounts of some neighbouring parishes*, (London, 1883)

Carlton, C. (ed.), *State, Sovereigns & Society in Early Modern England*, (Sutton Publishing, 1998)

Chalmers, C.R., & Chaloner, E.J., '500 years later: Henry VIII, leg ulcers and the course of history' in *Journal of the Royal Society of Medicine*. Volume 102: 12, 2009, pp. 514–517

Cherry, C., & Ridgway, C., *George Boleyn: Tudor Poet, Courtier & Diplomat*, (Made Global Publishing, 2014)

Clifford, H., Stevenson, J., and Estcourt, E.E. (eds.), *The Life of Jane Dormer, Duchess of Feria* (Burns and Oates, London, 1887)

Colvin, H.M. (ed.), *The History of the King's Works: Volume IV 1485–1660*, Part II, (Her Majesty's Stationery Office, London, 1982)

Cooper, H., *Annals of Cambridge*, Volume 1, (Cambridge, 1842–1853)

Cox, John, *The Royal Forests of England*, (Methuen & Co., London, 1905)

Craik, G., & MacFarlane, G., *The Pictorial History of England*, Volume 2, (New York, 1848)

Creighton, C., *A History of Epidemics in Britain*, Volume 1, (Cambridge: The University Press, 1891)

Cressy, D., *Birth, Marriage & Death: Ritual, Religion and the Life-Cycle in Tudor and Stuart England*, (Oxford University Press, Oxford, 2010)

Cunningham, S., *Prince Arthur: The Tudor King Who Never Was*, (Amberley Publishing, 2016)

Daybell, J., *The Material Letter in Early Modern England*, (Palgrave Macmillan UK, 2012)

DellaNeva, J. *The Story of the Death of Anne Boleyn – A Poem by Lancelot de Carle*, (Arizona Center for Medieval and Renaissance Studies, 2021)

Douglas, A. & Greenfield, P. (eds.), *Records of Early English Drama*, (University of Toronto Press, Toronto, 1986)

Dowling, M., *Fisher of Men: a Life of John Fisher, 1469–1535*, (Palgrave Macmillan UK, 1999)

Duffy, E., *The Stripping of the Altars: Traditional Religion in England 1400–1580*, (Yale University Press, 2005)

Dyer, A. 'The Influence of the Bubonic Plague in England' in *Journal of the History of Medicine and Allied Sciences*, July 1978, pp. 308–376

Ellis, Steven G., 'The Kildare Rebellion and the Early Henrician Reformation' in *The Historical Journal*, Vol. 19, no. 4, 1976, pp. 807–830

Elton, G.R., 'An Early Tudor Poor Law' in *The Economic History Review*, 6(1), 1953, pp. 55–67

Faulkner, Neil, '"A goodly howse": the rebuilding of Acton Court' in *Current Archaeology*. Issue 218, May 2008

Feuillerat, A. (ed.), *Documents Relating to the Revels at Court in the Time of King Edward VI and Queen Mary*, (Louvain, 1914)

Fox, J., *Jane Boleyn: The Infamous Lady Rochford*, (Weidenfeld & Nicolson, London, 2007)

Fuller, T., *The History of the Worthies of England*, Volume 3, (London, 1840)

Gray, J., *Oaths and the English Reformation*, (Cambridge University Press, 2018)

Gristwood, S., *The Tudors in Love: The Courtly Code Behind the Last Medieval Dynasty*, (Oneworld, 2021)

Grosvenor, B., 'Happy Birthday Katherine of Aragon' in *Art History News*, 16 December 2011

Grueninger, N., *Discovering Tudor London*, (The History Press, Stroud, 2017)

Guy, J., *A Daughter's Love*, (Harper Perennial, London, 2009)

Guy, J., *The Children of Henry VIII*, (Oxford University Press, Oxford, 2013)

Hawkyard, A.D.K., 'Thornbury Castle' in *Transactions of the Bristol and Gloucestershire Archaeological Society*, Vol. 95, 1977, pp. 51–58

Hayward, M., *Clothing and the Law in Henry VIII's England*, (Ashgate, 2009)

Hayward, M., *Dress at the Court of Henry VIII*, (Manley Publishing, 2007)

Hayward, M., 'Gift Giving at the Court of Henry VIII: the 1539 New Year's Gift Roll in Context' in *The Antiquaries Journal*, Vol 85, 2005, pp. 126–175

Head, D. M., '"If a Lion Knew His Own Strength": The Image of Henry VIII and His Historians' in *International Social Science Review*, 72(3/4), 1997, pp. 94–109

Howard, M., & Wilson, E., *The Vyne: A Tudor House Revealed*, (The National Trust, 2003)

Hurren, E.T., *King Henry VIII's Medical World*, (https://hrpprodsa.blob.core.windows.net/hrp-prod-container/11727/elizabethhurrenfinal.pdf)

Hurstfield, J., 'The Revival of Feudalism in Early Tudor England' in *History*, 37(130), 1952, pp. 131–145

Hutchinson, R., *Thomas Cromwell: The Rise and Fall of Henry VIII's Most Notorious Minister*, (St Martin's Griffin, 2014)

Huth, Henry, Ellis, Frederick Startridge, & Hazlitt, William Carew, *The Huth library. A catalogue of the printed books, manuscripts, autograph letters, and engravings*, (London, 1880)

Ives, E., *The Life and Death of Anne Boleyn*, (Blackwell Publishing, Oxford, 2004)

Ives, Eric W., 'Anne Boleyn and the Entente Évangélique' in Mettam, Roger, and Giry-Deloison, Charles (eds.), *François Ier et Henri VIII. Deux princes de la Renaissance (1515–1547)* (Lille: Publications de l'Institut de recherches historiques du Septentrion, 1995), pp. 83–102, (http://books.openedition.org/irhis/1478)

Johnson, C., *The Queen's Servants: Gentlewomen's dress at the accession of Henry VIII*, (Fat Goose Press, Surrey, 2011)

Jones, E.A., *England's Last Medieval Monastery: Syon Abbey 1415–2015*, (Gracewing, 2015)

Kisby, F., '"When the King Goeth a Procession": Chapel Ceremonies and Services, the Ritual Year, and Religious Reforms at the Early Tudor Court, 1485–1547' in *Journal of British Studies*, 40(1), pp. 44–75

Knowles, D., *The Religious Orders in England*, Volume 3, (The University Press, Cambridge, 1971)

Lawson, J.A., 'Rainbow for a Reign: The Colours of a Queen's Wardrobe' in *Costume*, Vol. 41, pp. 26–44.

Lehmberg, S.E., *The Reformation Parliament*, (Cambridge University Press, 1970)

Lennon, C., *Sixteenth Century Ireland: The Incomplete Conquest*, (Gill & Macmillan, Dublin, 1994)

Lerer, S., *Courtly Letters in the Age of Henry VIII*, (Cambridge University Press, Cambridge, 1997)

Levin, C., '"Would I Could Give You Help and Succour": Elizabeth I and the Politics of Touch' in *Albion: A Quarterly Journal Concerned with British Studies*, Vol. 21, No. 2 (Summer, 1989), pp. 191–205.

Lewis, D. (ed.), *Rise and Growth of the Anglican Schism by Nicolas Sander*, (London, 1877)

Licence, A., *In Bed with the Tudors*, (Amberley Publishing, Stroud, 2012)

Lipscomb, S., *A Visitor's Companion to Tudor England*, (Ebury Press, 2012)

Lipscomb, S., *1536: The Year that Changed Henry VIII*, (Lion Hudson, Oxford, 2009)

Livingstone, A., *Medieval Lives c. 1000–1292: The World of the Beaugency Family*, (Routledge, 2018)

Loades, D., *Six Wives of Henry VIII*, (Amberley Publishing, Stroud, 2014)

Loades, D., *The Boleyns*, (Amberley Publishing, Stroud, 2011)

MacCulloch, D., *Thomas Cranmer: A Life*, (Yale University Press, 1996)

MacCulloch, D. (ed.), *The Reign of Henry VIII: Politics, Policy & Piety*, (Macmillan Press Ltd., 1995)

MacCulloch, D., *Thomas Cromwell: A Life*, (Allen Lane, 2018)

Mackay, L., *Among the Wolves of Court*, (Bloomsbury Academic, 2020)

Mackay, L., *Inside the Tudor Court*, (Amberley Publishing, Stroud, 2014)

Marshall, P., *Heretics and Believers: A History of the Reformation*, (Yale University Press, 2017)

Mikhaila, N., & Malcolm-Davies, J., *The Tudor Tailor*, (Batsford, London, 2006)

Morris, S., & Grueninger, N., *In the Footsteps of Anne Boleyn*, (Amberley Publishing, Stroud, 2013)

Murphy, B., *Bastard Prince: Henry VIII's Lost Son*, (The History Press, 2001)

Naphy, W., *The Protestant Revolution: From Martin Luther to Martin Luther King Jr.* (BBC Books, London, 2007)

Neale, J.E., *Queen Elizabeth I*, (Academy Chicago Publishers, 2005)

Norris, H., *Tudor Costume and Fashion*, (Dover Publications, 1997)

Norton, E., *The Lives of Tudor Women*, (Head of Zeus, 2016)

Phillpotts, C., *Park Farm, Thornbury, South Gloucestershire Documentary Research Report*, (Cotswold Archaeology, 2010)

Prynne, William, *Aurum Reginae*, (London: Thomas Ratcliffe, 1668)

Reynolds, E.E., *Margaret Roper*, (P. J. Kennedy and Sons, 1960)

Ridgway, C., *The Fall of Anne Boleyn: A Countdown*, (Made Global Publishing, 2012)

Roberts, J., *Royal Landscapes: The Gardens and Parks of Windsor*, (Yale University Press, 1997)

Robinson, B., *The Royal Maundy*, (Kaye & Ward, London, 1977)

Robinson, J. (ed.), *Readings in European History*, Volume 2, (Ginn & Company, 1906)

Seyer, S. (ed.), *Memoirs historical and topographical of Bristol and its neighbourhood; from the earliest period down to the present time*, Volume 2, (John Mathew Gutch, Bristol, 1821)

Shaw, Anthony, N., *The Compendium Compertorum and the Making of the Suppression Act of 1536*, (PhD thesis, University of Warwick, 2003).

Shulman, N., *Graven with Diamonds: The Many Lives of Thomas Wyatt – Courtier, Poet, Assassin, Spy*, (Short Books, 2012)

Sim, A., *Food and Feast in Tudor England*, (Sutton Publishing, 1997)

Southworth, J., *Fools and Jesters at the English Court*, (Sutton, 1998)

St Claire Baddeley, W., *A Cotteswold Manor being the History of Painswick*, (Kegan Paul, Trench, Trübner & Co., London, 1907)

Starkey, D., *Elizabeth: The Struggle for the Throne*, (Harper Collins, New York, 2001)

Starkey, D. (ed.), *Henry VIII: A European Court in England*, (Collins & Brown, 1991)

Starkey, D., *Six Wives: The Queens of Henry VIII*, (Perennial, 2004)

Stevens, J. E., *Music and Poetry in the Early Tudor Court*, (Cambridge University Press, 1961)

Stevenson, W.H. (ed.), 'The Records of the Corporation of Gloucester' in *The 12th Report of the Manuscript Commission*, Appendix, Part 9, (London, 1891)

Streitberger, W.R., 'Devising the Revels' in *Early Theatre*, Vol. 1, 1998, pp. 55–74. JSTOR.

Strickland, A., *Lives of the Queens of England*, Volume 4, (Bell & Daldy, London, 1872)

Thornton, D., 'The Last Monks of Worcester Cathedral Priory' in *Midland History*, Vol. 43, no. 1, 2018, pp. 3–21.

Thornton, T., *Cheshire and the Tudor State: 1480–1560*, (St Edmundsbury Press, 2000)

Thurley, S., 'Henry VIII and the Building of Hampton Court: A Reconstruction of the Tudor Palace' in *Architectural History*, 31, 1988, pp. 1–57 (https://doi.org/10.2307/1568535)

Thurley, S., *Hampton Court: A Social and Architectural History*, (Yale University Press, New Haven & London, 2003)

Thurley, S., *The Royal Palaces of Tudor England*, (Yale University Press, New Haven & London, 1993)

Tremlett, G., *Catherine of Aragon*, (Faber & Faber, 2010)

Urkevich, L.A., *Anne Boleyn, A Music Book, and the Northern Renaissance Courts*, (PhD dissertation, University of Maryland, 1997)

Vasoli, S., *Anne Boleyn's Letter from the Tower: A New Assessment*, (Made Global, 2015)

Vincent, N., *The Holy Blood: King Henry III and the Westminster Blood Relic*, (Cambridge University Press, Cambridge, 2001)

Walker, G., (2002). 'Rethinking the Fall of Anne Boleyn' in *The Historical Journal*, 45(1), 2002, pp. 1–29

Walters, L., 'Monstrous Births and Imaginations: Authorship and Folklore in Shakespeare's *A Midsummer Night's Dream*' in *Renaissance and Reformation / Renaissance et Réforme*, 39(1), 2016, pp. 115–146

Warnicke, R.M., *Elizabeth of York and Her Six Daughters-in-Law*, (Palgrave Macmillan, 2017)

Warnicke, R.M., *The Rise and Fall of Anne Boleyn*, (Cambridge University Press, 1991)

Watkins, S.B., *Lady Katherine Knollys: The Unacknowledged Daughter of King Henry VIII*, (John Hunt Publishing, 2015)

Weir, A., *Mary Boleyn: 'The Great and Infamous Whore'*, (Jonathan Cape, London, 2011)

Weir, A., *The Six Wives of Henry VIII*, (Vintage Books, London, 2007)

Wilkinson, J. (ed.), *Anne Boleyn by Paul Friedmann*, (Amberley, 2010)

Wilkinson, J., *Mary Boleyn: The True Story of Henry VIII's Favourite Mistress*, (Amberley Publishing, Stroud, 2009)

Willis-Bund, J.W., & Page, W. (eds.), *A History of the County of Worcester*, Volume 2, (London, 1971).
Young, A., *Tudor and Jacobean Tournaments*, (Sheridan House, 1998)
Younghusband, G.J., *The Tower from Within*, (London, 1919)

Acknowledgements

I would like to offer my sincerest thanks to the many brilliant authors and historians that I've corresponded with over the course of researching and writing this book, who have so generously answered my questions and provided me with valuable resources. Among them are Dr Estelle Paranque, Dr Sean Cunningham, Dr Daniel Gosling, Adrienne Dillard, Graham Bathe, Dr Lauren Mackay and Brigitte Webster. Thanks are also due to Professor JoAnn DellaNeva for so kindly providing me with a copy of a number of chapters of her book, *The Story of the Death of Anne Boleyn*, while I awaited the arrival of the published work.

I'd also like to acknowledge the work of all of Anne Boleyn's biographers who have come before me, especially the late Professor Eric Ives, whose work has been invaluable. An immense thank you also to the many women historians who inspire me each and every day, including Professor Suzannah Lipscomb and Dr Tracy Borman.

A special thank you to my brilliant friends, Dr Owen Emmerson and Sandra Vasoli, for believing in me and cheering me on every step of the way, and for the many insightful chats that have helped me immensely to sharpen and refine my arguments. Any errors are my own, of course.

I am also grateful to James Peacock, Claire Ridgway, Kathryn Holeman, Sarah Morris and Gareth Russell for their friendship and ongoing support, which means so very much to me. A special thank you also to my wonderful podcast listeners and the online Tudor community for their endless enthusiasm and for never shying away from a friendly debate!

Deep gratitude also to my amazing sister, Karina, for reading the unedited manuscript and offering valuable feedback, and to my parents for instilling in me a love of words.

To my beloved children, Isabel and Tristan, thank you for your love and for never complaining about how much time I spend in the sixteenth century. My sincerest hope is that I've made you both proud.

Finally, I would like to offer a heartfelt thank you to my darling husband (and best friend), Chris, whose unwavering love and support have carried me through some challenging times. I could not have done this without you. Thank you for always believing in me and for so warmly welcoming Anne into our family, all those years ago.

Natalie Grueninger
November 2021

Index